René Rosenbaum

Mobile Image Communication Using JPEG2000

René Rosenbaum

Mobile Image Communication Using JPEG2000

Technology to Handle Large Visual Contents in Resource-limited Environments

VDM Verlag Dr. Müller

Imprint

Bibliographic information by the German National Library: The German National Library lists this publication at the German National Bibliography; detailed bibliographic information is available on the Internet at http://dnb.d-nb.de.

Cover image: www.purestockx.com

Publisher:
VDM Verlag Dr. Müller Aktiengesellschaft & Co. KG , Dudweiler Landstr. 125 a, 66123 Saarbrücken, Germany,
Phone +49 681 9100-698, Fax +49 681 9100-988,
Email: info@vdm-verlag.de

Zugl.: Rostock, University, Diss., 2006

Produced in USA and UK by:
Lightning Source Inc., La Vergne, Tennessee, USA
Lightning Source UK Ltd., Milton Keynes, UK

ISBN: 978-3-8364-5411-7

to my son Noah

Preamble

First of all I would like to express my gratitude to my mentor Prof. Dr. Heidrun Schumann for encouraging me writing this thesis and for supporting me with the perfect environment to do so. Without allowing room for my researches this thesis wouldn't be possible. Her social sense will always be a great example on how to support and bring together individuals.

I would like to thank Dr. David Taubman for providing the option to work in the front-line of image communication with JPEG2000. Being in his working group was definitely a great opportunity to enhance my horizon in research and culture. In this regard, I would also like to thank the DAAD for making this possible.

My thanks go also to Siemens Munich for a perfect collaboration and for supporting the first steps of my works to this thesis. I would like to stress the special contribution of Dr. Uwe Rauschenbach providing vision and assistance.

Over the years it has been my good fortune to encounter many people, to which I had the chance to talk about my current and future research plans. As representatives, special thanks go to Masayuki Hashimoto, Jérôme Meessen and my colleagues at University of Rostock. By the interactions and the feedback I received from their respective Final Year Projects or Master Theses, I would also like to thank the students Martin Tesche, Georg Fuchs, Sebastian Woyda, Thomas Schütze, Stefan Kolp, Volker Tesche, and Thorsten Seebahn.

I am, of course, particularly indebted to my wife for their monumental, unwavering support and encouragement on all fronts. She and my son Noah have changed and enriched my life so fundamentally. They have truly always been there for me, and without them none of this would have been even remotely possible. Together with my parents and my particular friends Christian and Steve, they have always reminded me that ...

"Mittler zwischen Hirn und Händen muss das Herz sein."
(The heart must serve as intermediary between the brain and the hands.)
THEA VON HARBOU (Metropolis)

Rostock,
May 2006

René Rosenbaum

i

Contents

List of Figures

List of Tables

Abbreviations

ADU	Application Data Unit
AET	Active edge table
BCQ	Bitwise Condensed Quadtrees
bpp	bit per pixel
CAT	Contrast Adaptive Thresholding
Codec	Coder&Decoder
dB	Decibel
DCT	Discrete Cosine Transform
DFT	Discrete Fourier Transform
DICOM	Digital Imaging and Communications in Medicine
DO	Detail&Overview
DoF	Depth of Field
DoI	Degree of Interest
DPCM	Differential Pulse Code Modulation
DWT	Discrete Wavelet Transform
EBCOT	Embedded Block Coding with optimized Truncation
EZW	Embedded Zerotree Wavelet
FC	Focus&Context
FITS	Flexible Image Transport System
FFT	Fast Fourier Transform
FGS	Fine Grain Scalability
GbZP	Grid-based Zoom&Pan
GDAL	Geospatial Data Abstraction Library
GIF	Graphics Interchange Format
GIS	Geographical Information System
GSM	Global System for Mobile Communications
HTML	Hypertext Markup Language
HVS	Human Visual System
IDCT	Inverse → DCT
IDWT	Inverse → DWT
IIP	Internet Imaging Protocol
ISO	International Organisation for Standardisation
ITU	International Telecommunication Union
JPEG	Joint Photographic Experts Group
JPIP	JPEG2000 Interactive Protocol
kB	Kilo Byte
kbps	Kilobit per second

LAN	Local Area Network
LBS	Location-based Services
LDV	Large Detail-View
LoD	Level of Detail
LSA	Limited spatial access
Mbps	Megabit per second
M-JPEG	Motion-JPEG
M-JPEG2000	Motion-JPEG2000
MRI	Magnetic Resonance Image
MrSID	Multi Resolution Seamless Image Database
NETCICATS	Network-Conscious Image Compression and Transmission System
NPR	Non-Photorealistic Rendering
OSI	Open System Interconnection
PDA	Personal Digital Assistant
PIT	Progressive Image Transmission
Pixel	picture element
PNG	Portable Network Graphics
PoI	Points of interest
rFEV	rectangular Fisheye-View
RD	Rate-Distortion
RoI	Region of Interest
RSA	Random spatial access
SBC	Subband Coding
SDK	Software Development Kit
SDoF	Semantic → DoF
SPIHT	Set Partitioning in Hierarchical Trees
SSROD	Screen Space Ratio between Overview and Detail
SVG	Scalable Vector Graphics
UI	User Interface
UMTS	Universal Mobile Telecommunications System
VRML	Virtual Reality Modelling Language
VTC	Visual texture coding
WAN	Wide Area Network
WC	Wavelet Coding
WIMAX	Worldwide Interoperability for Microwave Access
WLAN	Wireless → LAN
WoI	Window of Interest
WWW	World Wide Web
ZP	Zoom&Pan
ZUI	Zoomable User Interface

Identifiers

General identifiers

att	attribute tuple of a key element $\rightarrow k$ consisting of attributes $\rightarrow a_1$, $\rightarrow a_2$, $\rightarrow a_3$, $\rightarrow a_4$, $\rightarrow a_5$, and $\rightarrow a_6$.
b	A single subband $\rightarrow \mathrm{LL}_d, \mathrm{LH}_d$, HL_d or HH_d resulting from the DWT decomposition.
c_{pos}	Counter which stores the number of RoIs which have not already transmitted data for the current layer-resolution-component combination.
c_{neg}	Counter which stores the number of RoIs which have already transmitted data for the current layer-resolution-component combination.
$cb_{d,b,col,row}$	Single code-block determined by its relative position (col, row) within subband $\rightarrow b$ resulting from decomposition stage $\rightarrow d$.
$cbt_{col,row,r}$	Code-block triple determined by the relative position (col, row) at resolution level $\rightarrow r$ to thats reconstruction it is directly contributing to.
cm_r	number of code-block rows of a single subband directly contributing to the reconstruction of image resolution $\rightarrow r$.
cn_r	number of code-block columns of a single subband directly contributing to the reconstruction of image resolution $\rightarrow r$.
d	Decomposition level.
d_{max}	Highest decomposition level.
d_n	The nth level of distortion within a reconstructed image.
$[e_1, e_2]$	Offset of the image on the image canvas.
$[f_1, f_2]$	Spatial extension of the image canvas.
g	Specifies the applied scaling by 2^g.
$[goff_1, goff_2]$	Difference between image offset $\rightarrow [e_1, e_2]$ and the anchor of the partitioning grid.
img	Source image.
$\hat{img}$	Destination image (used for content exchange only).
img_a	Number of accuracy levels provided by the image.
img_c	Number of color components provided by the image.
k	Single generic key element.
$\mathcal{K}_{k,q}$	Partial data of key element $\rightarrow k$ residing at the ith quality layer.
l_n	The length of an encoded image truncated at the nth point.

$\ell_{\tilde{\imath}}$	The ith resequenced layer.
$LL_d, LH_d,$ HL_d, HH_d	Subbands $\rightarrow b$ resulting from the $\rightarrow d^{\text{th}}$ decomposition step.
$[\Omega_1, \Omega_2]$	Offset of the tile grid on the image canvas.
$[o_1, o_2]$	Offset of the image region that is to be handled.
$p_{col,row,r}$	Single precinct determined by its relative position (col, row) within the inherent image resolution $\rightarrow r$.
pm_r	number of precinct rows at resolution level $\rightarrow r$.
pn_r	number of precinct columns at resolution level $\rightarrow r$.
q	Number of quality layers of an image encoded with JPEG2000.
r	inherent image resolution.
r_{max}	highest resolution, refers to pixel domain.
$[reg_1, reg_2]$	Spatial dimensions of a region within the image which is to be handled.
$[s_1, s_2]$	Image dimensions.
$[screen_1, screen_2]$	Screen dimensions
s_n	The nth distortion-length slope.
S_k	Region of influence of key element $\rightarrow k$.
$t_{col,row,r}$	Single tile contribution determined by its relative position (col, row) within the inherent image resolution $\rightarrow r$.
tm_r	number of tile rows at resolution level $\rightarrow r$.
tn_r	number of tile columns at resolution level $\rightarrow r$.
t_i	Distortion-length slope thresholds.
w_k	The window scaling factor.
x_s	Intersection coordinate.
$*$ vs. $\hat{*}$	Identifier belonging to source ($*$) or destination image ($\hat{*}$). (Used for content exchange only)

LoD - attributes

accuracy	Numerical accuracy.
component	Number of color components.
x-resolution	Provided resolution in x dimension.
y-resolution	Provided resolution in y dimension.

Attributes of a generic key element

a_0	Element type of a generic key element $\rightarrow k$.
a_1	Column offset of a generic key element $\rightarrow k$ in resolution level $\rightarrow r$.
a_2	Row offset of a generic key element $\rightarrow k$ in resolution level $\rightarrow r$.
a_3	Number of columns of wavelet coefficients belonging to a certain key element $\rightarrow k$ with regard to a single subband.
a_4	Number of rows of wavelet coefficients belonging to a certain key element $\rightarrow k$ with regard to a single subband.
a_5	Number of pixel columns the belonging key element $\rightarrow k$ contributes to.
a_6	Number of pixel rows the belonging key element $\rightarrow k$ contributes to.

Relevant sets

CB_r	Set of all single code-blocks $cb_{d,b,col,row}$ directly contributing to the reconstruction of resolution r.
CBT_r	Set of all code-block triples $\rightarrow cbt_{col,row,r}$ directly contributing to.
$FIRST$	Set containing the top left elements from $\rightarrow VALID$ for each resolution level r.
KEY	Set of all key elements of a single type (code-blocks, precincts or tiles).
KEY_r	Set of all key elements $\rightarrow k$ of a single type directly contributing to the reconstruction of resolution level $\rightarrow r$.
$LAST$	Set containing the bottom right elements from $\rightarrow VALID$ for each resolution level r.
M	Set containing all key elements of a single image.
P_r	Set of all precincts defined at image resolution $\rightarrow r$.
$PAIRS$	Set containing the element pairs which are to be replaced.
T_r	Set of all tile contributions defined at image resolution $\rightarrow r$.
$VALID$	Set containing all elements contributing to the reconstruction of a particular region at a certain resolution $\rightarrow r$.
$*$ vs. $\hat{*}$	Set belonging to source ($*$) or destination image ($\hat{*}$). (Used for content exchange only)

Chapter 1

Introduction

1.1 Motivation

Visual information and imagery play an important role in almost all areas of daily life. However, compared to text, much more processing power and bandwidth for processing and retrieval is required.

A picture is worth a thousand words ... (but requires almost 500 times as much bandwidth). [Buc00]

Due to this, related applications and user tasks can only be supported by exploiting properties of modern hardware and infrastructure.

With the ability to access information *every time and everywhere* [Imi96], the enthusiasm for mobile computing is still unbroken. With 300 million new subscribers in 2004 alone, 27% of the world's population now has access to mobile communications [Sva05]. In the first quarter of 2006, worldwide PDA shipments grew 6.6 percent relative to the same period of 2005 [Gar06]. Due to its form factors and application environment, however, mobile devices are still limited by a number of factors. To overcome their influence, information contents must be adequately processed and adapted.

To bridge the gap between the limited resources in mobile environments and the demands required to handle imagery, this thesis is concerned with *mobile image communication*. This is achieved by appropriately combining properties of the different communication steps: *image compression, transmission* and *visual representation*. This has not been the case for related proposals, which usually consider each stage separately. By developing and combining basic technologies for compression and transmission, the influence of the most limiting issues – computing power and bandwidth – are significantly reduced. Moreover, of crucial interest is also the appropriate representation of the content on the small screens and the respective coupling to an appropriate image communication system.

To provide information independent of a certain application, it is important to use wide-spread and commonly supported media technology. Approaches for image communication systems proposed in this thesis are compliant to the new *JPEG2000*-image compression standard assumed to be accepted as one of the major internet standards in the near future. Thus, the presented thesis contributes to provide imagery in resource limited environments using State of Art technology.

1

1.2   Mobile environments

Mobile environments are determined by one or more portable computers (clients) connected with a stationary computer (server) via a wide area network (WAN). Due to its application area a single client is called a *mobile device*. This device class is diverse and spreads from very small gadgets like smartphones over Personal Digital Assistants (PDA) to tablet-PCs and laptops.

A typical characteristic of mobile environments are limited resources. Due to the small form factor, mobile devices suffer from insufficient screen space and resolution. The limited computing power directly related to energy consumption and weight is another constraint [Ros03c; Ros04d]. As each device type has its own application area, form factor and requirements, these limitations are more or less strongly pronounced.

Another point subject to strong limitations is the provided bandwidth needed to access remote contents. While stationary devices are often connected by a 100Mbit-ethernet, transmitting data to a nearly arbitrarily positioned mobile client is much slower. Furthermore, mobile connections are costly and not reliable. They are established by using WLAN, traditional modems or the data mode of the European GSM net. As the theoretical bandwidth can often not fully provided, the specified transfer speed (WLAN: 11%, Modem: 0.05%, GSM: 0.01% of 100Mbps) is even further decreased. Additionally, wireless connections are usually subject to bad transmission quality leading to lost or modified data. Although, there are emerging and more sophisticated technologies, as WIMAX or UMTS, limitations in bandwidth will still remain in the near future.

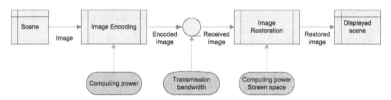

Figure 1.1: *Shannon's classic model of a communication channel[Sha48] applied to image communication together with critical limiting factors that constrain its performance in mobile environments.*

1.3   Image communication using JPEG2000

Image communication is a collective term for the different steps which must be passed from the supply of the image data at server side until its application at client side. A reasonable communication channel consists of at least three basic components – encoding, transmission and restoration. Figure 1.1 depicts the relation between these stages together with corresponding limiting factors in mobile environments.

Though there are rather different approaches to describe a *scene*, preparatory work of the author has shown that *raster imagery* is still the less demanding option to handle arbitrary contents in mobile environments [Ros03c; Ros04d; Ros06b]. Raster images describe graphical content by a regular 2D-grid, whereby a single grid cell is called pixel. Each pixel is assigned an independent color value.

To store or transmit such a 2D-structure, it is transformed into a 1D- or sequential data-stream. This process is called *image encoding*. As encoding is often bundled with a reduction in the amount of data needed to describe the image content, this step is often referred as *image compression*. Encoding is a requirement for *image transmission*. To transfer and assign image data at receiver side some kind of *signalization* is needed. It is often tightly bundled with image compression to support and provide properties of the encoding to the receiver. At receiver side, *image decoding* and *restoration* serves to re-transform the 1D-data-stream back into a pixel field. An important step often neglected in traditional communication systems is the appropriate *visual representation* of the decoded result. Depending on the respective *application*, the displayed scene may differ from the original scene.

Many reasonable approaches for each one of the steps have already been proposed. The general problem if used within a communication system is their loose coupling. This leads to a loss of performance at the interfaces from one stage to another. Often the majority of the costly transmitted and processed image contents are of little use at application side. In mobile environments, this is often due to the limited screen space preventing the display of all contents. A reasonable communication system omits or neglects irrelevant data and delivers missing contents on demand.

Contrary to the visual representation responsible for providing an appropriate user interface, compression and transmission are key technologies for the actual data handling. JPEG2000 [JPG02a] represents the State of Art in scalable image compression, and thus, is rather suited for the required demand-driven data handling. Beside a brilliant compression performance, a rich set of features to couple all stages of the communication channel to an appropriate system are provided. The foundation of these features is the property to generate a modular data-stream formed by certain key elements. As a consequence, single image parts can be independently accessed and processed.

1.4   Assignment of this work

1.4.1   An enhanced scheme for modern image communication

Due to new developments in the field of client/server-based image communication, it is reasonable to enhance the classic model shown in Figure 1.1 by a number of additional components. Such a model proposed by the author is shown in Figure 1.2. Since a respective task is usually performed at client side, this is the location where requirements for image communication are determined. A *display logic* receives these demands from a concrete *application*, manages and conveys them to one or more components.

The first opportunity to apply demands to image data is by *filtering* the data at server side (F_s) [Fox96; Rau96; Ort97; Ris02]. At this point the content is still represented by a pixel field enabling easy access and processing [IQW98; LTI05].

The next option for adaptation is during *image compression* (C). This step transforms the image content and refers to layer 6 (presentation) of the well known *OSI-reference model* [Day83] introduced and often applied to explicate generic data communication. Thereby, three different paradigms have been proposed: (1) the development, (2) selection, or (3) adaptation of the image codec. While the first approach targets on constantly new evolutions in image compression technology, the second is based on the reasonable assumption that the performance of a respec-

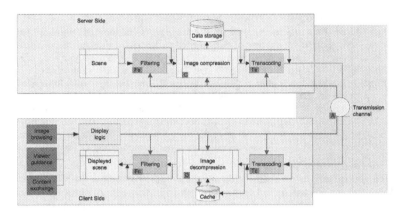

Figure 1.2: *The proposed processing scheme for modern client/server-based image communication.*

tive codec strongly depends on the characteristic of the image data [Rau96; Sai96b; Ire98]. The third point is mostly related to the utilization of provided codec features [Rau97; Ire98; Tau02b].

Once the image has been compressed it is stored or sent to the client. Storing already compressed data is a useful feature if similar requests of multiple clients are assumed. Nevertheless, before sending, the content may be further adapted.

Images transformed to a compressed representation are often understood as static and indivisible objects. However, modern compression schemes provide different features to select, access, and modify image content directly in compression domain. Thus, relevant image data can be dynamically retrieved or altered from still compressed streams. In the presented scheme this is accomplished by a *transcoding unit* (T_s). As an arbitrary selection and transmission of partial image data scrambles the order of the original data-stream, this component also serves to enrich the resulting data-stream with additional information required to reconstruct its original order at client side. Such a signalization basically corresponds to layer 5 (session) of the OSI-reference model designed to coordinate applications as they interact on different hosts.

Stage A of the proposed communication scheme is labeled *transmission channel*. More exactly, this term refers to layer 1 to 4 of the OSI-reference model. These layers are designed to handle arbitrary data and are especially interesting for real-time or demand-driven delivery [Ram00; Bar01; Sch03b], specialized hardware [Azu05; MOX05], energy efficiency [App01; Yu04], or error-resilience [DeB00; Thi04].

The most important challenge of the *transcoding unit* at client side (T_c) is to identify each received data chunk and to determine its position regarding the original ordering of the compressed data-stream. To achieve this, it is strongly coupled with its counterpart at server side.

After the received image data has been identified, it is cached or directly processed by the *image decompression* stage (D) transferring the compressed content back into a pixel field.

The final step and often the place where a reasonable content representation is created is client-side *filtering* (F_c). Regarding the classic model it is worth noting that the depicted image restoration process is represented by decoding and filtering.

As for its counterpart at server side, filtering is performed in pixel domain.

Once the image data has fully passed the communication pipeline and has been adapted by the components, its visual representation is shown on screen. Obviously, the resulting representation is required to satisfy the demands determined by the respective application used to achieve a certain task.

1.4.2   Problems with existing image communication systems

Due to the high relevancy of remote imagery in medical, geospatial and industrial applications, image communication systems have always been in focus of research and commerce, spreading from first works in 1955 [Fel55; Lin55], over simple [Ste95] or exotic systems [Sue03], to modern systems exploiting latest tendencies in image communication [Rau00; Des01; LIZ05; ER05; KAK05]. However, most of the proposals focus on single steps of the communication pipeline, as compression or transmission, and try to decrease the need for bandwidth only [Loh84; Rau00; Owe01]. Although some systems might be enhanced to reduce the computational efforts at client side [KAK05], no system has yet been proposed especially for mobile environments.

To stress the need for enhancements, Appendix A provides an overview to structure and design of relevant image communication systems supporting the dynamic adaptation to frequently changing demands. For easy comparison properties discussed in this thesis are listed in a concise scheme. Although there are more systems than discussed, some proposals lack on concrete statements to certain communication stages, and thus, have not been taken up. This especially applies for commercial products as [ER05; GDA05; LIZ05; LEA05; Lur05a; Lur05b]. Contrary, due to the many different system configurations supported by the standard *Digital Imaging and Communications in Medicine* (DICOM) [DI003], general statements can only hardly be derived.

However, all systems have been mostly designed for remote communication with stationary devices. The following problems likely appear if they are applied in mobile environments:

- Required computing power exceeds the capabilities of the client
- Generic design and loose coupling of single communication stages leads to an increased need for bandwidth
- Simple representation of the content makes its comprehension difficult
- Limited variety of supported user tasks limits mobile working

Each of theses points leads to a *decreased performance* of the communication system and *the satisfaction of the user* during working in mobile environments. Due to this, new ideas for mobile image communication significantly reducing the existing drawbacks are required.

1.4.3   Goals and main idea

This thesis is concerned with mobile image communication in *interactive client/ server environments*. To overcome the problems of existing communication systems in mobile environments, the main **goal** of this thesis is to *reduce the needs for resources* related to the most limiting factors – *computing power* and *bandwidth*. This leads to faster response times during interaction and less transmission costs.

Founded on the developed basic technology, a further goal is the supply of *multiple implementations for frequently appearing imaging tasks* partially paired with the reduction of the impact of the limited *screen size* of mobile devices.

Within this thesis, image communication is considered as a whole from the beginning to the very end. Depending on requirements specified by the task at hand, the main goal is achieved by a *dynamic adaptation of the communication pipeline to current demands*. To accommodate the fact, contents are often stored in compressed representation, in focus of proposed solutions is *already encoded imagery*. In consequence, server-side filtering (F_s) is neglected. This also applies for problems related to the transmission channel (A) and possible constraints at server side.

The **main idea** common to all strategies proposed in this thesis is the application of the following points:

1. Description of current demands and coupling of all communication steps by *Regions of Interest and Level of Detail*

2. *Application of JPEG2000* for image compression

3. *Exploitation of properties of JPEG2000* for an adapted *image streaming*

4. *Exploitation of properties of JPEG2000* for the uncomplex creation of the *content representation* at client side

Regions of Interest and Levels of Detail   It has been shown that demands at client side can be described by *Regions of Interest* (RoI) and the concept of *Levels of Detail* (LoD) [Rau99b]. Interesting image regions is assigned a high, irrelevant regions a low LoD. As shown in this thesis, these concepts allow for the unique description of the requirements at client side and lead to a highly adapted image handling at each communication stage. *Interactive environments require a dynamic RoI and LoD support.*

Application of JPEG2000   All modern communication systems apply the DWT as foundation for the used image codec (cf. Appendix A). Beside a high compression performance, the resulting data is *scalable*, supports RoIs and can be adapted to current needs. *JPEG2000 is the State of Art in scalable image compression* and assumed as codec (C, D) for proposed image communication systems. This also simplifies the migration of the introduced ideas into existing systems.

Exploitation of properties of JPEG2000 for image streaming   The beneficial properties of JPEG2000-encoded data are rather appropriate for flexible image streaming. This is shown in this thesis by *exploiting the modular structure of the encoded data* to limit the streamed data to that satisfying the current demands. By a *proper selection, transmission and identification* of data chunks, this is accomplished by the transcoding units at server (T_s) and client side (T_c).

Exploitation of properties of JPEG2000 for content representation   Selected properties of JPEG2000 are also exploited for the creation of sophisticated content representations. In existing systems this is often accomplished by client-side filtering (F_c), which usually requires strong computing power. By *exploiting the multiresolution-representation of the content and its modular structure* within the compressed datastream, this thesis proposes new ideas not requiring any pixel filtering. Due to the tight coupling between codec and representation, this also leads to the design of reasonable communication strategies for each of the covered problem fields – *image browsing, viewer guidance* and *content exchange.*

1.5   Structure and results of this thesis

This section outlines the structure and achieved results of this thesis. Thereby, the proposed communication pipeline shown in Figure 1.1 serves as foundation for the organization of the content. To emphasize the importance of the introduced ideas and to allow comparison to existing solutions, each chapter is provided with a discussion of related work. Thereby, JPEG2000-related approaches are reviewed in more detail.

Chapter 2 introduces a model for RoIs and LoDs and explores their support by scalable *image compression* schemes. As exploited for own developments, this section also serves to express the support for *dynamic RoIs* based on the modular structure of JPEG2000-encoded imagery. It is also proven if scalability compensates for the increased need of system resources.

Chapter 3 is concerned with *image streaming* and introduces new ideas for the compliant support of *dynamic RoIs* and LoDs within JPEG2000-encoded imagery. All stages of the streaming process are discussed and enhanced with new strategies. Overall, 6 new techniques to implement the proposed concept of dynamic RoIs are introduced. Statements to other application areas for dynamic RoIs close the contributions of this chapter.

Chapter 4 is concerned with *mobile image browsing*. An introduced generic classification scheme based on RoIs and LoDs serves to classify related strategies and to give transmission guidelines for current and future techniques. 2 new browsing techniques are introduced, classified and coupled to an efficient communication strategy. The option to design an appropriate image communication system founded on the proposed statements is also shown for an existing browsing technique.

Chapter 5 proposes 2 new approaches for *viewer guidance for raster imagery*. To achieve the respective image representations inherent features of JPEG2000 are exploited and no additional processing in pixel domain is required. For each strategy an efficient communication strategy is proposed.

Chapter 6 introduces a new approach for *content exchange between images* in JPEG2000 domain. This technique requires no decoding of the contents, and thus, reduces the complexity of the task significantly. It can also be coupled with the proposed streaming technology to an efficient communication system. The applicability of the approach is enormous. 5 potential remote applications are introduced, whereby 2 are discussed in detail.

Chapter 7 provides statements to *future work* and a *summary* of the results of this thesis. Beside others these are:

- A formal model for random spatial access in JPEG2000-encoded imagery
- A JPEG2000-compliant approach for dynamic RoIs and LoDs
- New and efficient strategies for image streaming
- A RoI/LoD-based classification scheme for image browsing techniques
- New and intuitive image browsing techniques
- New basic techniques for viewer guidance in raster imagery
- A flexible approach to content exchange in JPEG2000 domain
- The design of efficient image communication systems

The relevance of this thesis is underlined by the fact, that these results have been published in 18 international book, conference and workshop contributions. Within this thesis, own contributions are related to the respective context and described in-depth regarding their function, structure and properties. The next chapter is concerned with image compression and its capability to provide dynamic Regions of Interest.

Chapter 2

Image compression and dynamic RoIs with JPEG2000

This chapter is concerned with the image codec (cf. Figure 2.1) and shows that features provided by JPEG2000 lead to highly flexible modular data-streams. To describe their properties, a consistent concept for the support of dynamic RoIs and LoDs is introduced and serves in later chapters as the foundation for the design of appropriate demand-driven mobile image communication systems.

After revealing aims regarding compression (Section 2.1), a model to describe RoIs and LoDs is introduced (Section 2.2.1). The following review of related work also introduces foundations to JPEG2000 and its superior support for RoIs (Section 2.2).

New ideas for dynamic RoIs based on the provided options for random spatial access within JPEG2000-encoded data are introduced (Section 2.3). The respective key elements of the data-stream are carefully reviewed, unified, and discussed regarding their respective LoD-support (Section 2.4). Finally, the eligibility of JPEG2000 in mobile environments is shown (Section 2.5).

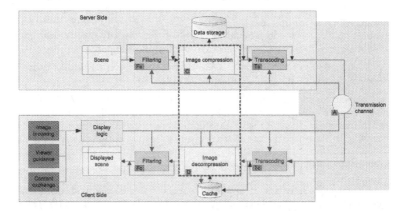

Figure 2.1: *Support for dynamic Regions of Interest is strongly related to features of the image codec.*

2.1   Aims and requirements

Mobile environments are subject to strong limitations regarding *computing power* and *bandwidth* (cf. Appendix B). The aim of image compression and dynamic Regions of Interest is to save these resources during image communication. Thereby, the reasonable assumption that not always all contents are of equal importance is exploited. This, however, requires detailed statements of the description to the respective requirements.

Paying attention to the small transmission bandwidth in mobile environments, contents are usually compressed before they are sent. To achieve this, numerous approaches have been proposed. To achieve a data transmission adapted to the demands at client side, however, the compression process must be either steerable or produce a data-stream which is of modular manner. Due to the reason, interactivity at client side may impose frequent changes of the respective demands, modular data-streams offer more flexibility. They are mostly produced by *scalable compression schemes*. As such schemes are often more complex than others, they must be suitably chosen so as not to exceed the capabilities of the client.

Overall, the requirements to achieve the strived aim can be summarized as follows:

- Suitable description of the requirements at client side
- Fulfillment of the requirements by partial image data
- Modular structure of the encoded data
- Low complexity at client side

To achieve the first point, the following section serves to introduce a model for Regions of Interest and Levels of Detail. Later chapters apply this model to show the implementation of the remaining points.

2.2   Fundamentals and discussion of related work

To achieve the adaptation of the communication to current requirements, the adaptation of the respectively used image codec is of crucial interest. Founded on an introduced model for RoIs and LoDs, this section serves to review selected image compression approaches to provide statements to the respective needs regarding computing power and bandwidth, and to show their RoI support.

"Scalable compression allows a single compressed bitstream to meet the needs of various users with different constraints." (ROBERS ET AL. [Rob98])

Due to their superior compression performance, the provided options to adapt the compression process, as well as the modular structure of the produced data-stream, in focus are scalable image transformation schemes.

2.2.1   Regions of Interest and Levels of Detail

The current requirements of an application at client side dealing with raster imagery can be appropriately described by the concept of *Regions of Interest* (RoI) and *Levels of Detail* (LoD). RoIs are an already accepted principle in image communication [Yin04; San04a; Hu04; JO04], but also in other research fields, as image rendering [VRM97; Lue02] or information visualization [Bed04; Gut04]. In general, the image respectively the information space is partitioned into multiple *Regions of Interest*. However, to determine the specific interest for a particular RoI, in literature often simple schemes founded on quality by predetermined [JPG02b] or adapted values [Wie01; Hu04], or specific image content [Dol01; EM02] have been proposed. In any event, such schemes are not sufficient for a detailed and generic description of the requirements.

To achieve a reasonable description, the term *Level of Detail* is applied. LoDs have their origin in 3D-image rendering, where they have been successfully applied to render objects far from the viewer with less detail [Lue02]. Although also used by FURNAS [Fur86] in a similar manner, the idea has been ported by RAUSCHENBACH [Rau98b; Rau98a; Rau99b; Rau00] to describe image transmission. As shown in this thesis, it is also appropriate to describe the requirements of other applications.

An LoD is basically a 4-tuple consisting of the attributes *x-resolution* ($0 \leq$ *x-resolution* ≤ 1), *y-resolution*, ($0 \leq$ *y-resolution* ≤ 1), numerical *accuracy* ($0 \leq accuracy \leq img_a$) and *component* ($0 \leq component \leq img_c$) located in a 4-dimensional euclidian *LoD-space*. An arbitrary combination of the four attributes indicates the particular interest to this region. The origin of the LoD-space refers to a RoI for which no belonging data is considered ($LoD(0,0,0,0)$). A *final-LoD* of $LoD(1,1,img_a,img_c)$ indicates that all available data is used to represent the RoI.

However, additional statements determining the manner of how to achieve a certain LoD are required. In interactive environments the LoD is subject to dynamic changes, which especially influences the transmission of image data. To regard this, an LoD is subdivided into a *target-LoD* determining the current interest and a *state-LoD* representing the already provided degree of detail. To avoid redundancies while switching from state- to target-LoD, *hierarchical LoDs* are of great importance. They are founded on the idea that starting from a certain hierarchy level, only incremental data, the *LoD-delta*, is needed to achieve higher LoDs. This principle leads to a *progressive refinement* of the content and is commonly called *detail on demand*. Contrary, a new target-LoD residing at a lower hierarchy level than the current state-LoD may easily be extracted from the available data.

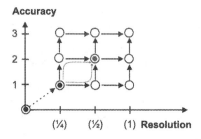

Figure 2.2: *Supported LoD-combinations (circles) and refinement paths (arrows) of a given LoD-hierarchy. To achieve a certain LoD different paths may be possible (arrows and dot).*

As progressive refinement only describes the ability to achieve a certain target-LoD, it does not provide statements for a deterministic proceeding of the enhancement. This is basically due to the structure of the provided LoD-hierarchy (cf. Figure 2.2) causing the following two problems:

1. Not all LoD combinations and refinement paths may be supported.

2. To achieve a certain LoD, different paths may be possible .

The first point strongly depends on the provided LoD-hierarchy and can only be solved by introducing a more suitable hierarchy. Thereby, the support increases with the number of supported values for each LoD-attribute and *orthogonality* between attributes. RAUSCHENBACH states that ambiguities imposed by the second point can be overcome by the prioritization of the LoD-axes. Based on this, the different refinement steps are always determined by a unique path through the hierarchy.

2.2.2   Brief history to scalable image compression

To reduce the long response rates in remote image browsing, *progressive image transmission* techniques (PIT) have been developed. The basic idea is to organize the data-stream in such a way that the decoding of a truncated stream leads to a restored image with less detail. Thus, content previews can be presented during a still running transmission. This principle is known as *streaming*.

First PITs have been proposed in the late 70s and 80s [Tan79; Sam84; San84]. At this time *Quadtrees* [Sam84] and their enhancement *Bitwise Condensed Quadtrees* (BCQ) [Dür91] providing progression with regard to resolution and accuracy were of main importance. In 1984, Lohscheller [Loh84] proposed the first progressive image communication scheme based on the selected transmission of DCT-coefficients.

After the focus of the research community shifted to achieve higher compression ratios by proposing *lossy* compression schemes, leading to the development of the *JPEG-standard* [JPG94; JPG96], *wavelet-* [Sha93; Sai96b] or *fractal-based approaches* [Bar93], the advent of the WWW drew back attention to progressive compression schemes. Due to their provided features especially wavelet-based approaches have been of main interest. They opened the horizon for *scalable image compression*.

A scalable compression technique is one that allows compressing the data once and then decompressing it at multiple data rates, spatial resolutions, and/or quality. (LIN ET AL. [Lin01])

Such a compression technique is very desirable from the communication viewpoint as it allows data delivery depending on the kind of service chosen by the user without having to pass the compression process for the image again. Thus, scalability is a property of the *embedded data-stream* itself [Sha93]. Common to all scalable codecs is the characteristic to place the most important information at the beginning of the stream followed by less important refinement data. Thus, all encodings of an image at low bit-rates are an integral part of the data-stream created for a higher bit-rate. However, to be able to take advantage of this property, it must be guaranteed that the bitstream can be decoded, even when truncated.

The challenge in scalable coding is to build a stream progressively decodable at different LoDs without any significant loss in performance by comparison to non-scalable streams. In other words, scalable coding is efficient if the stream does not contain data redundant to any of the strived LoDs. This has been achieved by sophisticated schemes such as SPIHT [Sai96b] or the modern image coding standard JPEG2000 [JPG02a], often stated as references for the evaluation of new techniques.

Nowadays, the research interest shifts more and more to *scalable video compression* schemes [Li01; Lin01; Yu02; Sec04; Mac05]. Beside embedded codecs [She99; Kim00], layered (MPEG-4 [Ebr00] and H.263+ [Cot98]) or hybrid scalability techniques (Fine Grain Scalability (FGS) mode of MPEG-4 [Li01]) are of interest.

The foundation of all valuable proposals to scalable image and video coding is the transfer of the source signal into another representation. Such transformations are reviewed in the following section.

2.2.3   Important image transformations

A reasonable image transformation transfers the pixel data into a domain in which they can be more efficiently encoded. The aim is to decorrelate the source data into parts with different properties, e.g. regarding their contribution to the visual perception of the content. The result are *transformation coefficients*. Although there are many approaches to transfer an image into a scalable representation [Fro03; Ven05], this section focusses on the two most accepted and applied transformations; *Discrete Cosine Transform* and *Discrete Wavelet Transform*.

2.2.3.1   Discrete Cosine Transform (DCT)

The DCT [Ahm74] may be regarded as a discrete-time version of the Fourier-Cosine series. It is a close relative of DFT, a technique for converting a signal into elementary frequency components. The DCT may be computed with a *Fast Fourier Transform* (FFT) like algorithm in $O(n \log n)$ operations. Unlike DFT, DCT is real-valued and provides a better approximation of a signal with fewer coefficients. A DCT represents a signal by a linear combination of cosine functions, and thus, transfers the signal from spatial to frequency domain. As complexity of the DCT increases with its scope, almost all known DCT codecs partition the image in 8×8 independent pixel blocks and apply a limited number of basis functions (64).

Within each block in transformation domain, coefficients at top left corner have the highest values and bottom right has the lowest. Thus, they provide a measure of the energy present at different spatial frequencies in the belonging region. The coefficient with lowest spatial frequency and highest variance value is considered as *DC coefficient*. It is proportional to the average brightness of the whole block. Arranged from top-left to bottom right, all other *AC coefficients* represent increasing spatial frequencies represented by the associated basis functions.

In principle, DCT (Equation C.1) introduces no loss to the source image samples, it only transforms the input data. However, a quantizer might then be applied to the coefficients to limit their range of possible value and to enhance compression efficiency. If quantization has been applied, coefficients are multiplied by the respective quantization value before reconstructing the original pixel values by applying the inverse DCT (IDCT) (Equation C.2).

Despite all the advantages of DCT transformation namely simplicity and widespread availability, these are not without their shortcomings. The most important may be the worse quality if strong quantization has been applied.

2.2.3.2   Discrete Wavelet Transform (DWT)

In recent years, image compression has been largely dominated by the use of wavelet-based transform coding techniques. However, first proposals have already been introduced in the beginning of the last century [Haa10]. In many applications wavelet-based schemes, also referred as *subband coding* (SBC), outperform other coding schemes like those based on DCT. Since there is no need to block the input image and its basis functions have variable length, wavelet coding schemes avoid blocking artifacts at higher compression ratios. In addition, they are better matched to characteristics of the Human Visual System (HVS). Because of their inherent multiresolution nature [Mal89], wavelet coding schemes have two main advantages: they are highly scalable and a fully embedded bitstream can be easily generated.

The main contribution of wavelet theory and multiresolution analysis is that it provides an elegant framework in which both anomalies and trends can be analyzed on an equal footing (SHAPIRO [Sha93])

Wavelets are functions that obey certain orthogonality, smoothness, and self-similarity criteria. Those properties are significant for image compression, because when applied to imagery, the resulting function is highly localized both in spatial and frequency content.

The fundamental concept behind *Subband Coding* is to split up the frequency band of a signal[1] and then to filter each subband accurately matching the statistics of the band. The process may also be iterated to obtain higher order decomposition filter trees. SBC has been applied in image coding due to its inherent advantage to access and handle subbands independently [Woo86]. In image compression separable transforms implemented by two 1D-filters instead of one 2D-filters are frequently used [Say00].

There are several ways to decompose a signal into various subbands. These include uniform decomposition, octave-band decomposition, and adaptive decomposition [Vet95]. Out of these, the non-uniform octave-band decomposition is the one most commonly used.

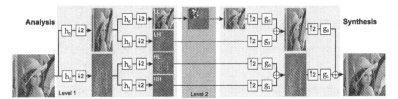

Figure 2.3: *Filter bank structure of a 2-level dyadic DWT. The structure of the second level is equal to the first level. Input of the second level is the sub-sampled image which has been low-pass filtered in both directions.*

Since 1990, methods very similar and closely related to SBC have been proposed by various researchers under the name of *Wavelet Coding* (WC) using filters specifically designed for this purpose. It can be thought of as a filter bank through which the original image is passed. The filters in the bank, which are computed from the selected wavelet function, are either low-pass (h_0) or high-pass (h_1) filters. The image is first filtered in the horizontal direction by both the low-pass and high-pass filters (cf. Figure 2.3). In case of the *dyadic DWT*, each of the resulting images is then sub-sampled by a factor of 2 in the horizontal direction. This can simply be accomplished by deleting alternate samples. These images are then filtered vertically by both the low-pass and high-pass filters. The resulting four images are then sub-sampled in the vertical direction by a factor of two. Thus, the transform produces four images: one that has been high-pass filtered in both directions (HH), one that has been high-pass filtered horizontally and low-pass filtered vertically (HL), one that has been low-pass filtered horizontally and high-pass filtered vertically (LH), and one that has been low-pass filtered in both directions (LL). This process may

---

[1] An image in this case.

be repeated by further processing the LL-image and leaving the high-pass output at each level without further modification. As for DCT, the transformation coefficients result may be quantized to reduce the overall amount of information.

This procedure can be reversed by applying the Inverse DWT (IDWT) with the respective reconstruction filters g_0, g_1. Up-sampling is performed by including a zero between two existing samples of the reconstructed image.

Such a transformation decomposes an image into a multi-frequency channel representation. The high-pass filtered images appear much like edge maps. They typically have strong responses only where significant image variation exists in the direction of the high-pass filter. The image belonging to the LL-band appears much like the original. In fact, it simply represents the image in reduced resolution and shares many of its essential statistical properties. The decomposed image may be represented by a multiresolution pyramid as shown in Figure C.1.

2.2.4   Selected scalable image compression schemes

This section reviews selected scalable image compression schemes founded on DCT or DWT. Due to the relevance for this thesis, their properties regarding the required *computing power* and achieved *compression performance* are in focus. To ease comparison, their respective qualities are stated in relation to the well established JPEG codec. The presented values represent results stated in [San00; SC02] for complexity and [Xio99; Foo00; San00; Yu02; SC02; Grg04] for compression performance. However, they may only be seen as a rough estimation and might differ for different hardware, implementations, and image contents [Chr00]. As the performance of DCT- and DWT-based approaches is often similar at bit-rates larger than $1bpp$, the provided performance values refer to a compression ratio of $0.25bpp$. They have been achieved by applying an objective quality measure (PSNR). However, similar results have been reported by conducting subjective tests [Grg04]. As some applications, e.g. in medicine [Clu00], demand the delivery of imagery without any loss in details, this property is also considered. Of crucial interest is also the respectively provided LoD-hierarchy. Possible values for *x-* and *y-resolution* are stated by sub-sampling factors.

2.2.4.1   The JPEG-standard

Transformation	Complexity		Performance	Lossy
DCT	100%		100%	yes

Level of Detail				
X	Y	Accuracy	Component	Orthogonality
1	1	1	usually Y, C_r, C_b	all

JPEG is the first established international digital compression standard for continuous-tone (multilevel) still images, both monochrome and color [Wal91; Pen93; JPG94] and has been developed to solve problems imposed by the emerging Multimedia-era regarding storage and transmission. This section addresses selected issues of the codec. A detailed explanation of the standard can be found in [Pen93].

The whole standard consists of different parts and basically describes 4 modes of operation: *sequential/baseline, progressive, hierarchical* and *lossless*. Unfortunately, the

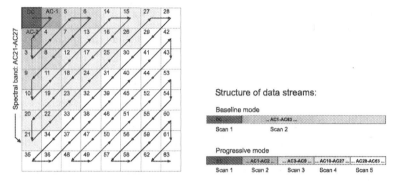

Figure 2.4: *ZigZag-traversing of the DCT coefficients (left) and the structure of the resulting 1D-sequence (right) for a single 8x8 block.*

respective codecs are founded on different approaches and cannot be arbitrarily combined. Of interest for this thesis are the first three modes, whereby statements regarding progressive and hierarchical mode can be found in Appendix C.3.

The JPEG - baseline mode   is the simplest of all modes and must be supported by all compliant decoders. The image is scanned from left to right and top to bottom and consists of the following incremental steps:

Intercomponent transform (optional): By assuming ordinary RGB color images as input their components are converted into a luminance component and two chrominance components. Additional sub-sampling of the color components is applied to enhance performance.

Transformation: JPEG applies the DCT as already described in Section 2.2.3.1.

Quantization: Each block of DCT-coefficients is quantized using a *uniform scalar quantizer*. Its quantization scheme involves frequency selectivity in the HVS model by incorporating it into the quantization matrix.

Traversing: To take advantage of coefficients quantized as zeros, each block is re-ordered using a ZigZag pattern to form a 1D sequence (cf. Figure 2.4). This rearranges the coefficients in approximately decreasing order of their average energies to create large runs of zero values. Each DC coefficient is separated from the AC coefficients and is coded with all other DC coefficients using *Differential Pulse Code Modulation* (DPCM).

Entropy coding: The final encoding step applies entropy coding such as Huffman coding on both AC and DC coefficients.

At the decoder side, this process is repeated in reverse order by applying the respective inverse operations.

Support for LoD: A baseline JPEG-encoded image is a data-stream consisting of separate sequences of DC and AC coefficients for each color component. Beside the inherent separation of the color components, it only supports one resolution and accuracy level. It does not produce flexible data-streams.

2.2.4.2   Embedded Zerotree Wavelet coder (EZW)

Transformation	Complexity	Performance	Lossy
DWT	$600 - 800\%$	$+6\%$	often

Level of Detail				
X	Y	Accuracy	Component	**Orthogonality**
$(1,...,2^n)$	$(1,...,2^n)$	number of bit-planes	-	$\frac{1}{2}Y \leq X \leq 2Y$, $\text{Å}{\rightarrow}(\text{X/Y})$

This coding technique proposed by SHAPIRO [Sha93] is a DWT-based scalar quantization scheme with successive approximation adaptive arithmetic coding. It provides excellent compression performance and takes advantage of self-similarity of wavelet coefficients in scale and space.

The main contribution of EZW is to efficiently encode the coefficients resulting from the DWT. To achieve this, EZW applies the idea of a significance map as an indication to whether a particular coefficient is more or less *significant* with regard to a given threshold T.[2] Due to the hypothesis of *decaying spectrum*, it is likely that for an insignificant wavelet coefficient at a coarse scale (*parent*), all coefficients of the same orientation at the same spatial location at next finer scales (*children*) are also insignificant with respect to T. The compression depends on the existence of *zerotrees*, which are exponentially growing *quad-trees* of coefficients that are insignificant according to T. If such trees are found, all coefficients are encoded by a single symbol assigned to the *zerotree root*. This gives considerable compression as compared to JPEG. The parent/child relationship is depicted in Figure 2.5/left.

The whole process is implemented by passes. For each pass, a single threshold for all the wavelet coefficients is chosen. If a wavelet coefficient is larger than the threshold, it is encoded and removed; if it is smaller, it is left for the next pass. When all the wavelet coefficients have been visited from coarser to finer subbands using a ZigZag scanning analogous to DCT-based transforms (cf. Figure 2.5/right), the threshold is lowered, and the image is scanned again to add more detail to the already encoded data. This process is repeated until the stopping threshold has been reached or all coefficients have been handled.

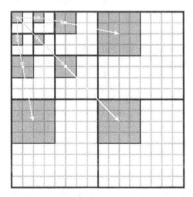 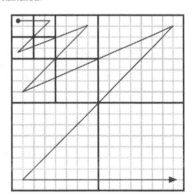

Figure 2.5: *Parent/Child relationships within zerotrees (left) and the traversing order of the DWT subbands (right).*

---

[2] A threshold might be chosen so as to correspond to a certain bit-plane.

Support for LoD: It is easy to see that this algorithm results in an embedded data-stream scalable at quality and resolution. Nevertheless, due to the application of the dyadic decomposition of the DWT there is a dependence between the LoD attributes *x*- and *y-resolution*. Due to bit-plane-wise traversal of all octave bands it is further not possible to limit the quality refinement to certain octave bands. Thus, the refinement order is determined by accuracy (A) →resolution (X/Y). Although EZW may be applied to multi-component images, SHAPIRO did not consider this in his original contribution [Sha93].

EZW laid the foundation of sophisticated wavelet coders as the *MPG-4: visual texture coding* standard (VTC) [Li01] or *Set Partitioning in Hierarchical Trees* (SPIHT) proposed by SAID AND PEARLMAN [Sai96b; Sai96a]. Especially SPIHT can perform better at higher compression ratios than EZW. Thereby the term "hierarchical trees" refers to similar tree structures as defined in EZW and "set partitioning" to an effective way of forming large sets of insignificant coefficients. Different increments supporting spatial [Dan03] or object scalability [Dan04] have been proposed.

2.2.4.3   The JPEG2000-standard

Transformation	Complexity		Performance	Lossy
DWT	$300 - 600\%$		$+15\%$	often

Level of Detail				
X	Y	Accuracy	Component	Orthogonality
$(1, ..., 2^n)$	$(1, ..., 2^n)$	number of quality layers	usually Y, C_r, C_b	$\frac{1}{2}Y \leq X \leq 2Y$

The success of wavelet-based image compression lead in 2000 to a new ISO/ITU-T standard for still image coding – JPEG2000 [JPG02a]. The codec is based on the DWT, scalar quantization, context modeling, arithmetic coding, and post-compression rate allocation of the source image. Although there are many parts of the standard, the review is constrained to the baseline mode.

JPEG2000 is much more than a compression algorithm, opening up new paradigms for interacting with digital imagery. (TAUBMAN AND MARCELLIN [Tau02b])

The JPEG2000-baseline mode   consists of 4 main steps: *color transformation, DWT, arithmetical encoding*, and *data-stream organization*. JPEG2000 also allows an image to be divided into smaller sub-images, known as *tiles*. If tiling is involved, each tile is disjoined from each other and is processed as an independent sub-image. The most important steps with regard to scalability is the encoding of each image component by applying the DWT, *Embedded Block Coding with Optimized Truncation* (EBCOT) [Tau99], and *data-stream organization*. The DWT decorrelates each image component by separating detail and approximation. EBCOT is applied to reduce remaining redundancies based on disjoint blocks. Each block can be efficiently accessed within the final data-stream.

Discrete Wavelet Transform: d_{max} analysis stages ($0 \leq d_{max} \leq 32$), labeled $d = 1, 2, ..., d_{max}$, decompose a component into $3d_{max} + 1$ subbands, labeled $LL_{d_{max}}$ and LH_d, HL_d and HH_d (cf. Figures 2.3 and C.1). A value of $d_{max} = 0$ refers to pixel domain, which means that no decomposition has been applied. Due to the underlying dyadic decomposition, subband dimensions at stage d are half the size of stage $(d - 1)$, which is $\frac{1}{2^d}$ of the image dimensions in pixel domain. Contrary, each synthesis stage increases the resolution of the reconstructed image by a factor of 2. This results in $(d_{max}+1)$ inherent image resolutions r, $0 \leq r \leq d_{max}$, whereby a value of $r = 0$ refers to the lowest resolution and r_{max} to pixel domain. Each inherent image resolution r is represented by the associated $LL_{d_{max}-r}$ subband of the decomposition scheme. To reconstruct a certain resolution level $r > 0$, all higher decomposition stages $d, d_{max} - r < d \leq d_{max}$, must be considered. Due to this, coefficients belonging to sub-bands at different decomposition levels interleave during the reconstruction of the image and have a different spatial influence. The DWT may be performed with either reversible filters, which provide for lossless coding, or non-reversible bi-orthogonal filters, for higher compression.

Embedded Block Coding with Optimized Truncation: For the sake of flexibility JPEG2000 encodes values of the wavelet coefficients for each subband independently. The applied principle is based on a proposal of TAUBMAN [Tau94; Tau99]. Thereby, each subband is divided into relatively small rectangular blocks of wavelet coefficients, known as *code-blocks*, and entropy coded using *context modeling* and *bit-plane arithmetic coding*. EBCOT generates finally embedded bitstreams separately for each bit-plane and code-block. These bitstreams contribute to the reconstruction of a limited pixel area and can be independently truncated to different lengths. Although each code-block is coded independently, their bitstreams are not explicitly identified within a JPEG2000 data-stream. Instead, code-blocks are collected into larger groupings known as *precincts*. This partition has no impact on the transformation or coding of image samples; it serves only to organize code-blocks.

Data-stream organization: The final data-stream is organized by applying the concept of *quality layers*. Each precinct is represented as a collection of *packets*, with one packet including an incremental contribution from each of its code-blocks assigned to a certain layer determined by a post-compression *rate allocation*. A final JPEG2000-encoded image consists of a concatenated list of packets and is independent of the encoder structure.

The compression performance of JPEG2000 for low bit-rates is much better than those achieved by JPEG or EZW. Although only a small objective increase compared to JPEG has been stated, even better results are achieved by considering subjective testing. As stated by CHINEN AND CHIEN [CC000] a performance enhancement of up to 53% (0.2bpp) has been quantified (36% (0.5bpp), 11% (1bpp)).

Support for LoD: Scalability is a central concept in JPEG2000. The baseline mode already supports the refinement of all LoD attributes. Due to the relevance of JPEG2000 for this thesis, support for LoDs is examined in detail in Section 2.4.

2.2.5   Regions of Interest in scalable image compression

Beside the ability to provide general scalability for the whole image, some compression schemes provide additional support for RoIs. The general idea is to place data contributing to the reconstruction of the RoI first in the data-stream. This results in an *interest ordered* data-stream where any valid stream termination leads to an image where the RoI is coded to a higher quality than the background.

All techniques proposed in literature can be basically assigned to one of two basic approaches – static or dynamic RoI coding. In case that a technique prioritizes the RoI data during the image compression process, it leads to *static RoIs*. This is due to the reason that these regions and their parameters are fixed and cannot be altered afterwards. Contrary, *dynamic RoIs* may be defined or re-parameterized as often as required. This is achieved by reordering the encoded data and implements the paradigm: *Compress Once: Decompress Many Ways* introduced by TAUBMAN AND MARCELLIN [Tau01, p.410]. Due to their flexible and modular structure, data-streams resulting from scalable compression are well-suited for such rearrange-ments. Thereby, properties of image compression and streaming are exploited. The literal rearrangements are mostly done by transcoding units[3]. As problems belonging to the rearrangement are discussed in the next chapter, the respective solutions are neglected for the following review.

Techniques to encode static or dynamic RoIs often apply same principles to achieve a target-LoD. Interestingly, common to many scalable compression schemes is the property that the image transform mainly influences the flexibility of the LoD-hierarchy. Support of RoIs is mainly achieved by exploiting features of the strate-gies used to further encode the resulting transformation coefficients. This also applies for data selection.

Data selection: To reconstruct a certain spatial image region the belonging trans-formation coefficients, further on labeled *RoI elements*, must be selected. To achieve this, in literature two different approaches have been proposed either based on (1) single or (2) groups of coefficients.

Due to the properties of block-based DCT transformations, all coefficients of a cer-tain block are needed to fully reconstruct the belonging pixel region. Thus, recon-struction must always be accomplished block-wise in either transformation as well as spatial domain. Amendment 3 of the JPEG standard [JPG96] describes such a technique for progressive mode. Here a single scan is limited to blocks belonging to the RoI. Similar concepts have been proposed for JPEG2000 for different stages of the compression pipeline, either based on code-blocks [Tau01; Tau02b; Tau02a] or packets [Des01; JO04; San04a]. Working on blocks is most effective when hand-ling large images with relatively small data containers [Tau01].

A finer approximation of the RoI shape can be accomplished by using single DWT-coefficients. As each coding scheme applies different principles for coefficient coding, RoI support strongly depends on the particular approach EZW [Sig97; Rau99a; Rau99b; Rau00; Alb00], SPIHT [Nis98; Par02; Wu02; Yin04], or JPEG2000 [JPG02a; JPG02b; Gro01; Ask02; Liu02; Liu03c]. Also hybrid schemes applying the coefficient- and block-based approach have been proposed for JPEG2000 [SC99; Ngu02a; Tai02]. However, accessing single coefficients is costly in terms comput-ing power and often imposes a redundant data handling [SC99].

X- and Y-Resolution: In literature only a few proposals address reduction in resolu-tion. This could be due to the limited applicability of the resulting visual represen-tation, as such single RoI would disrupt the regular arrangement within the pixel domain. However, certain applications require such a feature (e.g. the rectangular FishEye-View introduced in Chapter 4).

The proposal of RAUSCHENBACH [Rau99a; Rau99b; Rau00] is based on EZW and a coefficient-wise partition in one or multiple RoIs. Depending on current settings the RoI coefficients may only be refined up to a certain resolution. This principle is similar to the one proposed by SIGNORONI AND LEONARDI [Sig97] for static

---

[3]T_s, T_c in the proposed communication scheme.

encoding. Another technique based on SPIHT has been proposed by ATSUMI AND FARVARDIN [Ats98].

Refinement in resolution for imagery encoded with JPEG2000 has been shown by DESHPANDE AND ZENG [Des01]. Their approach is based in the selection of data packets. As each packet contains data contributing to the reconstruction of a particular image resolution, only certain packets must be selected to achieve the desired resolution.

Quality: Beside some rather different techniques based on DCT [JPG96; Zha96] and DWT [Sha96; Wu02], the most frequently applied approach for refinement of a RoI in quality is *bit-plane shifting*. This principle is based on the fact that quality increases with higher accuracy of the coefficients values and the idea that most significant bit-planes are handled and stored first in embedded bitstreams. Thus, RoI coefficients are up-scaled in a manner so as to be of higher value than remaining coefficients.

Especially for medical imagery, SIGNORONI AND LEONARDI [Sig97] proposed to multiply RoI elements by certain scaling factors before being encoded with EZW. ALBANESI ET AL. [Alb00] enhanced the resulting compression performance by applying adaptive quantization to RoI and background coefficients using *Contrast Adaptive Thresholding* (CAT).

To achieve a lossless RoI and lossy background, NISTER AND CHRISTOPOULOUS [Nis98] applied a combination of the *S+P transform* [Sai96b] and SPIHT. First the whole image is encoded and some bitplanes are truncated to achieve a certain data-rate. In a second step, the bit-planes of all RoI elements are encoded with a modified SPIHT algorithm. Because of the compression performance being not sufficient, PARK&PARK [Par02] mixed bit-planes of RoI and non-RoI coefficients by using large *multi-lists*. A method similar to this, but overcoming the need for such lists has been proposed by YIN ET AL. [Yin04].

Many different ideas for region-based quality-refinement for JPEG200-encoded imagery have been proposed. The standard itself describes two different techniques: *max-shift* [JPG02a; Ask02] and *scaling method* [JPG02b]. While the general principle to up-shift the RoI elements is basically the same, the principles to identify and down-shift them during decoding are completely different. A method how to select an optimal shifting value has been proposed in [Gro01]. This, however, leads to a decrease in compression performance [Gro01], and requirements regarding bandwidth can only be met if bit-planes belonging to background values are truncated [Bra03a; Bra03b]. A technique founded on max-shift and the adaptation of the data-stream order can be found in [Hu04].

An different approach proposed by TAUBMAN AND MARCELLIN is the *implicit method* [Tau01]. Here the distortion cost function of code-blocks is modified so as to render RoI code-blocks and their embedded bitstreams more important. This principle is similar to an upshift of the respective coefficient values. A combination of max-shift and implicit method considering only RoI coefficients, has been proposed in [Ngu02a] and [Tai02]. By truncating bit-planes belonging to background coefficients similar to [Bra03a], the approach of TAI ET AL. [Tai02] achieves even better bit-rates. Similar to the implicit method, DESHPANDE AND ZENG [Des01] and later on SANCHEZ ET AL. [San04a] proposed a method based on the handling of multiple instead of single bitplanes. Their proposal is founded on packets.

Beside the mentioned techniques compliant to the JPEG2000 standard, there are many other JPEG2000-based approaches [Ngu01; Ngu02b; Liu02; Wan02b; Wan02a;

Ngu03a; Ngu03b; Liu03c]. Because they require certain modifications to a compliant decoder, they are not further examined.

Component: Despite contributions dedicated to a certain standard [JPG96] or application subject [Yin04], many of the proposals to RoI coding do not consider multiple components. Nevertheless, many of the reviewed approaches seem to be able to process multi-component imagery by handling each component independently.

2.2.6   Summary of related work

Scalable compression is the key feature for adapted and flexible image delivery in interactive environments. Due to its beneficial properties, the majority of such codecs apply the DWT as image transformation. As a result the produced data-streams have a modular structure and provide flexible LoD-hierarchies. Although DWT-based schemes are more complex than DCT-based schemes [SC02], they provide better compression performance [Yu02; Grg04]. *The JPEG2000 standard represents the State of Art in scalable image compression.*

Regarding the support of RoIs, there are two different approaches: *static* and *dynamic RoIs*. Due to the reason their capability to adapt to changing demands, dynamic RoIs are more suited in interactive environments. However, both approaches apply similar concepts to support detail refinement: either single or blocks of coefficients are refined by single or multiple bitplanes at each transmission step. Due to the less demanding access, dynamic RoI support for JPEG2000-encoded imagery is mostly achieved by blocks of coefficients.

2.3   Higher-order spatial access in JPEG2000 data-streams

The goal of this chapter is to achieve an appropriate image compression paired with a demand-driven image streaming in mobile environments. As revealed in the discussion of related work, JPEG2000 provides besides best compression performance, the ability to support dynamic RoIs and a flexible LoD-hierarchy. Thereby, most of the reviewed RoI techniques for JPEG2000-data handle groups of wavelet coefficients included in key elements of the data-stream. This feature is commonly called *Random spatial access* (RSA) and can be defined as: *the option to independently access and process portions of a data-stream contributing to the reconstruction of a particular image region at a certain LoD.* Although, many of the RoI approaches exploit the option that the encoded data is encapsulated in *data containers*, a description of RSA based on properties common to all key elements is still missing.

The goal of this section is to uniformly describe the RSA feature for the 3 key elements of JPEG2000 data-streams: *code-blocks*, *precincts* and *tiles*. Thus, it will be possible to apply their properties regarding the RoI/LoD support by a higher-order *generic key element*. As shown later on, this element is a foundation of a set-based formalism to determine handling and streaming of dynamic RoIs.

2.3.1   Key elements for random spatial access

In addition to the brief description of the JPEG2000 standard in Section 2.2.4.3, in this section, the different key elements for RSA are further explained and logic structures enabling access and showing similarities are introduced. Since code-block-, precinct- and tile-partition strongly depend on the position of the image onto the image canvas, this principle is described first.

The spatial extent of an source image, img, is determined by values $[s_1, s_2]$ with $s_1 \geq 1$, $s_2 \geq 1$. For the sake of flexibility JPEG2000 applies the concept of an *image canvas* which may be described as a rectangular area with dimensions $[f_1, f_2]$ with $1 \leq f_1, f_2 < 2^{32}$. As depicted in Figure 2.6, the position of the image onto the canvas is determined by an image offset, $[e_1, e_2]$, with $0 \leq e_1, e_2 < 2^{32} - 1$, whereby $s_1 = f_1 - e_1$, $s_2 = f_2 - e_2$ applies. Canvas dimensions as well as image offset may vary depending on the applied intercomponent transform (cf. Section D.1).

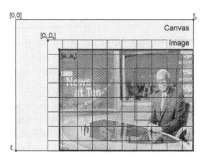

Figure 2.6: *The JPEG2000 image canvas.*

Code-blocks   Since each code-block has only a local influence and is coded independently, it contributes to a limited and predetermined region only. Thus, a RoI can be completely described by all belonging code-blocks residing at the different decomposition levels. As shown in Figure 2.7/left, certain code-blocks from subbands LH_d, HL_d and HH_d contribute to exactly the same region within image resolution LL_{d-1}. Because each takes a part of the information needed to fully reconstruct this region, it is reasonable to centralize the access to these structures. This can be done, by considering such a coherent code-block triple as one logical structure $cbt_{col,row,r}$, whereby r stands for the image resolution that can be reconstructed based on level $r - 1$ and details from subbands of decomposition level $d = d_{max} - r + 1$. Although there is only one subband $LL_{d_{max}}$ to reconstruct resolution level $r = 0$, this structure may also be used to access single code-blocks $cbd_{max,LL_{d_{max}},col,row}$ residing at the lowest level of the multiresolution hierarchy.

Based on this, the set of all code-block triples CBT_r directly contributing to the reconstruction of image resolution r may be described by:

$CBT_r = \{cbt_{col,row,r} | 1 \leq col \leq cn_r, 1 \leq row \leq cm_r\}$, with

$cn_r \ldots$ number of code-block columns of one belonging subband,

$cm_r \ldots$ number of code-block rows of one belonging subband,

Concrete values for cn_r and cm_r depend on image dimensions, resolution levels, and nominal code-block dimensions. Sections D.2 serves to provide statements for the determination of these variables for completeness.

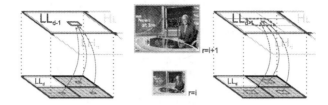

Figure 2.7: *Reconstruction of a local area in decomposition level (d-1) by using single code-block (left), or precinct structures (right) from level d. It can be seen that a precinct (dashed line) may contain more than one code-block.*

Precincts   Code-blocks are collected into precincts. These elements do not influence the transformation, and thus, share many code-block properties. However, there is the significant difference that a precinct is defined in that image resolution, which its comprised code-blocks from decomposition level d_{max} for $LL_{d_{max}}$ or d, $0 < d \leq d_{max}$, for LL_{d-1} directly reconstruct. This is illustrated in Figure 2.7/right for the later case. Despite the fact that a precinct may contain more than one code-block from each belonging subband, a single precinct appears as almost identical to the introduced code-block triple $cbt_{col,row,r}$. It contains all the data needed to enhance the resolution of the belonging region from $r - 1$ to r. To exploit this important similarity, a precinct structure $p_{col,row,r}$ for each precinct of the image is introduced. Since precincts are already defined in the belonging image resolution r, col and row represent the relative position of a precinct regarding other precincts at this resolution level.

A set P_r containing all precincts defined at image resolution r is determined by:

$$P_r = \{p_{col,row,r} | 1 \leq col \leq pn_r, 1 \leq row \leq pm_r\}$$

$pn_r \ldots$ number of precinct columns in resolution level r,

$pm_r \ldots$ number of precinct rows in resolution level r

As for code-blocks, precise values depend on image dimensions and encoding parameters and will be further explained in Section D.3. The general ability of precincts to support dynamic RoIs has been shown by the author in the contribution *"Flexible, dynamic and compliant region of interest coding in JPEG2000"* [Ros02].

Tiles   These elements are basically sub-images of the whole image. Each tile may be encoded with a different number of decomposition levels, code-block and precinct dimensions. Belonging data can be easily identified within the final bitstream.

To derive similarities from all element types, a tile is divided into its contributions to the reconstruction of the different inherent image resolutions. Thus, all tile data contributing to the reconstruction of resolution level r based on level $r - 1$, is labeled $t_{col,row,r}$. As already introduced for precincts, col and row represent the relative positions of a tile contribution regarding other tiles at level r.

We can refer to all tile contributions T_r for image resolution r by:

$$T_r = \{t_{col,row,r} | 1 \leq col \leq tn_r, 1 \leq row \leq tm_r\}$$

$tn_r \ldots$ number of tile columns in resolution level r,

$tm_r \ldots$ number of tile rows in resolution level r

The calculation of concrete values for tn_r and tm_r is further explained in Section D.4.

2.3.2   A generic key element for random spatial access

As each reviewed element type used to accomplish RSA, has been introduced with different intentions, it is seems impossible to derive higher-order statements valid for each type. However, regarding the support for RoIs, they have much in common. In this section a generic key element k with common properties regarding RSA is derived. For the remainder of this thesis, such an element is used wherever generic element properties are applicable.

The design of this element starts by forming sets of key elements, K_r, according to their contribution to the reconstruction of a certain resolution level r.

$$
\begin{aligned}
K_0 &= T_0 \ \cup \ P_0 \ \cup \ CBT_0 \\
K_1 &= T_1 \ \cup \ P_1 \ \cup \ CBT_1 \\
&\dotsi \\
K_{r_{max}} &= T_{r_{max}} \cup P_{r_{max}} \cup CBT_{r_{max}}
\end{aligned}
\tag{2.1}
$$

and a set for all key elements:

$$
M = K_0 \cup K_1 \cup \cdots \cup K_{r_{max}}.
\tag{2.2}
$$

Based on this, a *generic key element*, k, is defined as an element of M, $k \in M$.

Further on, each key element k is attributed in such a way as to allow the evaluation of these attributes and additional selection queries by using functions. Belonging to each key element k is an attribute tuple att consisting of attributes $(a_1, a_2, \ldots, a_6)$. Each attribute a_i is assumed to express nominal (a_0) or interval values $(a_1, \ldots, a_6)$ and is assigned its own domain A_i.

$$
\begin{aligned}
att \ &= \ (a_0, a_1, \ldots, a_6), \text{whereby} \\
&a_i \in A_i
\end{aligned}
\tag{2.3}
$$

Each attribute tuple consists of the following attributes:

a_0:   element type of the generic key element, $(A_0 = \{t, p, cbt\})$
a_1:   column offset of the reconstructed region in resolution level r
a_2:   row offset of the reconstructed region in resolution level r
a_3:   number of columns of belonging wavelet coefficients with regard to a single subband
a_4:   number of rows of belonging wavelet coefficients with regard to a single subband
a_5:   number of pixel columns in spatial domain the belonging wavelet coefficients contribute to
a_6:   number of pixel rows in spatial domain the belonging wavelet coefficients contribute to

Except for attribute a_0, range and definition of the attribute domains A_i depend on the respective key element and are basically determined by the definition of the elements within the standard. Appendices D.2-D.4 are dedicated to explain the influencing factors and to derive the respective domains for each element type independently. Due to the uniform description, values of attributes a_5 and a_6 can be easily calculated by using attributes a_3 and a_4 as follows:

$$
\begin{aligned}
a_5 &= 2^{r_{max}-r} a_3, \\
a_6 &= 2^{r_{max}-r} a_4
\end{aligned}
\tag{2.4}
$$

Although the calculation of their values is straightforward, the belonging attributes have been included to enhance the readability of related equations during the remainder of this thesis. It is also worth noting, that due to the properties of the applied wavelet kernels during synthesis, the spatial influence of code-blocks and precincts may be slightly larger than stated.

2.3.3   Functions on key elements for random spatial access

Although the generic key element is able to substitute elements of the data-streams, further considerations to the respective handling are required. This is covered in this section, which mostly consists in the introduction of basic functions able to identify and create sets of multiple elements. These functions are the foundation of a formalism, which, in the authors opinion, is the most compact and complete way to explain the selection of respective *data containers* in terms of key elements depending on a certain task. Based on particular sets of elements and their belonging attributes, containers of a given data-stream contributing to the reconstruction of a RoI at a certain LoD can be easily determined. As this process consists of multiple stages, functions to retrieve elements based on their attributes and vice versa must be provided.

To deliver the belonging attribute tuple att of a certain generic key element k, an attribute function $attrib$ is defined as follows

$$
att = attrib(k)
\tag{2.5}
$$

To be able to retrieve attribute tuples of more than one valid key element, this function is applied to sets. A set including all possible attribute tuples ATT may be stated as

$$
ATT = A_0 \times A_1 \times \cdots \times A_6
\tag{2.6}
$$

An enhanced function $attrib$, assigns to a set of key elements $K' \subseteq M$ the belonging set of attribute tuples $ATT' \subseteq ATT$.

$$
\begin{aligned}
ATT' &= & attrib(K') \\
&= & \{attrib(k)|\forall k \in K'\}
\end{aligned}
\tag{2.7}
$$

To be able to extract a set of key elements $K'' \subseteq M$ belonging to a given set of attribute tuples $ATT'' \subseteq ATT$, a function, *retrieve*, is defined as follows

$$K'' = retrieve(M, ATT'')$$
$$= \{k \in M | \forall attrib(k) \in ATT''\} \tag{2.8}$$

As shown in later chapters, only these basic functions are required to describe data selection for a variety of tasks. They are easy to implement.

2.3.4   Limited spatial access

One of the advantages of the EZW codec (cf. Section 2.2.4.2) is the exploitation of self similarity within the multiresolution decomposition scheme by zerotrees. A single tree with its anchor at $LL_{d_{max}}$ describes the full reconstruction of an independent and limited spatial region. As shown later on, this idea is the foundation for a number of effective operations in JPEG2000 domain and further on labeled as *limited spatial access* (LSA). To achieve LSA, however, elements belonging to a certain tree must be well selected (cf. Figure 2.5/left). Although JPEG2000 applies a different coding approach and does not inherently provide similar tree structures, LSA can also be supported by the reviewed key elements. This topic has been addressed by the author in *"Limited spatial access in JPEG2000 for remote image editing"* [Ros04a] and is now explained in detail.

The general characteristic of LSA in the dyadic DWT is that the amount of contributing wavelet coefficients decreases with each successive decomposition level by a factor of 2 in each direction. This is due to the multiresolution representation of the image (cf. Figure C.1) and may be depicted alternatively by a pyramid (cf. Figure 2.8). To construct such closed pyramid structures, the covered wavelet coefficients must be considered. Due to the different properties of the key elements, this is achieved in different manners and cannot described by the introduced generic element.

Code-blocks   The standard requires nominal code-block dimensions fixed across all resolutions. Thus, the respective number of coefficients for each pyramid level is accomplished by selecting one or multiple code-blocks. This basically leads to a pyramid with a decreasing number of blocks for each successive decomposition.

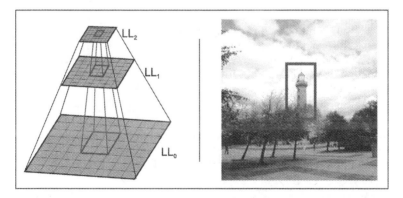

Figure 2.8: *Limited spatial access (left) applied to reconstruct a closed image region (right).*

Alternatively, the property that code-blocks are required to conform to precinct boundaries can be exploited. Thus, precinct dimensions are selected in such a way so as to control the actual code-block dimensions in each resolution. By assuming sufficiently large nominal code-block dimensions, it is, therefore, possible to construct pyramids with only one code-block per level by fully supporting LSA. Obviously, precinct dimensions must be chosen 2 times smaller for each successive decomposition step.

Precincts Similar to the second option to support LSA by code-blocks, the pyramid can be constructed by precincts only. To achieve this, a fixed spatial contribution in each direction is defined and required to be kept by all elements of a pyramid. As appropriate precinct dimensions may be selected for each resolution, this can be easily accomplished.

Tiles Each tile represents an independently processed rectangular region of the original image, and thus, inherently supports LSA without further modifications. However, contrary to code-blocks and precincts, each image tile may be decomposed with different parameters. Thus, the resulting multiresolution scheme of the whole image may be different from that shown in Figure 2.8 and C.1.

In either case, the result of introducing LSA into JPEG2000 is a collection of pyramids consisting of related data containers of a certain type, whereby each pyramid covers a different spatial region. This region can be fully restored by the belonging elements. LSA is an additional feature of the data-stream and must be introduced to be exploited. This can be achieved by steering the parametrization during the encoding of the image.

2.4   Levels of Detail in JPEG2000 data-streams

Dynamic RoIs for JPEG2000-encoded imagery can be implemented by exploiting the RSA feature of the standard. This section serves to show the provided LoD-hierarchy determined by valid LoD tuples and refinement paths between them. Thereby, the supported values of each LoD-attribute are of crucial interest.

X/Y-resolution: Possible values for these attributes depend strongly on the underlying transformation. Within the synthesis of the dyadic DWT, subbands resulting from decomposition stage $d + 1$ are required to be half the size of subbands at d. Thus, an image resolution LL_d represents the content at original resolution sub-sampled by factor 2^d in both directions. Due to this, image content can only be reconstructed at sub-sampling factors with powers of 2. JPEG2000 supports $0 \leq d \leq 32$ decomposition stages.

Accuracy: In JPEG2000 progressive refinement in terms of quality is accomplished by spreading encoded content of each code-block over q layers. The standard supports $1 \leq q < 2^{16}$ different layers, and thus, consecutive quality steps.

Components: JPEG2000 is able to process multi-component imagery. Legal values for the number of image components are $1 \leq components \leq 2^{14}$.

Scalability increases with the amount of supported values. However, this does not imply that they can be arbitrarily combined to valid LoD tuples. Unfortunately, there are dependencies between certain attributes.

Orthogonality: Within each consecutive decomposition step, the LL_d band is subdivided in both directions. Thus, x- as well as y-*resolution* strongly depend on each other. However, within the DWT information from subbands HL_d and LH_d has a strict orientation. Data belonging to one of this bands does reconstruct the image content in the respective direction only. This leads to a relaxation of the coupling, as x- and y-*resolution* are allowed varying by a factor of 2.

Data within a compliant JPEG2000 data-stream cannot be arranged in an arbitrary order. This imposes further dependencies between attributes. However, in image communication, data is often extracted and processed using arbitrary orders. In this case, those dependencies are resolved.

To be consistent with the defined LoD-space, it is also required that components are available at the same dimensions and encoded with equal parameter sets. Thus, we neglect a possible sub-sampling, or if applied to accomplish RSA, the option to encode tiles with different parameter sets.

Orthogonality is also the key for supported refinement paths, which only exist between adjacent and valid values of an LoD-axis (cf. Figure 2.2). Thereby each single refinement step must always lead to a valid LoD tuple. Violating this constraint would yield to tuples which cannot be assigned to the respective data-stream.

2.5   The performance of JPEG2000 in mobile environments

To justify the application of JPEG2000 in mobile environments, the codec must achieve better results compared to others. This especially applies for the two main limiting factors: the computing power consumed at client side and the required bandwidth during transmission.

Due to its complexity, JPEG2000 requires more processing power than JPEG. The first part of this section examines if this still applies for decompression considering the different options for scalability. Scalability, however, might also increase the size of the resulting data-stream. The second part provides additional measurements to compare the degree of scalability to compression performance. As the intercomponent transform is applied in a similar way for JPEG and JPEG2000, the LoD-attribute *component* is neglected for both kind of analysis.

2.5.1   Scalability vs. complexity

As scalability implies that often only partial data is processed, and thus less computing power is required, it is worth examining in detail. The provided measures refer to imagery encoded with JPEG2000 by applying a typical parameter set (5 decomposition stages, 8 layers, code-block dimensions: 2^6x2^6, precinct dimensions: 2^{15}x2^{15}, 1 tile). For fair comparison, images encoded with JPEG as well as JPEG2000 have been compressed at a target bitrate of approximately 1 bpp. For encoding images with JPEG, an implementation of the baseline mode provided by the independent JPEG group [Lan06] is used. The executed measurements have

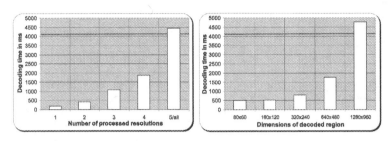

Figure 2.9: *Comparison of the complexity of the JPEG2000 decoding process considering spatial scalability regarding image resolution (left) and region (right). The solid line marks the constant performance of JPEG.*

been performed on a Dell Axim X50v (cf. Table B.1) to allow conclusions for current mobile hardware.

X/Y-resolution: These LoD-attributes strongly correspond to the number of reconstructed resolutions. If an image is to be restored at a certain resolution, the processing of data contributing to the reconstruction of higher resolutions is skipped. As shown in Figure 2.9/left, JPEG is only faster (6%) than JPEG2000 if the provided data-stream is fully decompressed. As soon as data belonging to higher resolutions is skipped, JPEG2000 achieves better results. It is already 2 times faster if only the highest resolution is omitted. Thereby decoding time increases exponentially with the numbers of processed resolutions. Only 5% of the time consumed by JPEG is needed to restore the smallest inherent resolution of the provided data-stream.

Accuracy: If only a limited number of layers is considered during decoding, data assigned to higher layers is not processed. The influence of partial decoding is depicted in Figure E.1, whereby a significant decrease in the required resources can be stated. JPEG2000 performs already 9% better for 7 and 35% better for 1 layer.

Random Spatial Access: A closed spatial region is restored by the synthesis of selected data containers contributing to the reconstruction of the respective region only. In the provided data-stream this is accomplished by code-blocks. As shown in Figure 2.9/right, decoding time decreases with the dimensions of the reconstructed image region. JPEG2000 requires only 50% of the resources consumed by JPEG, if a region spreading over half the original dimensions is to be decoded. For the smallest considered region the decoding is approximately 10 times faster. It can also be seen that the size of the region does not uniformly scale with decoding time. This is due to the nominal dimensions of code-blocks, which causes that often much more data than actually needed to restore a particular pixel region must be processed.

Another comparative review of the efforts needed to access spatial region within compliant JPEG2000 data-streams has been published in [Bra02]. The publication summarizes that for fast access tiles are the best opportunity followed by code-blocks and coefficients. Precincts have not been considered.

2.5.2   Scalability vs. performance

Scalability might increase the size of a data-stream. This is basically due to the fact that more data containers, each enriched with additional signalization information, are present. However, this does not imply, that data-streams supporting only a small number of valid LoD-attribute values are smallest. This section examines to which degree scalability can be included without significantly reducing compression performance. This also applies for the RSA/LSA feature. The provided results refer to the data-stream used for complexity measures.

X/Y-resolution: The number of inherent resolutions strongly influences the performance of the DWT. As depicted in Figure E.2 multiple decompositions are needed to efficiently decorrelate the image. Data-streams providing just the original resolution are by far larger than data-streams which are more scalable regarding resolution. However, the number of resolutions does not uniformly scale with the resulting performance. Above a certain threshold there is no further decrease in size. This is basically due to the properties of code-blocks which must cover a sufficiently large region to compress efficiently. Contrary, organization data within the stream increases with each additional resolution. This leads again to a decrease in compression performance and can be noticed by considering the differences between imagery with other dimensions. The respective threshold is reached faster for small images.

Accuracy: Contrary to the number of resolutions, the number of quality layers does not influence the decorrelation of data. However, with each additional layer the amount of data packets increases. As each packet includes additional header information, this leads to a slight decrease in compression performance. For many applications, this is negligible for the sake of scalability. For the layer range shown in Figure E.3 the size of the data-stream varies by only 0.6%. However, the amount of packets depends on the number of precincts and may be larger if more precincts are involved.

Random spatial access: Due to the fact that RSA can be achieved by each of the introduced elements, it is reasonable to examine their respective effect on the compression performance independently. As shown in Figure 2.10 and E.4 compression performance increases with element dimensions. The difference in the length of the resulting data-streams between code-blocks with small and large dimensions is approximately 40% (tiles: 60%). This shows that a suitable adjustment

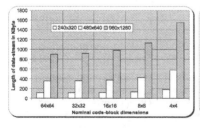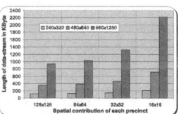

Figure 2.10: *Bandwidth required to reconstruct a spatial region of certain dimensions depending on the dimensions of code-blocks (RSA, left) or precincts (LSA, right).*

can heavily increase performance. Due to their strong relation, results achieved by code-blocks and precincts are similar. Small tiles compress significantly worse.

Although LSA can be achieved by all key elements, code-blocks must be sufficiently small to provide this feature. As shown in Figure 2.10, this goes along with a strong decrease in compression performance. Here, it is more eligible to accomplish LSA by precincts or tiles. Similar to RSA, it applies – *as larger element dimensions, as better the performance.* Thereby, the compression performance of precincts is similar to that of tiles (cf. Figures 2.10/right and E.4). However, precincts compress better than tiles at small spatial contributions required for granular spatial access (9% better for 16×16). Tiles are also susceptible to boundary artifacts at low bitrates [Tau02a; Tau02b], and thus, should only be applied where required.

2.6   Conclusion of the chapter

Scalable compression is the key feature for the creation of modular data-streams. Within these data-streams, the image content is separated in multiple dimensions. *JPEG2000 represents the State of Art in scalable image compression.*

The goal of a demand-driven image delivery can be achieved by *dynamic RoIs.* Thereby, the respective interest is determined by an *assigned LoD.* It is possible to progressively refine a certain LoD. To achieve this, the support of a flexible *LoD-hierarchy* is required.

The RSA feature of JPEG2000 is of crucial interest to access image content belonging to a certain RoI. It is achieved by certain *key elements* of the data-stream. These elements encapsulate data contributing to the reconstruction of a closed spatial region in multiple consecutive *data containers*, which can be easily accessed and independently processed. Each data containers adds to the LoD of the assigned RoI. Common properties of the key elements can be used to design a *generic key element* in order to ease the description of *higher-order spatial access.*

Scalability is required to benefit from JPEG2000 in mobile environments. Although granular LoD-levels slightly decrease the compression performance, in general *less computing power and bandwidth* is required to achieve an intermediate LoD. The following statements summarize the *relevant factors* for an appropriate encoding:

- Scalability can significantly reduce complexity at client side.
- Fastest processing times have been achieved for low resolutions or small RoIs (5-10% the complexity of JPEG).
- Reasonable numbers of inherent image resolutions are 4-8.
- It is meaningful to provide many layers.
- For RSA and LSA, code-blocks and precincts perform better than tiles.
- The best trade-off between compression performance and granularity are element dimensions (RSA) or spatial contributions (LSA) of 32×32 or 64×64.

This chapter has been dealing with the design of flexible and modular data-streams. The following chapter is concerned with the streaming of the currently relevant data portions. Thereby, the introduced generic key element serves to determine those elements contributing to the reconstruction of a certain RoI and LoD.

Chapter 3

Image streaming with dynamic RoIs

In the last chapter it has been shown that JPEG2000 data-streams are able to support dynamic RoIs. In this chapter, it will be shown how to take advantage of this feature to implement appropriate interactive streaming strategies. As a foundation, the streaming process is examined and requirements are derived (Section 3.1). The following discussion of related work reveals existing problems and the need for new developments (Section 3.2).

Within the proposed image communication scheme (cf. Figure 3.1), the support of dynamic RoIs is accomplished by transcoding units at server (T_s) and client side (T_c). Due to the fact that appropriate image streaming consists of multiple stages, new solutions for *calculation* (Section 3.3), *sequencing* (Section 3.4), and *signalization* (Section 3.5) of relevant image parts are introduced. The proposed basic technology serves as the foundation to design efficient communication systems for the applications introduced in later chapters.

By applying some of the streaming technologies to other problem fields, the chapter closes with *further applications for dynamic RoIs* (Section 3.6).

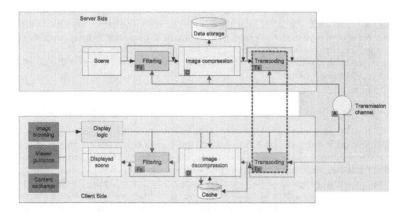

Figure 3.1: *The calculation, dynamic sequencing and appropriate signalization of relevant elements is accomplished by transcoders at server and client side.*

3.1   Aims and requirements

The main goal of image streaming is to efficiently deal with provided resources. More exactly, it is strived to sent as little data as possible from server to client (*bandwidth*) and to disburden the client from complex operations (*computing power*). To achieve this, a strong adaptation to the respective requirements at client side is required. It is assumed that they are described by RoIs and LoDs.

In image streaming, the determination of relevant data is mostly accomplished by a *calculation of elements*. Especially for JPEG2000 imagery, this process requires the selection of all RoI elements of the data-stream contributing to the reconstruction of a particular LoD. It is desirable to select as little data as needed to satisfy current demands. However, the resulting element sequence is usually not optimal. This problem is solved by an appropriate *sequencing of the calculated elements*. This step also allows for prioritization between elements and enhance flexibility. The final streaming step consists in the suitable *signalization of the sequenced elements*. This step basically serves to ensure that received data is appropriately identified at client side.

The requirements to image streaming can be summarized as follows:

- **Overall:** Transmission of as little data as possible.
- **Overall:** Little complexity at client side.
- **Calculation:** Selection of as little image contributions as possible.
- **Sequencing:** Introduction of means for prioritization.
- **Signalization:** Introduction of means to identify received data at client side.

After a review of related work proposed in literature, the following sections introduce new technology addressing each of these points.

3.2   Discussion of related work

Data streaming is a huge topic in a variety of application areas [Mil98; Ahr01; San04b]. Especially for raster imagery, the interest has significantly increased with the introduction of first PIT systems. Due to their relevance to own proposals, this section reviews the particular approaches applied to imagery process by JPEG, EZW, SPIHT and JPEG2000. Thereby, detailed statements to all stages of the streaming pipeline are provided.

3.2.1   Calculation of elements

Different options for the determination of RoI elements have been proposed for static and dynamic RoIs. Due to the reason, the calculation of RoI elements is disjoint from the dynamic handling, the proposed solutions, however, do not strongly vary. All techniques may be described by using a partitioning grid. This grid separates the elements used for RoI coding, more exactly single or blocks of coefficients (cf. Section 2.2.5). By projecting the shape of the RoI on the grid, all cells that are at least partially covered by the RoI are assumed to contribute to its reconstruction. Interestingly, some approaches require the RoI to be of certain shape, such as rectangles [JPG96; JPG02b; Yin04] or ellipses [Sig97; JPG02b].

Due to the properties of block-based DCT transformations, all coefficients of a certain block are needed to fully reconstruct the belonging pixel region. Amendment 3 of the JPEG standard [JPG96] describes an approach for static RoI coding. A single scan is limited to blocks contributing to the RoI. As the partitioning grid is identical to the block partition, the calculation of these blocks is straightforward.

Due to the multiresolution representation of data transferred by the DWT, element determination is more complicated. This has been solved by creating an independent partitioning grid for each inherent resolution level and adapting its cell dimensions to the respectively used elements. It is also required to adapt the shape of the RoI to each resolution [SC99; JPG02a; JPG02b]. For single coefficients, such a doing has been proposed for EZW [Sig97; Rau99a; Rau99b; Rau00; Alb00], SPIHT [Nis98; Par02; Wu02; Yin04] and JPEG2000 [SC99; JPG02a; JPG02b]. Due to the inherent support of the partition, calculation of contributing blocks of coefficients is mainly found in JPEG2000-based schemes [Tau01; Des01; JO04; San04a].

3.2.2 Sequencing of the calculated elements

Sequencing changes the data order within the compressed images. Due to progressive transmission and decoding at client side this allows for *prioritization* and leads to an *interest ordered* data-stream. Applied to RoIs, sequencing places RoI elements first into the stream and handles less interesting elements later.

Common to many techniques is the application of a bit-plane offset. Depending on the current prioritization, this offset is calculated for all coefficients of the image. As all codecs start the data handling on the most significant plane, RoI coefficients are assigned a smaller offset than others. For single elements and static RoIs this has been shown by SIGNORONI AND LEONARDI [Sig97] (EZW) and ATSUMI AND FARVARDIN [Ats98] (SPIHT), and for dynamic RoIs by RAUSCHENBACH [Rau99a; Rau99b; Rau00]. However, an offset can also be dynamically applied if some bitplanes of a coefficient have already been handled. To keep track of the systems state, FRAJKA ET AL. [Fra97] (SPIHT), uses three different counters (inactivity, importance, number of already handled bit-planes) for each coefficient. This, however, requires much system resources at server and client side.

Bitplane offsets have also been adopted for sequencing RoI elements in JPEG2000-encoded imagery. The standard itself introduces two different techniques [JPG02a; JPG02b]. Contrary to the max-shift technique, which allows only a single offset value for all RoIs, an independent offset is assigned to each RoI within the scaling-based method. In consequence, this allows for prioritization between RoIs. Based on these ideas, many similar approaches have been proposed [SC99; Wan02b; Liu02; Liu03c].

To JPEG2000-encoded imagery often block-based RoI schemes are applied. To achieve prioritization, TAUBMAN AND MARCELLIN [Tau01] propose to modify the distortion cost function of code-blocks so as to render RoI code-blocks and their embedded bitstreams more important. This principle is very flexible for static and dynamic RoIs. Although sequencing is only briefly discussed, DESHPANDE AND ZENG [Des01] and ORTIZ ET AL. [JO04] achieve prioritization based on precincts. NGUYEN ET AL. [Ngu03b] propose a hybrid approach, applying principles from [Tau01] for code-block and [JPG02a] for coefficient prioritization.

3.2.3   Signalization of the sequenced elements

The goal of signalization is the proper identification of transferred image parts at client side without significantly enlarging the data volume to be transmitted. To accomplish this, 3 different approaches have been proposed in literature: *Inherent, synchronized* and *external signalization*. Due to their rather different characteristics, these approaches are explained separately.

Inherent signalization   In inherent signalization the element sequence follows a certain *predefined progression order*. As this order is a-priori known at client side, each element can be easily identified. Due to the rather simple manner, this mechanism is part of many modern image standards supporting PIT as *JPEG* (progressive and hierarchical mode), *JPEG2000* (5 different modes), *GIF89a* (interlaced mode) [GIF89] or *PNG* (interlaced mode) [PNG04]. JPEG2000 provides the most flexible support for inherent signalization.

Due to the fact inherent signalization usually leads to data-streams compliant to the respectively used codec, all reviewed techniques providing static RoI support apply this type of signalization. Some techniques also signal additional information, e.g. the shape of the RoI [JPG02b], to restore the original data values. Due to the strong alignment to a certain progression order, however, arbitrary requirements can not always be satisfied. By exploiting the option of an internal switching from one order to another (JPEG2000), a certain degree of independence can be achieved [Hu04]. However, there is no approach for dynamic RoIs supporting arbitrary element sequences.

Synchronized signalization   Synchronized signalization is more flexible and appropriate for interactive environments than inherent signalization. It is based on the assumption that the transcoding units at server and client side *run synchronously from beginning to end of the streaming process*. If both parts can keep the same state regarding the traversal of the image data, proper element identification at client side is always guaranteed. Depending on the case the transcoder at server [Rau00] or client side [Des01; JO04] takes over the part of selecting the data to be transmitted, different strategies have been proposed in literature.

RAUSCHENBACH [Rau00] applies synchronized signalization to provide dynamic RoI support for EZW-encoded imagery. To ensure synchronization, server and client react in exactly the same manner to current demands. Thereby, the server selects and transmits the values of relevant elements. As this strategy is the foundation of own developments, more details can be found in Section 3.5.2.

Contrary to the former approach, DESHPANDE AND ZHENG [Des01] propose a fully client-driven method founded on the *Vfile*-mechanism proposed by LI ET AL. [Li99]. All required calculations are executed at client side. As the client also initiates data transmission, the transcoder at server side only serves to transmit the requested data. As long as data transmission is in sync with the respective requests, all elements can be identified at client side. To be able to determine relevant RoI elements, however, a virtual JPEG2000 file must first be transferred to the client. In a later proposal ORTIZ ET AL. [JO04] enhanced this approach by deriving the internal file structure from elements of the JPEG2000 data-stream. As a fully client-based approach is likely too complex to be applied in mobile environments, however, new developments are required.

External signalization The foundation of external signalization is the attachment of additional ID markers to transmitted data. Thus, an unequivocal assignment at client side can be guarantied even if image parts arrive in a different order than they have been sent. Such an approach is the most frequently applied strategy for signalling data and often labeled *protocol* [Hew97; JPG04]. Nevertheless, the additional overhead imposed by the identification marks increases the transmitted data volume.

Forced by Hewlett Packard, Live Picture and Eastman Kodak, in 1997 the *Internet Imaging Protocol* (IIP) [Hew97] has been developed. The protocol is strongly bundled with the belonging *FlashPix-codec* [FPX97] and a virtual FlashPix-file which must be available by the client to requests parts of the image. Although similar to the synchronization approach of DESPANDE ET AL., additional markers are attached to the transmitted data. Applied in astronomy, the *Flexible Image Transport System* (FITS) [Han01] provides a means of transporting image data stored in arrays and tables. Thereby each structure corresponds to a certain image region and is signaled with a certain mark. Especially for JPEG2000-encoded images, SANTA CRUZ ET AL. [SC99] proposed the application of specific *RoI switching markers* within the data-stream to signal image data belonging to certain RoIs. Beside the fact those markers have not been adopted for the JPEG2000 standard, this approach does not exploit many opportunities and features of the standard.

The *JPEG2000 Interactive Protocol* (JPIP, Part 9) [JPG04] is an evolving standard for efficient interactive communication of JPEG2000-encoded content. One of the main goals during its design was *to exploit the modular structure of JPEG2000-encoded data, to standardize a means of interacting with the data in an efficient and effective manner* [Tau03a]. Thereby, JPIP applies principles of external signalization. Precincts and tiles are the predominant structures for transmission. Considerably more flexibility regarding the refinement of an LoD is achieved by applying precincts. Contrary, using tiles offers simplicity in the order in which data is transmitted [Tau03a]. Although less functionality is provided, MEESSEN ET AL. [Mee03] propose a protocol similar to JPIP.

3.2.4   Summary of related work

Appropriate streaming must ensure that the handled data is reasonably calculated, sequenced and signaled. Although, there are also techniques which combine these 3 stages to a single strategy [Fra97; Rau99b], there are many single approaches to either step.

Due to the multiresolution-representation of JPEG2000-encoded imagery, the *calculation* step requires exact statements to determine all relevant elements. Although, there are many proposals to achieve this for a certain element type, no publication describes a single strategy for the handling of different element types.

Sequencing allows prioritization of the calculated RoI elements. Most of the proposed strategies exploit the bitplane-wise refinement of the image. By introducing an offset to elements of minor interest, their respective values will be shifted to the end of the resulting data-stream. Due to the little efforts required for content access, techniques based on the re-ordering of blocks of coefficients are most suited for mobile environments.

There are 3 different approaches for the *signalization* of image data, each with certain advantages and drawbacks. It applies: *as more flexible a strategy as more complex and demanding its application*. Inherent signalization usually means save of computing power and bandwidth at the expense of the ability to dynamically react to changing demands. Contrary synchronized or external signalization is flexible, but more costly in terms of required resources. Thus, a trade-off best matching the requirements of an application must be found for practical implementations. No reasonable approach for inherent and synchronized signalization supporting dynamic RoIs for JPEG2000-encoded imagery in mobile environments has yet been proposed. As external signalization is efficiently covered by JPIP, there is little need for own developments.

3.3   New ideas for the calculation of elements

To be able to fully reconstruct a RoI, it is required that all RoI elements are determined. How to accomplish this, is the topic of this section. The challenge and innovation here is to determine all but those elements contributing to a certain RoI for all possible element partitions, key elements, and LoDs. To achieve this, the introduced generic key element and its attributes are used. Thereby, the proposed strategy is not limited to a certain RoI shape and is able to deal with the multiresolution-representation of an image. To disburden the client from complex operations, related calculations are performed at server side.

The sections starts with a basic technique for rectangular RoIs. The provided procedure is able to determine all elements required to restore a RoI at a certain target-LoD. For the sake of simplicity, the statements are limited to the LoD attributes *x-* and *y-resolution*. However, the procedure can easily be enhanced by an extended attribution of the generic key element.

To cope with the strongest drawback of working on blocks of coefficients – the coarse approximation of the demands –, furthermore, two different adaptations of the basic approach are proposed and motivated.

3.3.1   The basic approach

Due to the reason calculations are basically the same for each type of key element, the following procedure consequently makes use of the generic key element introduced in the last chapter. To be able to state a generic description of the selection procedure, a set $KEY \subseteq M$ serves to collect all available RoI elements of a single type. Thereby, the property that elements reside at different decomposition levels must be considered.

$$KEY = \begin{cases} T_0 \;\; \cup \;\; T_1 \;\; \cup \ldots \cup \;\; T_{r_{max}} & : \;\; \text{if using tiles} \\ P_0 \;\; \cup \;\; P_1 \;\; \cup \ldots \cup \;\; P_{r_{max}} & : \;\; \text{if using precincts} \\ CBT_0 \cup CBT_1 \cup \ldots \cup CBT_{r_{max}} & : \;\; \text{if using code blocks} \end{cases} \qquad (3.1)$$

To be able to retrieve elements resolution-wise, the set of all elements is divided into sets containing only elements belonging to a certain resolution level.

$$\begin{aligned} KEY_0 \;\; &= KEY \cap K_0, \\ KEY_1 \;\; &= KEY \cap K_1, \\ &\ldots \\ KEY_{r_{max}} &= KEY \cap K_{r_{max}}, \end{aligned} \qquad (3.2)$$

The spatial contribution of an element strongly depends on the underlying partition. As it may happen that the respective grid anchor ($[0,0]$ for code-blocks and precincts, $[\Omega_1, \Omega_2]$ for tiles) does not correspond to the image anchor, $[e_1, e_2]$, an possible offset, $[goff_1, goff_2]$, between those values is determined in pixel domain.

$$goff_1 = \left\{ \begin{array}{lll} e_1 & : & \text{if using code-blocks or precincts} \\ e_1 - \Omega_1 & : & \text{if using tiles} \end{array} \right.$$

$$goff_2 = \left\{ \begin{array}{lll} e_2 & : & \text{if using code-blocks or precincts} \\ e_2 - \Omega_2 & : & \text{if using tiles} \end{array} \right.$$

It is worth noting that in the case of code-blocks or precincts, this might lead to elements which do not overlap with the image. Although they have no counterpart within the data-stream, they are handled as valid elements in order to be conform with the standard.

Within the source image a particular rectangular RoI is specified by its dimensions, $[reg_1, reg_2]$, with $1 \leq reg_1 \leq s_1$ and $1 \leq reg_2 \leq s_2$, and offset, $[o_1, o_2]$, regarding the top left corner of the image, $0 \leq o_1 \leq s_1 - reg_1, 0 \leq o_2 \leq s_2 - reg_2$. As all RoI elements are determined by these values, a set $VALID$ containing all RoI elements can easily be extracted from the set KEY. This is accomplished by evaluating the offset and spatial extent of each element via its belonging attribute tuple collected in ATT. This results in a new set $ATTV \subseteq ATT$.

$$
\begin{aligned}
ATTV = \ & \{attrib(k) | \forall k \in KEY_0 \cup KEY_1 \cup \ldots \cup KEY_r : \\
& o_1 < (a_1 + 1)a_5 - goff_1 \cap a_1 a_5 - goff_1 \leq o_1 + reg_1 \cap \\
& o_2 < (a_2 + 1)a_6 - goff_2 \cap a_2 a_6 - goff_2 \leq o_2 + reg_2 \}
\end{aligned}
\tag{3.3}
$$

$$VALID = retrieve(KEY, ATTV) \tag{3.4}$$

The set $VALID$ represents all elements of the data-stream contributing to the reconstruction of a given RoI at resolution r. Each of these RoI elements may consist of more than one contribution, e.g. multiple packets for a single precinct, which are now resequenced and signalled by the subsequent processing steps of the communication pipeline.

3.3.2 Adaptations

Working on blocks of wavelet coefficients has the significant drawback that a single group contributes to the reconstruction of a whole pixel field. Thus, the RoI can only be approximated. Due to the reason it is always assumed to fully reconstruct a RoI at a certain LoD, more data than actually required is handled. This section proposes two approaches to cope with that. The main idea of the first adaptation is to consider the spatial extent of RoI elements in a manner so as they do not exceed certain dimensions. The second improvement is dedicated to LoDs with different values for x- and y-resolution. Both improvements may be arbitrarily combined.

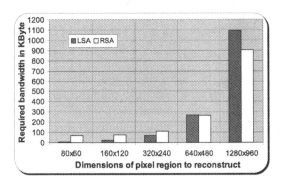

Figure 3.2: *Required bandwidth to restore a pixel area of different dimensions for RSA based on code-blocks (dimensions: 64×64) and LSA based on precincts (spatial contribution: 64×64).*

3.3.2.1   Applying Limited Spatial Access

In arbitrary streams the contribution of some RoI elements might be quite large and even spread over the whole image. Due to the reason that elements are not subdivided, much more data than required must be handled. Contrary, within data-streams enhanced with the LSA feature, the spatial contribution of each RoI element is well defined, and thus, can better adapt to the respective RoI shape. As the LSA feature only influences the element partition, the introduced calculation procedure may be applied as described.

Results and conclusions: LSA enabled data-streams are larger than their pendants (approx. 18% in the given example). However, experiments (cf. Figure 3.2) revealed that much less bandwidth ($< 10\%$) is required if data transmission is limited to a small pixel region. The selected RoI elements at each resolution level are smaller, and thus, much less data is transferred. In the provided example, this statement is valid for RoIs up to a size of 480x640. For larger regions the increased compression efficiency outperforms the advantages of smaller elements.

Due to this, LSA is of advantage especially if only small image regions are to be reconstructed. Although this feature can always be applied to increase efficiency in early transmission stages, the decreased compression performance leads to slightly more transferred data if the whole image is streamed.

3.3.2.2   Applying subband-wise selection

Flexible adaptation to an LoD also requires the ability to handle different values for x- and y-*resolution*. This can only be achieved by code-blocks. Blocks defined at subbands LH_d and HL_d contribute to the reconstruction of a certain orientation only, and thus, have the ability to reconstruct a RoI defined in resolution level r, $r = d_{max} - d + 1$, in half of its dimensions in the respective direction only. However, x- and y-*resolution* can only vary in a factor of 2.

Most of the related proposals found in literature do not cope with that. In [Rau99a], RAUSCHENBACH describes a technique which is able to support refinement in resolution even if x- and y-*resolution* differ in a factor of 4. As this is achieved by proposing a new decomposition scheme, it is not applicable to JPEG2000. This section presents techniques to overcome this. They have been part of the publication *"Remote display of large raster images using JPEG2000 and the rectangular FishEye-View"* [Ros03b] proposed by the author.

Handling single code-blocks requires a subdivision of the introduced code-block triple $cbt_{col,row,r}$. Such a code-block is labeled $cb_{d,b,col,row}$, whereby col and row represent its relative position within subband $b \in \{LL_{d_{max}}, HL_d, LH_d, HH_d\}$. Due to strong similarities to the code-block triple it can still be described by the generic key element. However, to keep consistency the attribute domain A_0 must be enhanced to $A_0 = \{t, p, cbt, cb\}$.

As depicted in Figure 3.3/left, to each of the belonging subband LH_d and HL_d a scaling factor $x_b : y_b$, with $x_b = 2^{d-1}, y_b = 2^d$ for HL_d, $x_b = 2^d, y_b = 2^{d-1}$ for LH_d $(d > 0)$, in both directions is assigned. These factors basically mean that image content reconstructed by all lower image resolutions r, $r < d_{max} - d + 1$, and subband b can be scaled by these values without loss of information.

If CB_r is a set of single code-blocks directly contributing to the reconstruction of resolution r, a set of all single code-blocks is defined by $KEY = CB_0 \cup CB_1 \cup \cdots \cup CB_{r_{max}}$. Equation (3.4) can still be applied to extract RoI elements. A slight modification of Equation (3.3), however, ensures only code-blocks corresponding to scaling factors $x : y$ ($x = \frac{1}{x-resolution}, y = \frac{1}{y-resolution}$) are selected.

$$
\begin{aligned}
ATTV = \quad &\{attrib(cb_{d,b,col,row}) | \forall cb_{d,b,col,row} \in CB_0 \cup CB_1 \cup \ldots \cup CB_r : \quad (3.5) \\
&o_1 < (a_1 + 1)a_5 - goff_1 \cap a_1a_5 - goff_1 \le o_1 + reg_1 \cap \\
&o_2 < (a_2 + 1)a_6 - goff_2 \cap a_2a_6 - goff_2 \le o_2 + reg_2 \cap \\
&x_b \ge x \cap y_b \ge y\}, \text{ with } \tfrac{1}{2}x \le y \le 2x
\end{aligned}
$$

In some applications larger differences 2^n, $n > 1$, in x- and y-resolution are required. As those scalings are not directly supported by the dyadic decomposition scheme of the DWT, it seems impossible to accomplish. However, some subbands contribute more to the reconstruction of a certain orientation than others. While this property has yet only been applied within a certain resolution, it is proposed to also be applied to subbands at higher decomposition levels. This is reasonable, as performed experiments have revealed that this improvement does not significantly

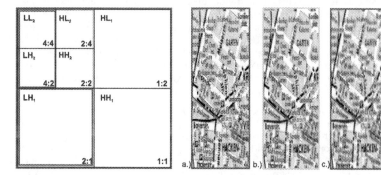

Figure 3.3: *Three different strategies for subband-wise data handling. Even if not all available data is used (b/c), results identical to the original (a) are achieved if image content is scaled by the respective values (this example: 4 : 1).*

change the visual appearance of the content after scaling (cf. Figure 3.3/right).

To select such code-blocks again Equation (3.5) is applied. However, to omit data from nonrelevant subbands, the selection criteria $(x_b \geq x \cap y_b \geq y)$ must be enhanced to $((x_b \geq x \cap y_b \geq y) \cup ((x_b > y_b) \cap (y_b \geq y)))$ for $x > y$ or $((x_b \geq x \cap y_b \geq y) \cup ((x_b < y_b) \cap (x_b \geq x))$ for $x < y$. Valid pairs of scaling factors may now differ by larger values: $\frac{1}{2^n}x \leq y \leq 2^n x$.

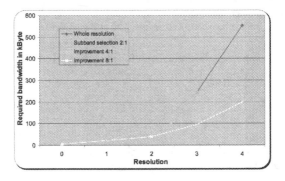

Figure 3.4: *Comparison of different strategies regarding the bandwidth required to achieve a scaled version of the image content without loss of information.*

Results: Working on subbands instead of whole resolutions has an significant impact on the required bandwidth to reconstruct a RoI with different scaling factors in both directions. This is shown in Figure 3.4 for an image with dimensions of 1280x960 encoded by applying 4 decomposition steps and different scaling factors.

If the content is to be scaled by equal factors in both directions, the scaling properties of code-blocks are of no use. As the whole code-block triple must always be selected, this leads to an equal performance compared to the ordinary approach.

For all scaling factors at least the data available for lower resolutions must be selected. As shown in Figure 3.4, there is no difference in the need for bandwidth for all strategies. However as soon as the region must be scaled by different scaling factors, the requirements for bandwidth decrease with an increasing difference between the factors. The proposed removal of subbands not exclusively contributing to the reconstruction of a certain orientation has the least impact if scaling factors differ by a factor of 2 (orange line). However, a saving of up to 38% has been achieved. Obviously, the proposed improvements of the code-block approach perform better on higher differences (yellow and beige line). While up to 58% of the available bandwidth to reconstruct the whole resolution is saved if the image is to be scaled by factors 4:1, this value increases to 64% for the 8:1 case.

Even though the presented results suggest that significant gains in transmission efficiency can be obtained, it is worth noting that this scheme is still unable to fully remove redundant information for regions with certain scaling parameters. This applies for horizontal and vertical scaling parameters which differ by a factor greater than 2. Consider, for example, a region with scaling parameters 4 : 1. Such a region must be reconstructed at $\frac{1}{4}$ the original resolution in the horizontal direction, but at full resolution vertically. This suggests that only the subbands marked 4 : 4, 4 : 2 and 2 : 1 in Figure 3.3 need to be sent to the decoder. The total number of transmitted subband samples in this case is $\frac{3}{8}$ of the original image samples, while a perfectly efficient scheme would send only $\frac{1}{4}$ the original samples. This requires a transmission of $\frac{1}{8}$ more image samples, but ensures that the approach is still compliant to the JPEG2000 standard.

Conclusions: Working on code-blocks leads to a more granular access to encoded data, and thus, decreased need for bandwidth. By assuming the application of sufficient decompositions during analysis, the proposed code-block selection strategy provides differences in the scaling factors of 2^n, $n > 0$, and thus, allows much more granular data delivery. Thereby the benefit of the proposal increases with larger difference in x- and y-direction. Only 36% of the data required for the traditional approach are needed if a RoI is to be scaled by a factor of 1:8.

3.4   New ideas for the sequencing of calculated elements

The result from the calculation step is a set of RoI elements. Although, the original sequence of those elements is often optimal if the whole image is to be streamed, this might not be the case for RoIs. The option to handle multiple regions with different interests requires prioritization mechanisms.

If multiple RoIs are specified, it is often useful to interleave the RoI elements based on a *global sequencing* strategy. Such a strategy must allow flexible prioritization between the RoIs depending on the belonging LoDs. Furthermore, it must be able to dynamically adapt to changing demands and to handle overlapping RoIs. This flexibility is often not available in RoI schemes proposed in literature [JPG02a; Des01; Ask02]. An appropriate sequencing strategy fully satisfying these requirements is introduced in Section 3.4.1.

However, even if only a single RoI is present, an adapted handling of contributing elements can achieve better results. As shown in Section 3.4.2, *local sequencing* can increase the speed of the refinement by keeping the required bandwidth constant. To achieve this, elements contributing more to the refinement of the RoI are determined and optimally sequenced in the R-D sense. Such an approach has not been proposed in literature before.

To consider the critical factors in mobile environments, all operations are accomplished at server side. Limited bandwidth is considered by ensuring a non-redundant and adapted data-transmission even if requirements frequently change. In case of overlapping RoIs, elements contributing to multiple RoIs are assigned to the RoI with highest priority. Local and global sequencing may also be combined to a single strategy.

3.4.1   Prioritization-based global sequencing

Support for multiple RoIs requires mechanisms for prioritization. This can be accomplished by an appropriate sequencing strategy. Applied to precincts, this topic has been part of the contribution *"Flexible, dynamic and compliant region of interest coding in JPEG2000"* [Ros02] proposed by the author. However, it is also applicable to code-blocks or tiles.

Prioritization between multiple RoIs can be accomplished by granting elements of a more important RoI a certain advantage over elements of less interesting RoIs.

Once elements from other RoIs are ready to be handled, they are interleaved with the remaining elements belonging to the first RoI.

The most general manner to describe priority is achieved by exploiting the available LoD-hierarchy and the current LoD values of each RoI. As the refinement of the image consists of multiple and successive refinement steps, prioritization of a more important RoI can be accomplished if its refinement starts n steps earlier than that of a less interesting RoI. The parameter n may basically be understood as a *prioritization delta* between these two RoIs. If refinement is limited to accuracy only, this is the difference in the number of already sequenced quality layers for each RoI element [Ros02].

Due to the reason an LoD is defined in a 4D space, however, more than one attribute is available. Thus, prioritization by a single value is not sufficient. To handle this, a prioritization tuple $prio(x, y, accuracy, component)$ is introduced. As this tuple strongly corresponds to an LoD tuple, it can be applied to determine the respective nose for each LoD dimension independently. Data from a lower prioritized RoI is only handled, if the LoD-delta to a RoI of higher priority is higher or equal for all single values of the prioritization delta. An example of this principle is depicted in Figure 3.5. The strategy is able to handle complex (all tuple values > 0) as well as simple prioritization (one tuple value > 0).

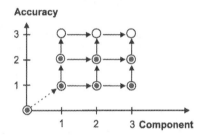

Figure 3.5: *Global prioritization between two RoIs. By assuming no elements have yet been handled, first data belonging to a RoI prioritized by $prio(0, 0, 0, 0)$ will only be served if a higher prioritized RoI ($prio(0, 0, 2, 1)$) has achieved one of the upper marked LoDs.*

To decide which RoI is ready to be handled at a particular sequencing step, the global sequencing scheme compares the different LoD- and prioritization deltas at each successive step. Reference for the calculation is always the RoI with highest priority. RoIs which have reached their target-LoD are not considered.

Conclusions: Prioritization of multiple RoIs by applying a prioritization tuple is flexible and intuitive. As prioritization tuples and target-LoDs may be dynamically changed during image streaming, it is also well suited in interactive environments. Such changes directly influence the next sequencing step. Nevertheless, this strategy does not consider the image content itself. A local sequencing scheme taking this into account is introduced in the next section.

3.4.2   Rate-Distortion optimized local sequencing

Due to the coarse spatial access of the key elements, the shape of a given RoI can often only be roughly approximated. Some elements contribute more to its reconstruction than others. Thus, it is reasonable to consider them earlier during streaming, whereby the overlap serves as a prioritization criteria. In "*Rate-Distortion optimized interactive browsing of JPEG2000 images*" [Tau03b], a joined work, the author considered this by proposing an algorithm for sequencing data in such a way so as to maximize the received image quality within the RoI, at each point during image delivery.

To service a RoI, perhaps the most natural way to stream elements from a JPEG2000 data-stream is to send them in quality progressive fashion. That is, each element collected in *VALID* is subdivided in incremental contributions for each quality layer. The first contribution of each element is sent first, followed by the second contribution, and so forth. As each element has been divided by using an R-D optimization algorithm applied to the whole image, however, this can be far from the optimal sequencing policy for a RoI.

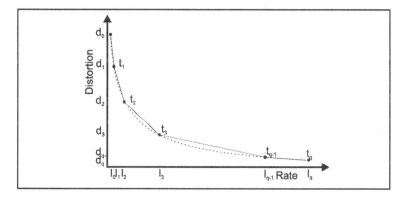

Figure 3.6: *Typical R-D curve in image compression (dashed) and selected layer thresholds t_i.*

R-D properties of quality layers   During encoding of the image, embedded bitstreams belonging to the respective elements $k \in KEY$ of the data-stream are spread over a number of layers, so as that distortion within the reconstructed image decreases with each handled layer during decoding. Thereby layers are best formed by a post compression R-D optimization process [Tau99] briefly reviewed here. A detailed description can be found in [Tau02b].

During encoding, element contributions to each of the q quality layers, $i = 1, \ldots, q$, are determined from a convex hull analysis and thresholding. While the first step ensures that R-D slopes decrease monotonically with increasing i (cf. Figure 3.6), the second stage serves to determine the respective layer contributions. A distortion-length slope, s_n, is determined by

$$s_n = \frac{d_n - d_{n-1}}{l_n - l_{n-1}}, \quad n = 1, 2, \ldots, \mathbb{N} \tag{3.6}$$

Thus, a layer i is formed by incremental element contributions of $l_i - l_{i-1}$ codebytes (l_1 if $i = 1$), whereby distortion-length slopes of included contributions must conform to $t_{i-1} > s_n \geq t_i$ ($s_n \geq t_i$ if $i = 1$). Distortion-length slope thresholds t_i are selected during compression so as to achieve suitably spaced layer bit-rates or quality increments.

This layering strategy has the property that truncating the data-stream to any whole layer boundary results in a compressed representation which is optimal in the rate-distortion sense. Specifically, discarding all but the first i contributions from each element in the image results in a compressed representation with the smallest distortion amongst all representations with the same or smaller length. This property holds for all layers q, and also holds for the reduced resolution representations formed by discarding one or more highest resolution levels.

However, an important observation is that the original layers were generated so as to minimize distortion over the whole image, rather than just the RoI. Element contributing only partially to the reduction of distortion within the RoI are handled at their full rate. This is not optimal in R-D sense.

R-D optimal resequencing   To a sequencing policy is referred as optimal if at each point in the sequence the distortion within the RoI is as small as it can be, given the total number of bytes which have been sent. This can only be achieved if the respective contributions at each layer are changed. As the goal is to deliver existing compressed content with dynamically changing requests, such doing is not available without decoding and re-doing the layer assignment. For this reason, the attention is restricted to a resequencing of elements.

To achieve this in the absence of any specific knowledge concerning the original values used to calculate the R-D slopes of each element, a *window scaling factor*, w_k, representing the fraction of pixels in the region of influence, S_k, of element $k \in VALID$ which also lie within the RoI represented by *reg*. Thereby, S_k can easily be determined from attribute values of k.

$$w_k = \frac{\|reg \cap S_k\|}{\|S_k\|} \tag{3.7}$$

Ideally, one would regenerate the data-stream layers, replacing d_n with $w_k d_n$ or, equivalently, replacing s_n with $w_k s_n$ in Equation (3.6). This is not generally possible, however, since the individual rate-distortion slopes are not retained after the image has been compressed. Nevertheless, it is possible to attach such information in a very efficient way, without significantly increasing the length of the data-stream.

Let $\mathcal{K}_{k,i}$ denote partial data of an element k residing at the ith layer. Noting that the rate-distortion slopes are in the range t_{i-1} to t_i, and hence scaled slopes in the range $w_k t_{i-1}$ to $w_k t_i$, it is reasonable to demand that $\mathcal{K}_{k_1,i_1}$ should be sequenced earlier than $\mathcal{K}_{k_2,i_2}$ whenever $w_{k_1} t_{i_1} \geq w_{k_2} t_{i_2}$.

To keep the layer principle, the notion of *resequenced layers*, $\ell_{\bar{i}}$, with corresponding slope thresholds, $\bar{t}_{\bar{i}}$ is introduced. Resequenced layer $\ell_{\bar{i}}$ consists of all element contributions $\mathcal{K}_{k,i}$ for which $\bar{t}_{\bar{i}-1} \geq w_k t_i > \bar{t}_{\bar{i}}$, where $\bar{t}_0 = \infty$. If the thresholds $\bar{t}_{\bar{i}}$ are spaced sufficiently finely, the resulting sequence of element contributions $\mathcal{K}_{k,i}$ will be ordered strictly on the basis of $w_k t_i$, and the aimed R-D optimized sequencing is achieved.

In practice, however, often a compliant ordering is required (e.g. for inherent signalization based on precincts described in Section 3.5.1). Thus the number of layers is of crucial interest. To this end, the proposed resequencing algorithm constructs the smallest number of resequenced layers, such that each layer contains at most one contribution from each element. This is accomplished by selecting

$$\bar{t}_1 = \max_{k \in VALID} w_k t_2, \quad \text{and} \quad \bar{t}_{\bar{i}} = \max_{\mathcal{K}_{k,i} \in \ell_{\bar{i}-1}} w_k t_{i+2} \text{ for } \bar{i} > 1$$

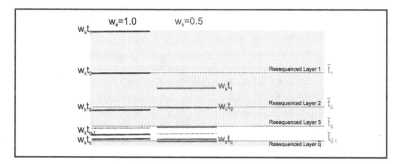

Figure 3.7: *Corresponding layer thresholds $w_k t_i$ of two elements k with different window scaling factors. New layer thresholds $\bar{t}_{\bar{i}}$ determine the contributions for each resequenced layer $\ell_{\bar{i}}$.*

This strategy is depicted in Figure 3.7, where $\bar{q}$ resequenced layers are created from two elements with different window scaling factors. While the element on the left hand side fully contributes to the RoI, the second element has only a partial overlap. This results in scaled threshold values and resequenced layers. It can be seen that the proposed determination of the new threshold values $\bar{t}_{\bar{i}}$ leads to single contributions for each involved element only.

Results: As shown in Figure 3.8, a high gain in performance can be achieved by the R-D optimal sequencing. The measures are based on precincts of dimensions 32×32 at each resolution level and packets as belonging layer contributions. The presented values are based on a JPIP signalization and represent the required communication bandwidth. The experiments are performed in the context of multi-component imagery measuring 980×1280 pixels. The imagery has been compressed with 3 decomposition levels. The data-stream has 16 quality layers, representing compressed bit-rates logarithmically spaced between 0.04 bpp and 4 bpp.

Figure 3.8 plots the luminance PSNR, measured within a requested RoI of dimensions 128×128, as a function of the amount of data received, for two different RoI locations. In the left figure, the RoI has an offset of 176×176 and is such that

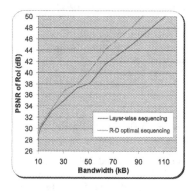
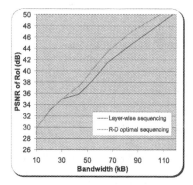

Figure 3.8: *Comparison of R-D optimal vs. layer progressive sequencing of packets regarding need for bandwidth for a RoI where many precincts have little (left) or strong overlap (right) with a RoI.*

the RoI contains the maximum number of relevant precincts, many of which have relatively little overlap with the RoI and are thus strongly affected by the window scaling factor. In this case, R-D optimal resequencing yields massive improvements of more than 3 dB in reconstructed image quality at most points of interest in the received packet sequence. In terms of bandwidth this often leads to the advantage that 10-16% less data must be transmitted to achieve a similar quality to the ordinary layer-wise sequencing.

The second RoI location, corresponding to Figure 3.8/right, the RoI has an offset of 96×96 and involves fewer precincts and more window scaling factors which are close to 1. In this case, the improvement due to R-D optimal sequencing is smaller, but still significant, on the order of 2 dB.

The performance gain strongly depends on the element partition and the content, and might be even higher [Tau03b]. The LSA feature has no significant impact on the performance of the approach.

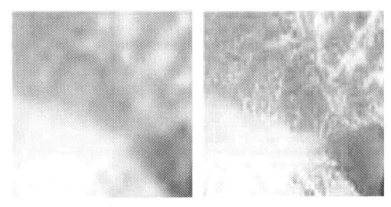

Figure 3.9: *Visual comparison of the reconstruction of a* 128×128 *RoI at 6.4kB from a layer-wise (left) and R-D optimized (right) sequenced data-stream.*

Conclusions: By applying R-D optimal sequencing to the elements selected by the basic approach higher efficiency is achieved than by handling those elements in original layer-wise order (cf. Figure 3.9). Thereby improvements of up to 3dB have been accomplished. To be applied only the thresholds t_i used to determine original layer contributions are required. The sequencing strategy retains its desirable rate-distortion properties even across multiple spatial resolutions and image components. This comes not without a slight increase in the need for computing power at server side, but does not affect the limited client side.

3.5   New ideas for the signalization of sequenced elements

After the all RoI elements have been calculated and sequenced depending on current needs, they are sent. The biggest challenge of this task is to ensure that each individual contribution can be unequivocally identified at client side. Thus, strategies for signalization are needed. This is shown in this section for *inherent* and *synchronized* signalization of JPEG2000-encoded imagery.

Although *inherent signalization* has mostly been adopted by approaches introducing static RoIs, the proposed technique is able to dynamically adapt the streamed data. As the applied strategy creates compliant streams, the identification of each sent data container can be easily derived. All required operations are accomplished at server-side.

The proposed approach for *synchronized signalization* is founded on a polygonal description of the RoI shape and a span-based traversal. As the shape of the RoI and the processing order is known to server and client, synchronization during image streaming ensures that each container can be identified. As only the original image data is sent, this approach is especially suited for low-bandwidth environments.

External signalization of image data is rather efficiently covered by JPIP (cf. Section 3.2.3), and thus has not been subject to own developments.

3.5.1   Inherent signalization

The main idea of the proposed inherent signalization strategy is the server-side sequencing of the data in a compliant progression order. This leads to a datastream which can be partially or completely processed by any compliant decoder. The strategy has been published by the author as part of the contribution *"Flexible, dynamic and compliant region of interest coding in JPEG2000"* [Ros02]. None of the related approaches is able to support dynamic RoIs to that extent. Although a strategy quite similar to that proposed by the author has been published in 2004 [San04a], the originality of the author's proposal is founded on a related patent [Ros01] in 2001 and conference contribution in 2002 [Ros02]. Due to the reason, the transcoder at client side is fully disburdened from the computational efforts required to identify received image chunks, this strategy has strong relevance for resource-limited mobile hardware.

Within a compliant stream, each data container is identified by its position. Depending on the respective progression order, elements are always traversed in a particular and unique manner. A simple example showing a typical distribution of image data and the resulting ordering in layer-progressive mode is shown in Figure 3.10/left. Thereby, data available at each resolution is spread over 4 different data containers, one for each element and layer.

The foundation of the proposed signalization strategy is the option to include empty element contributions wherever needed. With regard to RoIs this is the case for all containers which do not contribute to a currently handled RoI. For the given example, a corresponding data-stream taking advantage of this feature is shown in Figure 3.10/right.

So as not to limit the refinement of a certain RoI, a reasonable signalization strategy must support all valid refinement paths defined in the LoD hierarchy. Thereby, the respective progression order is of crucial interest. It has been found that the layer-wise progression is the only compliant order able to achieve this. Although it might be assumed this progression refines in quality only, it offers considerable flexibility. As shown in Figure 3.10 a single layer covers contributions from all resolutions. This also applies for components. Thus, a single layer might serve to refine in each of the LoD dimensions, either exclusively or in arbitrary combination.

As packets have a strong relation to layers, the dynamic construction of a compliant data-stream is best explained using precincts. A packet represents a partial contribution of a precinct at a certain layer. Empty contributions are represented by *empty header packets*.

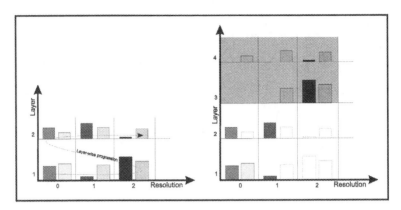

Figure 3.10: *Distribution of data containers within the original (left) and modified data-stream (right). The marked area indicates data on layers not contributing to the current LoD.*

The data-stream is constructed layer-wise. For a given sequence of packets, the proposed procedure inserts empty contributions as long as the belonging position of the next packet to be sequenced is reached. This process stops if the currently strived LoD for all RoIs has been achieved, and ends if all packets of the original data-stream have been handled. For the given example shown in Figure 3.10, this can be observed at the first 2 layers of the modified data-stream. By assuming the reconstruction of a RoI (blue containers) up to resolution 1 and two levels of accuracy, empty contributions are inserted at related positions of higher resolutions. The same applies for the background (yellow containers), which is to be reconstructed at the lowest resolution and one accuracy level only.

Once a part of the RoI-enabled data-stream has been constructed it is no longer subject to changes and may be transmitted to the client. There, it is processed in the same order allowing for an easy identification of each packet. This procedure is unambiguous and may be applied to any compliant data-stream.

This method can be implemented by all types of key elements. However, for code-blocks and tiles additional statements are required. As tiles are handled as independent sub-images, for each tile a similar principle as explained for precincts can be applied. This is due to the property that a tile may be divided in *tile-parts*, which can be interleaved at will. Since each tile-part is assigned a compliant ID mark, no empty tile contributions must be signalled. However, the size of the modified data-stream increases significantly if many tile-parts are present.

To apply inherent signalization to code-blocks, the property that a precinct basically consists of belonging code-blocks is exploited. Thus, a packet represents the incremental contributions from each of its code-blocks to a certain layer. Thus, an empty contribution of one or more code-blocks is signalled by modifying the respective packets. Due to this, the strategy can be applied as described. However, to access code-block contributions packetization must be un- and re-done. The principle is similar to the implicit method proposed by TAUBMAN AND MARCELLIN [Tau02a; Tau02b], but is designed to handle already encoded imagery.

Results: The proposed strategy produces RoI-aware data-streams, which can be processed by any compliant decoder without further modification. This is a benefi-

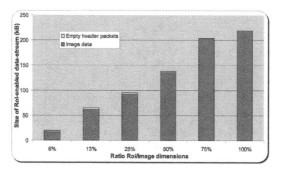

Figure 3.11: *Example for the resulting stream length depending on the ratio between RoI and image dimensions if the proposed inherent signalization based on precincts is applied (LSA: 32 × 32).*

cial property especially in mobile environments, as no transcoding but only decoding must take place at client side. This significantly reduces complexity. Such RoI-enabled data-streams might also been stored at server-side to satisfy frequently appearing demands. The strategy is easy to implement; just knowledge of the decomposition scheme and the progression order are required to calculate the respective position of each data container. Empty contributions are either pre-created (precincts) or part of the used data containers (code-blocks).

The proposed idea is based on the fact of including empty contributions. Although they are rather small (1Byte for empty header packets), their accumulated length can reach a threshold where their influence is not longer negligible. Similar statements apply for tiles. However, concrete values for the increase in stream size depend on various factors influenced by user interaction and the respective demands. For a single RoI the most influencing factor is the ratio between RoI and image dimensions. This is depicted in Figure 3.11. It generally applies: *the bigger the RoI, the less empty contributions, the better the performance of the strategy.* However, a decrease in compression performance is a common property of all RoI-enabled data-streams [JPG02a; Gro01; Ask02].

If small RoIs are estimated to appear often, it is reasonable to apply a hybrid strategy combining properties from tile and precinct-based signalization. If an image is tiled before the described signalization based on precincts is used, empty contributions must only be included on a tile instead of image basis [Fuc01, p.25]. This significantly decreases the number of empty header packets to be included, and thus increases the performance of the approach [Fuc01, p.43]. If the number of tiles is well-defined, the increased number of tile-parts is negligible.

3.5.2   Synchronized signalization

In [Rau00] RAUSCHENBACH proposed an approach for image transmission with dynamic RoIs. Due to its provided flexibility, it has been adapted by the author to JPEG2000 and extended to handle multiple overlapping arbitrarily shaped RoIs. Thereby many enhancements to handle the unwieldy properties of concave RoI shapes have been developed. The proposed strategy is based on a synchronized signalization and also contains parts dealing with element calculation and sequencing. It has been published by the author and RAUSCHENBACH in *"A Flexible Polygon Representation of Multiple Overlapping Regions of Interest for Wavelet-based*

Image Coding" [Rau01b]. Due to its generic manner, the strategy may also be applied to other wavelet-based image codecs.

3.5.2.1   The main idea

The foundation of the proposed signalization strategy is that server and client know shape and current prioritization of the RoIs and run synchronous during image streaming. Depending on prioritization, the transcoder at server side selects one or multiple RoIs as active, determines their next incremental contribution, and sends this data. Due to equal processing and element traversal, the transcoder at client side is able to exactly identify each data container of the received sequence.

Calculation of relevant data containers is founded on a *span-based scanline algorithm* applied to a multiresolution grid. The term *"scanline"* means that the element grid at each resolution is traversed in scanline order. Here, the original scanline algorithm [Fol90] used in computer graphics to solve the problem of discretization in raster images is adopted to describe the shape of RoIs and to efficiently handle the common problem of overlapping RoIs. RoIs are represented geometrically by regular polygons. *"Span-based"* stands for the beneficial property that RoI elements generally form easily manageable spans at relevant scanlines. For sequencing, a prioritization scheme similar to that described in Section 3.4.1 is applied. Calculation and sequencing are combined to one strategy, which ensures a redundancy-free transmission of image data belonging to one or multiple RoIs.

3.5.2.2   Calculation and sequencing

Calculation and sequencing is performed by a multi-pass procedure visiting each position of the DWT-hierarchy multiple times. Each time a belonging element is about to be handled, the next LoD contribution to the element is accessed and sequenced. As described for the inherent signalization strategy, the procedure traverses the DWT-hierarchy in *layer-resolution-component-position* order.

The shape of a RoI is represented by a polygonal *footprint*, whereby complex shapes are approximated. As the element partition may be different at each resolution level r, this footprint is handled for each level separately. This is achieved by scaling the RoI footprint by $2^{d_{max}-r}$ in each direction.

In the proposed solution, an element contributes to a RoI if it intersects the footprint of that RoI. This differs from the original scanline algorithm, which approximates the shape of an object and may omit elements with a small overlap.

For a particular resolution all elements covered by a RoI are traversed scanline by scanline (cf. Figure 3.12). A sequence of consecutive elements on a scanline which contribute to the same set of RoIs is labeled *span*. A span may be started or terminated only at elements intersected by an edge of a RoI. For appropriate span computation all edges intersecting a scanline must be considered.

To avoid redundancy, each data container is at most handled once. That means, when accessing a data container contributing to a RoI, it must be checked if it also belongs to a higher prioritized RoI already handled. This is done by checking the attributes of the state-LoD of all RoIs which overlap the element. The span-based algorithm has the beneficial property this check has to be done only once per span.

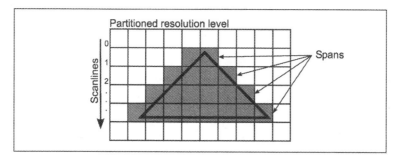

Figure 3.12: *At a certain resolution level, all elements covered by the footprint are considered to contribute to a RoI. These elements form spans at each scanline.*

3.5.2.3   Span computation

It is now described how spans are computed for a single scanline. All polygon edges which intersect the current scanline are stored in a data structure called the *active edge table* (AET). This structure is updated from scanline to scanline to ensure that it contains all valid edges. Each edge in the AET holds the intersection coordinate x_s of that edge with the current scanline. A fast incremental update of x_s from one scanline to another is supported by separately storing the edge slope, the whole-numbered and the fractional component of x_s as three integers. The AET is sorted in ascending x_s order.

In a preprocess, all edges are classified as *opener*, which means that the area left of the edge does not belong to the polygon but the area right of the edge does, *closer*, which means that the area left of the edge belongs to the polygon but the area right of the edge does not, or *horizontal*. If this cannot be accomplished, a footprint is replaced by its convex hull.

For each edge in the AET, the algorithm checks whether this edge opens or closes a span. Furthermore, two counters evaluating the state-LoDs of the RoIs overlapped by the spans of the currently handled scanline are maintained. The counter c_{neg} contains the number of RoIs which did already transmit data for the current layer-resolution-component combination, and c_{pos} stores the number of RoIs which did not. If a span is opened or closed, the algorithm evaluates these counters in order to decide whether the elements on the span have to be handled. This is the case for spans with $c_{neg} = 0$ and $c_{pos} > 0$.

Because of the coarse element grid, two or more edges may intersect the same cell. To handle this case correctly, the edges which intersect a particular grid cell are evaluated using a three-pass algorithm. The first pass considers only edges classified as *opener*, the second one edges classified as *closer*. A third pass must be added to handle the special case that two *opener*-edges of the same polygon intersect the current grid cell. These three passes are sufficient to handle regular concave polygons, i.e. polygons in which vertices are the only points where two edges intersect.

3.5.2.4   Intersection point computation

The correct computation of the intersection coordinate x_s is crucial to consider all elements contributing to a RoI. It is important to decide whether the intersection

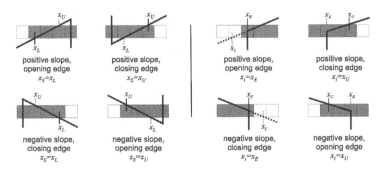

Figure 3.13: *Computing the intersection coordinate x_s with a non-vertical edge (left) and at joins (right).*

of the edge with the upper or lower element boundary is used. Figure 3.13/left shows the four possible cases.

When computing the intersection coordinate at joints of two edges, one of the edges is assumed as vertical for simplicity and two values x_i ($i \in \{1, 2\}$) are computed. x_1 is determined as depicted in Figure 3.13/right, assuming the lower edge as vertical. x_2 is computed analogously, assuming the upper edge as vertical and modifying Figure 3.13/right as follows: both edges are mirrored about the x-axis and "positive" resp. "negative" slope are swapped. As the resulting value for x_s, the minimum, if both edges are openers, or the maximum of x_1 and x_2, if both edges are closers, is used.

In contrast to the classical scanline algorithm, where they are ignored, horizontal edges require special handling within the proposed algorithm. This is due to the property of concave polygons to locally affect the well-defined behavior of the introduced opener and closer logic. Thus, horizontal edges are handled by temporarily replacing them by zero, one or two auxiliary vertical edges which intersect the current scanline only. Figure 3.14 shows the possible cases. It is worth noting that, non-horizontal edges may become horizontal at coarser grid resolutions.

Results: The deterministic element traversal leads to synchrony at server and client. Thus, at each time during image streaming the client can identify received data containers. No additional ID is required to be attached.

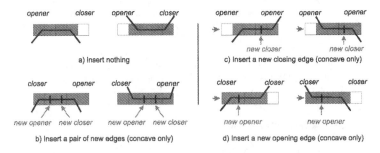

Figure 3.14: *Handling a horizontal edge by inserting auxiliary vertical edges at the current scanline.*

As shown in Figure 3.15, this significantly reduces the need of bandwidth and outperforms inherent and especially external signalization for all RoI dimensions. However, it can also be seen that the performance gain to inherent signalization decreases with increasing RoI dimensions.

Signalization without attached ID marks, however, also requires that beginning and end of each data container can be determined. This is only possible for packets. Partial contributions of code-blocks and tiles require additional marks.

An additional advantage of the proposed streaming strategy is the ability to handle arbitrarily shaped and overlapping RoIs without redundancies. In case of multiple RoIs, it is also possible to prioritize RoIs. Such a flexibility is generally not provided by related techniques proposed in literature. The more complex determination of RoI elements, however, also slightly increases complexity.

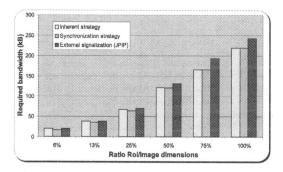

Figure 3.15: *Bandwidth required to deliver an equal amount of image data for the proposed strategies for inherent and synchronized signalization. External signalization is represented by JPIP. (Image dimensions: 480×640, LSA: 32×32)*

3.6   Further applications for the proposed approaches

The proposed ideas for the flexible processing of valid image parts are not interesting for image streaming only. They may also be applied to the creation and compliant storage of data-streams modified to visually represent the content in a certain manner, e.g. as shown in Figure 5.4, p. 94. In this section, it will be shown how to accomplish this with or without the ability to fully reconstruct the content.

As shown in previous sections of this chapter, data contributing to a certain RoI can be appropriately sequenced. Thereby, it has been shown that it is reasonable to move less interesting contributions for each RoI element to higher layers $l > m$. If it is assumed that a strived visual image representation can be achieved by the first contributions residing at layers $1 \leq l \leq m$, this representation is permanently kept and can always be restored by decoding the first m layers only. If there is another successive image representation, which is required to be restorable, this process might also be repeated for layers $m < l \leq q$ and so forth. As shown in later chapters this is useful for a number of applications and can be easily implemented.

The full decoding of all available data leads to the full reconstruction of the image content. This might not always be desired. To save storage space, it is often useful to keep the data contributing to a particular image representation only. Especially for medical data, such a representation is the exact reconstruction of RoIs at a reduced background [Kim95; Str97; Tai02]. This can be achieved by removing all contributions at layers $l > m$. Although the creation of such reduced representations has already been accomplished by techniques for static RoIs [Bra03a; Bra03b] using the proposed approach does not require the definition of the representation at encoding time.

To store the respective layer contributions, the application of the proposed inherent signalization strategy can be applied. It ensures the result may be handled by any compliant decoder.

3.7   Conclusion of the chapter

As they are able to significantly reduce the needs for computing power and bandwidth, developments in image streaming based on dynamic RoIs and JPEG2000 are important for mobile environments. Thereby, the streaming process may be divided into the 3 major stages *calculation, sequencing* and *signalization*.

The aim of *calculation* is the determination and access of data contributing to the reconstruction of a RoI at a certain LoD. Introducing a *scheme able to handle all types of key elements* has shown this for rectangular RoIs and the LoD attributes *x-* and *y-resolution*. To cope with the general drawback of a coarse approximation of the RoI shape and its assigned LoD, *2 adaptations* of the basic scheme have been proposed: *Limited Spatial Access* and *subband-wise selection*. Both approaches are able to *significantly reduce the amount of data* required to reconstruct a RoI at a certain LoD.

Simply transmitting the calculated elements, however, might not lead to optimal results or provide sufficient flexibility during streaming. This has been overcome by adapting the *sequencing* stage and introducing *new ideas for the prioritization* between multiple RoIs (global sequencing) and the R-D optimal refinement of a single RoI (local sequencing). For *global sequencing* new means for determination and implementation of flexible prioritization have been proposed. They are simple, intuitive and enhance the streaming process by new functionalities. *Local sequencing* exploits spatial properties of each RoI element to adapt the element sequence to an optimal refinement of the RoI. As a result a better image quality of up to 3db can been achieved.

Streaming also requires mechanisms for the *signalization of each image part*. This is often achieved by attaching additional external ID marks, which require further bandwidth. To overcome this, *a new inherent signalization strategy* has been proposed. It *requires little computing power* at client side and is especially applicable for larger RoIs. As it produces compliant data-streams, the general idea can also be applied to permanently store certain visual image representations.

Especially for low-bandwidth environments, *a new synchronized signalization strategy* combining ideas from calculation, sequencing, and signalization within a single approach has been proposed. It is based on a scanline traversal of the transformed image in DWT domain and *requires only the transmission of the image data* without further ID marks.

Common to all of the proposed strategies is their *compliance to the JPEG2000 standard*. However, they can also be applied for other codecs with similar properties. Thus, they are a valuable contribution to modern image communication, and due to their reduced requirements, especially suited for mobile environments.

Chapter 4

Mobile image browsing

If an image cannot be completely shown to the user, it must be browsed to allow for exploration of its contents. Especially for mobile environments, this imposes a number of problems. After declaring the aim of mobile image browsing, these issues are identified and requirements to overcome them are derived (Section 4.1).

Probably the most important part of browsing techniques is the representation of the content [Bjo00]. To stress the need for new developments, related work is reviewed and discussed (Section 4.2). Founded on their respective properties a new classification scheme is introduced, which also serves to give guidelines for an appropriate application of dynamic RoIs as proposed in the last chapters (Section 4.3).

This chapter also introduces new browsing techniques for the *Zoom&Pan* (Section 4.4), *Detail&Overview* (Section 4.5) and *Focus&Context* (Section 4.6) approach. Contrary to many other techniques, they have been developed especially for mobile environments and designed to overcome their multiple limitations. To show this, they are evaluated regarding the introduced requirements. This chapter is concluded by a summary of the achieved results (Section 4.7).

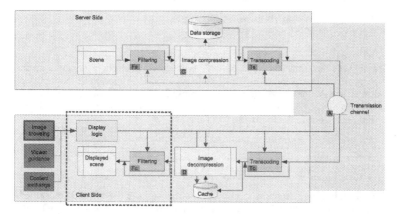

Figure 4.1: *Creation of the visual representation is accomplished by the filtering step at client side. The display logic serves to determine and signal the respective demands to relevant components.*

4.1   Aims and requirements

Browsing a single image on a small screen is still a demanding task. As large contents exceed the provided screen space and the eyes are still considered as the only User Interface (UI) for visual information [Ebr03], consequentially, this leads to problems. Although there are approaches to overcome the screen space barrier by using external [Wan02c] or multiple [Joh01] displays, it is questionable if these strategies can be applied to mobile environments. Due to this, the content must be adapted to the screen space.

To achieve this, it is reasonable to divide the image in interesting and uninteresting regions. Thus, a small *image representation* can be achieved by removing negligible content. Although there are some approaches to guess the user's intentions [Che03; Liu03a; Liu03b; Xie05], the determination of interesting regions is in general accomplished by *user interaction*. During interaction the image representation is dynamically adapted to the current needs. In all systems known to the author this is achieved by the *filtering* component at client side (F_c in Figure 4.1).

If not suitably adapted, this process is bundled with high requirements for computing power and bandwidth. To overcome this, it is proposed to exploit the benefits of a demand-driven image streaming. Thus, the streaming process is always adapted to the current image representation. Data not required is not transferred. Beside a save of bandwidth, this also reduces the complexity of the decoding process (cf. Section 2.5). Within the proposed communication system, the adaptation is accomplished by the *display logic*, which only requests data passing the filtering process.

Summarizing, *the aim of mobile image browsing* is to enable the viewer to comprehend contents by progressive and interactive exploration overcoming the limitations of mobile environments. This can be achieved by the appropriate implementation of the following three points:

1. Spatial representation of the original image content

2. Means for interactive content exploration

3. Adaptation of the image streaming process

To be able to evaluate the solutions proposed in this chapter, the next sections derive requirements for each problem area.

Spatial image representation   The content representation strongly depends on the demand-driven partition of the image into regions. However, to fit the representation to screen some content must be removed. This gives rise to problems in *locating* and *interpreting* contents, and in *relating* it to others [Leu94]. Especially for images, this leads to the following requirements:

- **Locating:** to show information to the currently most interesting region

- **Interpreting:** to show interesting regions in detail

- **Relating:** to show information to important image properties

To prevent loss in orientation, location, and dimensions of the currently most interesting region regarding the whole image must always be deducible. Thereby, the interpretation of the belonging content must be supported by the display of this region in *sufficient detail*. The provision of *spatial relationships* has always been proven to be of crucial interest for content browsing [Car97b]. Especially for images they might be supported by *providing important image properties*, as proportions and dimensions of the image as well as context information.

To create image representations it is important to consider the consumed *computing power* and the *bandwidth* required to transmit the shown content.

Means for interaction   Browsing also means interaction. An appropriate browsing technique provides intuitive mechanisms for dynamic content exploration. *Interaction* can be described in terms of the *balance of control* [Twe97] between user and device. A technique is *intuitive* if the user does not require long practice to understand and use a technique. This is especially given for real-world interactions adapted by the browsing technique. The following list identifies most common browsing tasks:

- **Roaming** means *selection and immediate display of a certain image region*. Roaming interaction is a discrete jump between two distinct regions. It corresponds to the real-world task of looking up a certain page or image section. Roaming zones do often not overlap.

- **Panning** means *slight spatial adjustment of the most interesting region* and is related to the real-world expression of exploring contents on a continuous path. Contrary to roaming, old and new region strongly overlap.

- **Scaling** means *content presentation at different scales*. Browsing by simply changing the image region is often not sufficient and does not provide the option of showing the image at once. Like in real life, scaling allows a hierarchical view of the image and gives the user a better understanding of the content. If the image is provided in different scales, its comprehension is enhanced.

The manner in which these tasks are supported plays a crucial role for the evaluation of a certain technique. Thereby, it is desirable to support the information seeking mantra [Shn96] – *Overview first, zoom and filter, then details-on-demand* – without requiring extensive user interaction. This is especially important in mobile environments, where hands-free working is essential and the input is rather simple.

Common to modern mobile hardware are touch-sensitive screens allowing pen-based interactions. Almost all current devices also provide an easy to handle 2D-rocker allowing for navigation if pen-based interaction is not appropriate or possible. It is desirable for all tasks to be accomplished by these two inputs only.

Image streaming   Although the most interesting region might be the same, each particular browsing technique provides another image representation. As they strongly vary in the presented image regions and detail levels, an *adaptation of the streaming process* to the respective representation is required.

This can be achieved by applying the RoI/LoD-based streaming technology introduced in the last chapters. Bundled with a redundancy free-transmission, the proposed strategies are even able to react to dynamically changing requests. Due to the spatial partition in more and less interesting regions, they are rather suited for remote image browsing.

The needs, however, must be specified. This can be achieved by formulating and delivering requests to the respective communication components. The most important are:

- **RoI/LoD partition:** The partition of the image in RoIs and the assignment of LoDs

- **Applied streaming technology:** Methods to select, sequence and signal RoI elements

- **Applied streaming strategy:** Methods to increase the progressive refinement

Statements regarding the first point are often similar for related representations. The remaining strongly depend on the respective layout or task.

4.2 Discussion of related work

The browsing of data sets has also been a typical problem in *Information Visualization* [Poo00; Suh02; Bau04; Xie05] and *Geographic Information Systems* (GIS) [Chu95; Kea99] over years. As images are a specific kind of data, it is reasonable to adopt basic principles proven to be useful in those application areas. Nevertheless, as in raster imagery content is described by single pixel values and their spatial relation to others, there is a significant difference to the abstract multidimensional data often handled by information visualization: *the original spatial relations must be kept within alternative image representations.* If this cannot be guaranteed, the content of raster imagery is lost.

The following sections review and classify approaches for the representation of the content. Thereby, related approaches from other research fields dealing with information visualization are also considered. Due to the variety of different application scenarios and contents, none of these approaches outperforms all others on all kind of data [Hor01; Gut04], device [Xie05], or application [Kap95; Chi01; Bau02]. As shown in Section 1.4.2, there is only little work on remote content browsing.

As mechanisms for interaction are of minor interest for image communication, they will be neglected. For an explicit overview regarding browsing interaction the interested reader is referred to [Eis96; Twe97; Poo00; Hor02; Gut04].

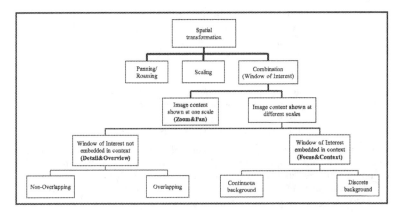

Figure 4.2: *A new classification scheme for image browsing techniques founded on the spatial representation.*

4.2.1 A new classification scheme for image browsing techniques

The variety of different techniques proposed to solve the problem of limited screen space requires statements for a meaningful classification and taxonomy. Different publications have addressed this issue for general visualization tasks [Leu94; Twe97; Chi00; Sto03] or image browsing [Bea90; Pla95]. The proposed schemes, however, cannot handle modern techniques [Bea90; Pla95], lack on statements to spatial representation [Twe97; Chi00; Sto03], or focus on specific approaches [Leu94]. Furthermore, they often do not utilize current terminology or do not provide exact definitions. This led to the problem that some techniques could not be unequivocally classified or equal terms are applied differently.

The complexity of two-dimensional browsing suggests that more careful analysis, design, and evaluation might lead to significant improvements. (PLAISANT ET AL. [Pla95])

One contribution of this thesis is the introduction of a new classification scheme for image browsing techniques based on RoIs and LoDs (cf. Figure 4.2). It allows a clear determination in disjunct and hierarchical classes and can handle all techniques known to the author. It has been published by the author as part of the contribution *"JPEG2000-based image communication for modern browsing techniques"* [Ros05b]. The scheme is founded on the assumption that not the whole image, but only a certain region, the *Window of Interest (WoI)* [Tau02a; LM02], is of main interest at a single browsing step. More concrete, a WoI is a RoI assumed to be shown in final-LoD. This is reasonable and considers the introduced requirement of interpretability. Thus, the different techniques mainly differ in the manner they represent the remaining *background*. Thereby, the layout of WoI and background as well as the particular LoDs are of crucial interest to classify a technique. Without loss of generality, the following statements assume only one WoI.

Contrary to other classification approaches, only the consideration of the spatial image representation at a certain browsing step is required for taxonomy. As we will see later on, this is also of crucial importance to derive statements for appropriate image streaming. Nevertheless, the author agrees that to fully characterize an image browsing technique, interaction is an additional point to consider. This can be accomplished by including the proposed scheme as an independent module into a more general classification as that proposed by CHI [Chi00].

By assuming a limited screen space with static dimensions and a large image exceeding the provided display space, there are basically two main approaches to represent the image: (1) by a certain image region only (*Panning/Roaming*), or (2) by a downsized version (*Scaling*). While for the first approach the displayed region is represented in final-LoD, for the second case the LoD is inherently lower. Since usability of both approaches is rather inappropriate for browsing imagery of arbitrary dimensions [DMM82; Bea90; Kap95; Pla95], nowadays they are of little practical use. Most of the proposed techniques apply the WoI approach as a combination of both. From the variety of such displaying techniques, one can clearly divide two kind of representation:

1. **WoI only:** content is shown at one scale

2. **WoI and background:** content is shown at multiple scales

While for techniques belonging to the first group only one classification criteria is required, many different techniques presenting WoI and background at the same time have been proposed. They are often labeled *distortion oriented* [Leu94] and apply the fact that perceptual learning of object recognition is size-invariant [Suh02]. This requires another classification criteria for an appropriate assignment: *the spa-*

tial layout of WoI and background. The following subsections review the different approaches in more detail.

4.2.2   The Zoom&Pan approach

The combination of Panning/Roaming and Scaling (cf. Figure 4.3) is commonly called *Zoom&Pan* (ZP) [Bed94; NS997; Com99] or *Zoomable User Interface* (ZUI) [Com99; Poo00]. Due to their simplicity such representations can easily be classified by the following criteria:

- Information is represented by the WoI only (background is truncated)

- The WoI is shown in final- or lower LoD to fit on screen

Although it is assumed to display the WoI in final-LoD, it may happen that it exceeds the available screen space (e.g. to get a content overview). Thus, its LoD must be reduced to fit the region on screen. However, zooming not always means a simple change in dimension or scale as during magnification (*Graphical zoom*). By zooming, objects may also change fundamentally in their appearance and presence (*Semantic zoom*) [Bed94; Fur95; Kea98]. To achieve this, content representations for each zoom level are required (cf. Figure 4.3/right).

As within ZP-based techniques the provided screen area is fully occupied by the WoI, it is not possible to display relevant micro and macro information at the same time. The content must be sequentially explored. However, it has been shown that the information seeking mantra is well supported [Pla95; Chi01; Gut04].

Zoom&Pan is the most widespread technique for a variety of tasks in the field of data [Kea98; Poo00] and image browsing [Bed94; NS997; Com99]. Beside being simple and intuitive, this might be due to its support by the *Windows* desktop metaphor. Other representatives from the field of visualization applied to browse structured contents are *Pad++* [Bed94] and its successor *JAZZ* [Bed00b]. Zoom&Pan is very popular in image browsing, and the application areas spread from stationary systems [GIMP05] over handhelds [Ima05] to very small devices such as smart phones [DR04].

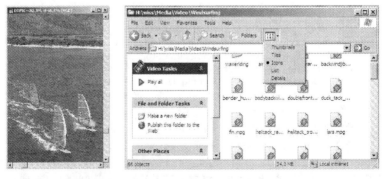

Figure 4.3: *Two examples applying the Zoom&Pan approach. In the right representation, semantic zoom is achieved by showing different data representatives at each zoom level.*

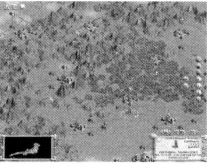

Figure 4.4: *Application of the Detail&Overview approach in visualization of diagnostic data (left, src:[Gho99]) and computer games (right, src:[FIR05]).*

4.2.3 The Detail&Overview approach

Some work has been conducted on how to classify *Detail&Overview*-approaches (DO) [Pla95; Smi98; Car99; Bjo00; Hor01; Lec03; Gut04] using various analogies, including *single coordinated pairs* [Gho99], *coordinated views* [NS997; Ols00], or *specialized multi-window arrangement* [Bau02]. BAUDISCH ET AL. [Bau02] describes such representations as follows: " ... *one window shows the overview, which always represents the entire document, and the other window shows the detail displaying a close-up version of the data.*" However, a clear definition is still missing. This additional criteria is the representation layout defined as follows: *A technique applies an DO-approach, if the WoI may be placed at arbitrary positions without to affect the representation of the background and vice versa.*

Regarding the spatial representation DO is basically a multi-window ZP with a certain zoom level for each window. To create the overview, however,the whole content must be shown in very low detail. As not all available data fits into a very small view, JERDING AND STASKO introduced the *Information mural* [Jer98] basically proposing to apply principles from the field of computer graphics, as shading and anti-aliasing, to solve this problem (cf. Figure C.3). This underlines that it is not required to show all data in all views in the same way. Interestingly, within DO-representations data belonging to the WoI is actually shown twice, once within the WoI and in low detail within the overview. This also applies if more than one overview is provided (cf. Figure C.4).

Spatial properties of Detail&Overview-techniques can be summarized as:

- The image representation consists of a WoI and one or multiple overviews.
- WoI and overview may be placed at an arbitrary position of the available screen space, without influencing each other.
- The overview is spatially distorted to fit on screen.

The DO-based approach covers numerous varieties depending on the fact overview and WoI do overlap [GVS05; MSM05] or not [Gho99], the number of overviews [Pla95], or the manner detail and overview are blend together [Lie97] (cf. Figures 4.4 and C.4). Although especially for small screens more space is reserved to show the WoI, it is not mandatory [War95]. To indicate the position of the detail within the overview, both windows are coupled by a visual marker, usually labeled *viewfinder*.

Although extensively applied to 2D- [Sku03; GVS05] and 3D-GIS [SMP05; MSM05], information visualization [Gho99; Suh02] (cf. Figure 4.4/left), or combinations of both [POL05; SAG05; SPF05], DO has been of little interest for raster image browsing so far. Here, the main application areas are still computer games [WES04; FIR05] (cf. Figure 4.4/right) and image processing products [Ado05] (cf. Figure C.5/left). DO has yet not been applied to mobile devices.

A unique DO technique has been proposed by LIEBERMAN's [Lie97] *Macroscope* system. One or more overviews are spatially covered by the detail view. Due to the application of transparency, however, their content is still visible (cf. Figure C.5/right). Although this technique can only be applied to certain image contents, as maps, it has the valuable benefit of not requiring additional space for the overview.

 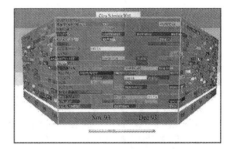

Figure 4.5: *Implementation of the Focus&Context approach in visualization of map data (left, lens function, src:[Kea97a]) and time dependent data (right, perspective wall, src:[Sta03]).*

4.2.4 The Focus&Context approach

Many different terms for *Focus&Context* techniques, including *Rubber sheets* [Sar93], *multiple dimensions of transformation* [Spe93], *space-scale diagrams* [Fur95], *non-linear magnification fields* [Kea97b], *higher-order visualizations* [Bjö98], *interactive external- izations* [Twe97], and *FishEye views* [Fur81; Rau99a] have been applied. If there exists a definition that is accepted by researchers, it is implicit in literature. How- ever, the following description comes rather close to being such a definition:

[Focus&context] starts from three premises: First, the user needs both overview (context) and detail information (focus) simultaneously. Second, information needed in the overview may be different from that needed in detail. Third, these two types of information can be combined within a single (dynamic) display, much as in human vision. (CARD ET AL. [Car99, p. 307])

While the first two points also apply for DO, the third point is the crucial distinc- tive feature for FC. It mimics our natural vision systems more closely than DO and can be basically seen as a *magnification lens* [Car97a] embedded into remain- ing background (cf. Figure 4.5/left). For the proposed classification scheme this property may also be related to the spatial layout of the representation: *Within FC-techniques, the WoI is combined with the background by keeping its relative position within image and representation.*

Due to the power of this paradigm, FC techniques are widely spread in the field of visualization. There are even proposals for specific FC hardware displays [Bau01; Bau02] or for browsing multiple images (*PhotoMesa* [Bed02]). There are also some applications for common user tasks as *FishEye-Menus* [Bed00a], the *Fisheye-Calendar* [Bed04] or HTML-browsers [Hoi03; Bau04]. In the review, however, the author concentrates on techniques of crucial interest for image browsing. An exhaustive overview of FC-techniques can be found at the *Nonlinear Magnification InfoCenter* from KEAHEY [Kea02], or in the publications of BJOERK AND REDSTROEM [Bjo00] and TWEEDIE [Twe97].

The *Bifocal Display* [Spe82], invented in 1980, was arguably the first demonstration of the use of distortion to provide a FC view. While in this technique distortion has only been applied to one direction, FURNAS [Fur81; Fur86] went one step further and applied 2D distortion. The result was the first proposal for a *Fisheye-View*. Interestingly, he applied a *Degree of Interest* (DoI) function analogue to the proposed LoD to determine the distortion for a particular part of the representation. In his works, KEAHEY [Kea97a] generalizes this idea and presents many possible distortions (cf. Figure C.6).

The general description of spatial distortions introduced by KEAHEY can also be applied to images. Nevertheless, it is reasonable to substantiate the given statements. To compensate the space consumed by the embedded and detailed WoI, the background is strongly squeezed. Thereby, the background is distorted by using a continuous or discrete function [Rau01a] applied locally [Dar04] or globally [Rau99a; Rau01a] (cf. Figure C.6). The simplest approach is to apply *uniform distortion*, but this imposes discontinuities at the transition from WoI to background (cf. Figure C.7/left). To solve this, the background may be further partitioned and shown at different detail (cf. Figure C.7/middle and right). This has been proposed within the *Rubber sheets* paradigm (SAKAR ET AL. [Sar93]) and applied to raster imagery by RAUSCHENBACH [Rau99a; Rau01a].

The spatial properties of Focus&Context-approaches can be summarized as:

- The image representation consists of a WoI and background regions
- The WoI is embedded into the background, whereby its position is crucial
- The background may be further partitioned and differently represented

4.2.5 Summary of related work

There are 3 main approaches for browsing graphical contents: *Zoom&Pan*, *Detail&Overview*, and *Focus&Context*.

ZP is the most widespread approach for representing information on limited screen space. It is simple, intuitive, and little demanding to system resources. However, it is commonly understood that when Zoom&Pan is used to gain detail, memory of the context is quickly lost [Poo00]. This imposes usability problems. To overcome this, it is reasonable to show micro and macro information at the same time and to exploit the ability of the HVS to perceive multiple texture scales simultaneously [DeV88].

DO techniques display relevant micro and macro information at the same time in different views. While this approach helps users to orient themselves in large spaces, is has two crucial drawbacks: the additional screen space and computing power to provide the overview. It also requires users to visually switch back and forth between the two distinct views and to reorient themselves within the representation every time they do so.

FC can display relevant micro and macro info at the same time on a single view and is for many tasks better suited than DO or ZP [Bau02]. However, to achieve a lens effect the background must be further divided. This is by far more costly in terms of processing power. Techniques applying equal distortion to large image regions, as *Rubber sheets* [Sar93] or the *rectangular Fisheye view* [Rau99a], are less demanding than other FC techniques.

Little work has already been done on remote image browsing (cf. Appendix A). Almost all related techniques apply the ZP approach. There is only one proposal applying FC.

4.3   Adaptation of the image streaming process

As shown by the introduced classification scheme, many image browsing techniques share common properties regarding content representation. In this section, these properties are exploited to formulate concrete requests for image streaming. The goal is to provide general transmission guidelines for a certain browsing technique. As the given statements are founded on RoIs and LoDs, the requests can be implemented by the introduced streaming technology. Most of the presented ideas have been proposed by the author in *"JPEG2000-based image communication for modern browsing techniques"* [Ros05b]. Beside some strategies for Zoom&Pan [Des01; JO04; IDE05; KAK05] and Focus&Context [Rau99a], this topic has been of minor interest so far. If considered, however, massive improvements regarding the need for bandwidth make it especially suited for mobile environments.

To specify the data required by a browsing technique, the structure of the classification tree is of crucial interest. Each node can be basically seen as a representant of characteristics valid for the belonging subtree. As single techniques reside at the leafs of the hierarchy, belonging properties can be easily determined. The following sections state the respective requests for every level and node of the classification hierarchy. Thereby, in focus are *RoI partition* and the *target-LoD* of each RoI. As the taxonomy is based on the spatial representation of the image, statements are limited to LoD attributes *x*- and *y-resolution*. Detail for the remaining attributes vary strongly on user interests, the respective task, and output device and will therefore be neglected. They are assumed to be restored up to the final-LoD values. Due to their dependence on a single browsing technique, of minor interest are also the respectively applied *streaming technology* and *strategy*.

4.3.1   First tree level

The first level of the hierarchy serves to provide statements to the most fundamental image representations: *Panning/Roaming*, *Scaling*, and their combination.

Panning/Roaming: This technique shows a fixed section of the image only. Content belonging to the remaining areas is truncated.

- **RoI partition:** The image is divided into two RoIs spatially aligned with the shown region and the background.

- **Target-LoDs:** The presented section is shown in final-LoD ($LoD(1, 1, img_a, img_c)$). Since no background is displayed, the belonging attributes values *x-/y-resolution* are 0.

Scaling: Within Scaling the image is downsized to fits on screen. Thus, the whole image is shown at less detail.

- **RoI partition:** There is only one RoI covering the whole image.

- **Target-LoDs:** Image dimensions must be reduced to fit the image to screen. If scaling factors are assumed as $x : y$, with $x, y \geq 1$, the target-LoD may be stated as $LoD(\frac{1}{x}, \frac{1}{y}, img_a, img_c)$. If screen respective image dimensions are stated as $[screen_1, screen_2]$ and $[s_1, s_2]$ with $screen_i \ll s_i$, $i = 1, 2$, the respective scaling values are determined by $\max_{i=1,2} \frac{s_i}{screen_i}$.

Using a Window of Interest: The application of a WoI is more a paradigm than an independent branch of representation techniques; it mostly combines properties of Roaming and Scaling. This results in hybrid techniques applying these fundamental techniques to two (ZP) or more RoIs (DO, FC). Common to all techniques, however, is the property that one RoI is assumed as WoI.

4.3.2   Second tree level

Using the paradigm of a WoI, one can clearly divide into techniques displaying the content at one or multiple scales. This has direct consequences to RoI partition, leading to more or less RoIs to be handled.

Zoom&Pan: This technique represents the consequent combination of Roaming and Scaling. The WoI may be placed at arbitrary positions within the image and may also be scaled. No background is displayed. The visual result may also be equal to one of the fundamental representations. In any event, always only the WoI is shown.

- **RoI partition:** The image is divided into the WoI and a single background RoI.

- **Target-LoDs:** In case the WoI is not scaled, the same statements as for Roaming apply. If scaled, the LoD of the WoI is reduced to $LoD(\frac{1}{x}, \frac{1}{y}, img_a, img_c)$ with $\frac{1}{x}, \frac{1}{y} < 1$. Similar to ordinary Scaling, scaling factors are determined by $\max_{i=1,2} \frac{reg_i}{screen_i}$. Thereby, $[reg_1, reg_2]$ refers to the dimensions of the WoI. As typical for panning, attribute values x-/y-resolution$= 0$ lead to the visual removal of background regions.

Content shown at different scales: The property to show the content at different scales opens up for the meaningful application of multiple RoIs with varying LoD. This implies that beside the WoI, at least a second RoI with target-LoD values x-/y-resolution> 0 is used.

4.3.3   Third tree level

If multiple RoIs at different LoDs are shown, the embedding of the WoI is used for further differentiation. Embedding (FC) leads to more RoIs than an arbitrary positioning (DO). As belonging techniques mostly differ in their representation of the background, the following statements do not consider the WoI. This region is always assumed to fit on screen and to be presented in final-LoD. For applications requiring a scaled WoI, statements given for Scaling can be applied as described.

Detail&Overview: This class of techniques applies Roaming and Scaling to different content views. In addition to the WoI, these are 1 to n overviews. The coarsest view may also cover the whole image.

- **RoI partition:** For each overview, the image is divided into two RoIs, one covering the shown area around the WoI and one the background. Due to the reason some views may *overlap* within the visual representation, a RoI may be partially hidden. Further dividing a shown RoI and considering such parts as background offers further potential for the save of bandwidth. Of course, this does not apply for *non-overlapping* representations.

- **Target-LoDs:** To create a tiny overview of a large RoI, the content must be strongly scaled and shown in very low detail ($\frac{1}{x}, \frac{1}{y} \ll 1$). To keep the original ratio of the image dimensions, $x = y$ applies. Regions belonging to the background are simply truncated (cf. to *Roaming*).

  In case n overviews are used, the same statements may be applied. If overview dimensions are assumed to correlate with n, and x_o represents the scaling value of a RoI belonging to overview o ($1 \leq o \leq n$) in x dimension (y dimension respectively), the belonging LoD attributes must be chosen to satisfy: $x_1 > \ldots > x_n$. The fact all overviews show the content around the current WoI can be exploited to avoid a redundant data transfer.

Focus&Context: In this class of techniques the consistent embedding of the WoI into the background plays an important role. To achieve this, a sophisticated RoI partition and LoD assignment is crucial.

- **RoI partition:** Common to many techniques is the definition of a WoI, and the partition of the background in *belts*. To achieve the typical lens effect, these belts surround the WoI and are self formed by multiple RoIs. Thereby, *discrete backgrounds* are characterized by large rectangular RoIs.

  Although this concept can also be applied to *continuous backgrounds*, it would lead to a number of problems. Such representations contain in general no uniform regions. A large number of small belts and RoIs is the consequence.

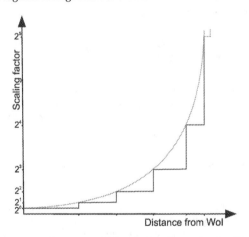

Figure 4.6: *Approximation of an exponential function by a discrete function. The characteristic of the approximating function is based on refinement steps supported by a dyadic DWT.*

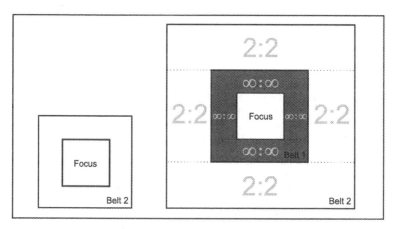

Figure 4.7: *To achieve the local FC-technique (left) requiring only a quarter of the original space, the image is partitioned in a focus and 2 belts (right). The save of screen space is achieved by omitting regions covered by belt 1 and scaling regions belonging to belt 2 accordingly.*

Due to the variety of valid continuous distortion functions it might not even be possible to achieve such a partition.

In such cases, it is proposed to apply a second, discrete, belt partition. This partition does not influence the distortion of the background, and serves only to determine the respective demands for image transmission. It is designed in such a manner so as to approximate the continuous distortion function and to ensure that at least the required LoD is provided. This again leads to a partition into larger and regular RoIs and allows a determination of the desired demands. Figure 4.6 shows an example of the approximation of an exponential function by a discrete distortion function considering LoD values supported by JPEG2000-encoded data. The large uniformly scaled areas mark the spatial extent of the respective RoIs.

- **Target-LoDs:** Within FC representations to each RoI a well-defined scaling factor is assigned. The respective attribute values strongly depend on the association of a RoI to a certain belt and its position within the representation. As techniques for distorting the background vary strongly, general statements cannot be given.

As an example for LoD assignment, the following statements refer to a local lens technique proposed by DARLING ET AL. [Dar04]. The spatial layout has been adopted by the author for image browsing and published in *"Interfaces for mobile image browsing"* [Ros07a]. The spatial representation and partition is shown in Figure 4.7. To achieve a local lens effect, the additional space occupied by the WoI is compensated by belts very close to the focus. Thus, their LoD is much lower than the LoD of RoIs belonging to remaining belts at image borders. In the provided example, strong scaling ($x, y = \infty$) even leads to an omission of these RoIs. This causes the visual appearance as if the WoI covers adjacent image areas. To belts close to image borders an identic scaling factor is assigned.

For such a representation the distribution of LoDs can be easily determined. Thereby, n denotes the number of all belts and i the number of belts used for compensation. If x_b represents the scaling value of a RoI belonging to a belt

b used for compensation ($1 \leq b \leq i$, starting from the WoI) in x dimension (y dimension respectively), the respective detail value conform to $1 \gg \frac{1}{x_1} \geq \frac{1}{x_2} \geq \cdots \geq \frac{1}{x_i} \geq 0$. For the remaining belts c ($i < c \leq n$) it applies: $\frac{1}{x_i} \ll \frac{1}{x_{i+1}} = \frac{1}{x_{i+2}} = \cdots = \frac{1}{x_n} \leq 1$.

Contrary to local lenses, global lens techniques apply the reasonable assumption that the interest of the user decreases with increasing distance from the focus. Statements to the RoI/LoD partition of such a technique are provided in Section 4.6.

Conclusions: Based on the introduced classification scheme, general requests to the adaptation of the image streaming process can be formulated. This allows appropriate coupling of streaming and browsing for all image browsing techniques known to the author. Due to the foundation on fundamental principles, this also applies for new browsing techniques as long as they can be classified by the adopted scheme. As based on RoIs and LoDs, the given guidelines can be realized by the streaming technology already introduced. This leads to an easy and modular coupling of the different components to an efficient JPEG2000-based communication system.

Generality also imposes space for improvements. Thus, the general guidelines assigned to a single technique might be further refined. Due to the variety of the approach, this especially applies for techniques representing the content at different scales. How to achieve this, is part of the next sections dealing with the introduction of new image browsing techniques.

4.4   Grid-based Zoom&Pan (GbZP)

This section introduces a new Zoom&Pan-based image browsing technique. It has been proposed by the author in *"Grid-based interaction for effective image browsing on mobile devices"* [Ros05a] and varies from related methods in its provided features for user assistance and interaction. The new idea to achieve this is the use of an transparent grid structure representing important image and browsing properties, and providing innovative means for interaction. This grid can be basically seen as an image overview with the following inherent features.

1. The grid outline represents the displayed image and its proportions.

2. Each transparent grid cell has the shape of the available screen space and represents position and dimensions of the belonging image region.

3. Grid-based navigation substitutes sliders and menus, and brings fast and intuitive interaction to Zoom&Pan techniques.

Grid-based Zoom&Pan (GbZP) exploits the fact that more than one "screen" is required to display a large image completely. This is directly adopted to the provided grid structure (cf. Figure 4.8). While the grid outline represents the whole image, each grid cell stands for an image region which fits on screen. Since a viewfinder always indicates the current position within the image, the user is relieved from complex mind maps and well assisted during exploration.

The grid also introduces intuitive ways for image exploration. Although there are single enhancements [Pla95], the common means via sliders and menus are too complicated and time-consuming for mobile working. To overcome this, a

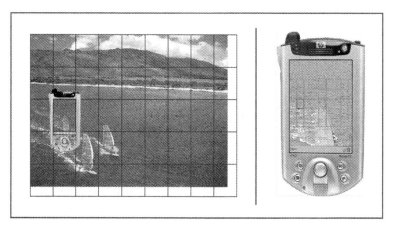

Figure 4.8: *A certain number of "screens" is needed to show a large image completely (left). This is directly adopted to the layout of the navigation grid (right).*

completely new paradigm has been developed. The next sections will explain this in more detail. It will also be shown how to achieve an adapted image streaming.

4.4.1   Image browsing

4.4.1.1   Spatial image representation

The image representation of GbZP consists of two different parts: the *image view* and the *navigation grid*. The image view shows the image content belonging to the current WoI at a particular LoD. Thus, the introduced approach clearly belongs to the class of Zoom&Pan. Nevertheless, to enhance the browsing process and to disburden the user from complex mind maps, an intuitive navigation grid is provided. This grid is not only used for interaction. It also communicates several properties of the image and the browsing task, and thus is an important part of the image representation.

The *navigation grid* basically consists of the *grid outline* and a well-defined number of regular transparent *grid cells*. While the grid outline has been designed to represent the whole image, a single cell stands for an individual presentable region. The entirety of the cells again represents the whole image. They can be basically seen as a representation of a number of screens laid down side by side, each showing another section of the image.

The navigation grid is directly rendered on the presented image region to save screen space and maximized to simplify interactions. Depending on the ratio between image and screen, to the grid outline is assigned a certain orientation (anchored at top/bottom or left/right or both). Grid dimensions $[grid_1, grid_2]$ may vary depend on the orientation and can be calculated by:

$$grid_1 = \begin{cases} screen_1 & : & \frac{screen_1}{screen_2} \leq \frac{s_1}{s_2} \\ \left\lceil \frac{s_1 \cdot screen_2}{s_2} \right\rceil & : & \frac{s_1}{s_2} < \frac{screen_1}{screen_2} \end{cases}$$

$$grid_2 = \begin{cases} screen_2 & : & \frac{s_1}{s_2} < \frac{screen_1}{screen_2} \\ \left\lceil \frac{s_2 \cdot screen_1}{s_1} \right\rceil & : & \frac{screen_1}{screen_2} \leq \frac{s_1}{s_2} \end{cases}$$

(4.1)

As these values do not change, the outline is considered to be constant during the whole browsing task. This is not the case for grid cells, whose dimensions and shape carry interesting information. Each cell has the shape of the available screen area. As image dimensions are usually larger, and thus, more than the provided screen space is needed to display the whole image, the number of cells depends on image dimensions (cf. Figure 4.8/left). As for larger images more screens are needed as for smaller images, the physical image dimension can be easily determined by the user. This also applies if the image is presented in different scales, since the virtual dimensions of the image ($\tilde{s}_1, \tilde{s}_2$) become larger (magnification) or smaller (diminution) (cf. Figure 4.9/left and right). The number of cells in each direction required to display the whole image can be calculated by

$$cols = \left\lceil \frac{\tilde{s}_1}{screen_1} \right\rceil , rows = \left\lceil \frac{\tilde{s}_2}{screen_2} \right\rceil$$

(4.2)

Due to the reason a whole number of "screens" cannot always be used to represent an image, some cells might be truncated at the grid outline (cf. Figure 4.8/left). Thus, the determination of cell dimensions must be split into the calculation of nominal cell dimensions [$cell_1, cell_2$] and dimensions of smaller *border cells*. To accomplish this, it is proposed to calculate the nominal cell dimensions by considering the ratio between the available screen and image dimensions only. Again, the orientation of the grid must be regarded.

$$cell_1 = \begin{cases} \left\lceil \frac{screen_1^2}{\tilde{s}_1} \right\rceil & : & \frac{screen_1}{screen_2} \leq \frac{\tilde{s}_1}{\tilde{s}_2} \\ \left\lceil \frac{\tilde{s}_1 \cdot cell_2}{\tilde{s}_2} \right\rceil & : & \frac{\tilde{s}_1}{\tilde{s}_2} < \frac{screen_1}{screen_2} \end{cases}$$

$$cell_2 = \begin{cases} \left\lceil \frac{screen_2^2}{\tilde{s}_2} \right\rceil & : & \frac{\tilde{s}_1}{\tilde{s}_2} < \frac{screen_1}{screen_2} \\ \left\lceil \frac{\tilde{s}_2 \cdot cell_1}{\tilde{s}_1} \right\rceil & : & \frac{screen_1}{screen_2} \leq \frac{\tilde{s}_1}{\tilde{s}_2} \end{cases}$$

(4.3)

Afterwards, dimensions of border cells can be derived from the grid outline, nominal cell dimensions, and their respective number in a particular direction.

4.4.1.2 Means for interaction

The advantage of using the proposed navigation grid becomes even more apparent if interaction is considered. The interaction scheme has been designed to adapt real world image handling to mobile devices. To give the user an immediate feedback and feeling about what he is doing, each task is directly accomplished by

Figure 4.9: *The proposed navigation grid supports important image browsing tasks as panning (left), the selection of cells for downscaling (middle), and downscaling (right).*

interacting with the grid. It can be basically understood as the virtual equivalent of the related physical tasks – moving or folding maps. As in real world, they are necessary to locate a desired image section. Although, a related grid-based technique has been proposed in ZONEZOOM [DR04], it only applies the grid paradigm and lacks of interactive features for interaction. As shown in the following, this can be fully achieved by GbZP:

Roaming: Since each grid cell represents a disjunct image region, roaming is inherently supported. To change the current WoI, the user just taps the cell belonging to the next WoI on the touch-screen display. While switching between two different regions, an optional "fly-over"-animation shows the content located between them.

Panning: Since panning is assumed to only be used if local adjustments to the displayed region must be made, it has been implemented via the 2D-navigation rocker rather than the pen. Thereby, each panning operation is tracked via the highlighted viewfinder. It is worth noting, the viewfinder might not always be aligned with the navigation grid during panning (cf. Figure 4.9/left).

Scaling: For scaling, user-friendly mechanisms have been developed. Scaling basically means a split of cells for magnification, and a fusion for an overview. As simple and intuitive interaction was one of the main goals, a single perspicuous action for either task has been developed.

To get an overview of an image region, the user simply selects multiple cells by a quick drag movement of the pen. Cells highlighted this way form a *super cell*. As the same downscaling factor is applied to both dimensions, this super cell has the beneficial feature of having the same shape as a current nominal grid cell (cf. Figure 4.9/middle). By counting the number of covered cells in one direction, it is easy to determine the downscaling factor. After finishing the action, all selected cells are fused into one (cf. Figure 4.9/right).

Magnification is done the opposite way around dividing a single cell into four cells (magnification factor 2 in each direction). To achieve this, the user simply keeps pressing after the cell selection. Depending on some adjustable time delay, a cell split occurs, and the image is shown in a resolution which is two times higher than the resolution before. The user may now keep pressing the pen down to further increase resolution.

Based on the fast and intuitive support for these three basic interaction techniques, a user is well assisted to manage the different tasks appearing during browsing an image on a small display. All available interactions are summarized in Figure 4.10.

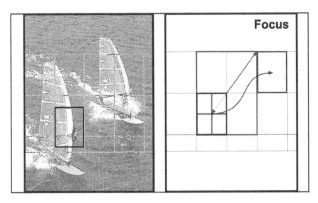

Figure 4.10: *Image representation (left) and provided interactions on the navigation grid of GbZP (right / roaming, zoom in, zoom out).*

4.4.2   Adaptation of image streaming

GbZP belongs to the group of ZP approaches, and thus, applies their principles regarding image streaming. Due to the reason that their spatial representation is simple, high-level statements already given in Section 4.3 can easily be applied. This section serves to summarize and enhance these statements regarding the application of related streaming technology and strategy.

RoI/LoD partition   As for all ZP-based techniques, the respective image content is shown at one scale only. Thereby, it may be represented at final- or reduced LoD. The background is removed. If $x : y$ represent possible scaling factors of the WoI, the respective specifications are depicted in Table 4.1.

	GbZP representation	
	WoI	**background**
target-LoD:	$LoD(\frac{1}{x}, \frac{1}{y}, img_a, img_c)$	$LoD(0,0,0,0)$

Table 4.1: *RoI/LoD partition of an image represented by GbZP.*

Applied streaming technology

Calculation of contributing elements: Due to the rectangular shape of the display area, especially the proposed technique for *calculation of RoI elements for rectangular RoIs* is of interest. Although not mandatory, *Limited Spatial Access* can be applied to limit the amount of data required to reconstruct the WoI. *Subband-wise selection* is of minor interest to ZP-based techniques.

Sequencing of calculated elements: As it is highly possible there are truncated RoI elements at the WoIs borders, *R-D optimized local sequencing* can be applied to accomplish a better refinement of the WoI. Due to the reason that there is only one displayed region, *prioritization-based global sequencing* is not required for ZP-based techniques.

Signalization of sequenced elements: There is no specific requirement for the signalization of elements contributing to a GbZP representation.

Applied streaming strategy   As there is only a single region of relevance, there is no need for sophisticated streaming strategies.

4.4.3   Discussion

In this section, the properties of GbZP regarding its intended use in mobile environments is discussed. Here, the introduced requirements for spatial representation (*providing information* during browsing and need for *computing power*), *intuitive interactions* and image streaming (need for *bandwidth*) are of crucial interest.

Providing information   ZP-based techniques do not provide context in terms of image content to a current WoI. Thus, it is rather difficult to determine its position and further desirable browsing information. This is overcome by the proposed navigation grid. Like the overview component of Detail&Overview-based techniques, the grid outline is defined to represent the proportions of the image to explore. Thus, a user gets an immediate and permanent feedback for this image property. Furthermore, the nominal cell shape is well designed. Thus, the physical extension of an image region can be determined not only by the number of grid cells but also by the dimensions of the hardware display as physical representative of a single cell. Important information to the focus is also provided by the viewfinder indicating position and ratio between WoI and image.

Computing power   The complexity of presenting the image content is the same for GbZP as for traditional ZP representations — low. This is due to the fact that only the WoI is shown with none or uniform distortion. The additional navigation grid does not increase the efforts. Most of the required calculations must only be done once and are inexpensive. If the used mobile hardware provides sufficient power, even optional transitions and animations may be provided.

Intuitive Interactions   GbZP inherits all advantages of ZP-based techniques, e.g. the full usage of the available screen space for the WoI, suitability for very small screens, or the property to keep spatial relationships within the shown content, often not available for distortion based techniques [Car97b]. It also introduces intuitive means for interaction. To overcome the slider/menue paradigm, all interactions are applied to the image grid.

ZP-based browsing has proved to be generally effective if the user moves the WoI by small increments only [Com99]. To support this, rather simple and intuitive interactions for panning have been developed. This also applies for roaming, which can be achieved by one single action. The navigation grid also supports the vertical movement of the WoI, another drawback of related techniques [Pla95]. Zooming is often considered to be the bottleneck for the ZP approach [Dan03]. Here, the proposed navigation grid achieves another substantial simplification. By a single interaction the user may scale the image at different values. This is a strong relief compared to related techniques.

Based on the provided means for interaction, the information seeking mantra is easy to achieve. To get an overview the user executes a single zoom out operation, pans/roams to a desired location and zooms in to get details, overall accomplished by 3 simple interactions only.

Bandwidth   To state the requirements for bandwidth it is reasonable to distinguish a WoI shown in final- or reduced detail. By assuming a spatially equally distributed amount of data, the save of bandwidth for the first case directly correlates with the ratio between region and image and can be approximated by

$$100 - \frac{screen_1 \cdot screen_2 \cdot 100}{s_1 \cdot s_2} \tag{4.4}$$

In case the WoI covers 10% of the whole image, 90% of all image data can be neglected during streaming.

If the WoI has been downscaled, only data contributing to the reconstruction of lower image resolutions must be transmitted. To give an approximation for the save of bandwidth, the general assumption that the need for bandwidth increases exponentially with the enhancement in resolution is exploited. If $2^{2 \cdot 0}$ represents the data required to restore the image in the lowest inherent resolution and $2^{2r_{max}}$ the amount of data for the whole image, the data required to reconstruct an image downscaled with factors $x : y$ $(x, y = 2^r, x = y)$ can be stated as $2^{2(r_{max} - \log_2 x)}$. Thus, the estimated save of bandwidth is

$$100 - \frac{100}{2^{2 \log_2 x}} \tag{4.5}$$

which is already 75% for a scaling of $2 : 2$. The influence of other scalings is shown in Figure E.5. The calculation for both cases may also be combined if required.

4.5   The largeDetail-View (IDV)

All ZP-based techniques suffer from the drawback of not providing context in terms of image content. This is overcome by the *largeDetail-View* proposed in this section. This browsing technique has been published by the author in *"Information presentation on handheld devices"* [Kar04] and varies from related methods in its application to raster imagery, the spatial representation, means for interaction, and its alignment to mobile hardware.

The technique applies the DO approach and represents the image by a *detail view* and an additional *content overview* (cf. Figure 4.11). The overview is smaller than the detail and is superimposed on the WoI to save screen space. A rectangular viewfinder within the overview indicates position and dimensions of the WoI. Interaction is accomplished by manipulating the viewfinder or the overview and allows for intuitive exploration. The features of IDV can be summarized as follows:

Figure 4.11: *As the available screen space does not allow to show the whole image in full detail (left), within the largeDetail-View (right) two different views provide access to the WoI in high (red) and the whole content in low detail (green).*

1. The overview represents content and proportions of the image.

2. The displayed viewfinder has the shape of the available screen space and shows properties of the WoI in relation to the whole image.

3. Fast and intuitive navigation provided by viewfinder and overview.

The following section serves to explain the browsing components in more detail. Statements to appropriate image communication and the discussion of the achieved results will be provided in later sections.

4.5.1   Image browsing

4.5.1.1   Spatial image representation

The largeDetail-View consists of two different content views: the *detail view* and the *overview*. The *detail view* shows the image content belonging to the current WoI. To be able to represent the WoI in high detail, it occupies the largest screen space. The *overview* represents the content of the whole image, and thus, provides context and serves for orientation. The belonging content is downscaled and displayed in low detail. As the WoI is not embedded in the context, this technique clearly belongs to the Detail&Overview-approach.

Contrary to the dimensions of the detail view, which are aligned with the available screen space, the dimensions of the overview may vary and must be suitably determined. The resulting Screen Space Ratio between Overview and Detail (SSROD) [Pla95] heavily influences the applicability of the approach. Due to the variety of influencing factors, however, generally valid statements are difficult to give. Experiments have revealed that the overview should not cover more than a forth of the whole detail view, whereas its should not exceed a third to a half of the available display space in each direction. The overview should be as small as possible so as not to hide large parts of the WoI and to prevent further interactions. Thereby, it must be ensured that the content displayed in viewfinder and WoI can still be matched. As this may vary even during the exploration of a single image, interaction is mandatory.

Dimensions of detail and overview are determined by the used hardware and external factors. Position and dimensions of the presented viewfinder, however, vary and must be suitably determined. If the current WoI is specified by its spatial dimensions $[reg_1, reg_2]$ and a certain offset $[o_1, o_2]$ regarding the top left corner of the image, and the overview by its dimensions $[ov_1, ov_2]$, the top left position of the viewfinder within the overview, $[pos_1, pos_2]$, is determined by

$$pos_i = \frac{o_i \cdot ov_i}{\tilde{s}_i}, i = 1, 2 \qquad (4.6)$$

Thereby, $[\tilde{s}_1, \tilde{s}_2]$ represents the virtual dimensions of the image in case the WoI is presented in lower detail. Similarly, the dimensions of the viewfinder $[dim_1, dim_2]$ are determined by

$$dim_i = \frac{reg_i \cdot ov_i}{\tilde{s}_i}, i = 1, 2 \qquad (4.7)$$

Although there is no real-world pendant to the DO approach – two different views of the same content at the same time – the principle is easy to understand and does not require extensive learning. Each view is examined independently. However, appropriate means for interaction are required to link them.

4.5.1.2 Means for interaction

Within the IDV, the overview not only provides context for orientation but also serves for navigation. Most of the interaction is accomplished via the viewfinder. As this structure is directly linked to the detail view manipulating its position and size influences the WoI and its belonging content. This is a reasonable concept also applied in other systems [Smi98; Lec03]. The introduced basic interactions are implemented as follows:

Roaming: To accomplish the fast jump between regions, the user just taps within the overview on the position belonging to the new region. This leads to an according update of the position of the viewfinder and the detail view.

Panning: Small adjustments to the spatial position of the WoI can be accomplished by either a pen- or rocker-based displacements of the viewfinder. Panning using the 2D-rocker is especially useful if the intended changes are small or if exact adjustments cannot be accomplished by pen.

Scaling: During scaling smaller or larger spatial regions are displayed within the detail view. As the current WoI is linked to the viewfinder, its dimensions must also be adapted during scaling. This has been applied as the foundation for scaling interaction. Inversely, the user resizes the viewfinder to adapt the detail level of the WoI (cf. Figure 4.12). Downsizing leads to a small WoI displayed in higher detail, enlarging to an extended but less detailed WoI. To accomplish this, the user just selects and drags one of the viewfinders borders. Intermediate rendering steps give a direct feedback to the result of the current manipulation.

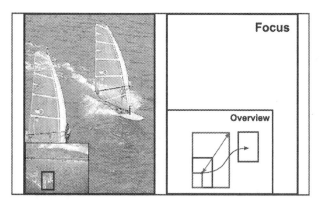

Figure 4.12: *Image representation (left) and provided interactions on the viewfinder of the IDV (right / roaming, zoom in, zoom out).*

These actions are able to accomplish all basic image browsing tasks. Nevertheless, additional interactions to modify the spatial layout of the image representation are required to further enhance usability:

Overview move: The overview is superimposed on the detail view. To allow discovery of these areas, it is reasonable to offer options for its interactive placement. This is achieved by providing a small *Drag-Rectangle* displayed at its top left corner. The position of the overview is adjusted by dragging this tool. Simple tapping completely hides or recovers the overview.

Overview resize: An option to resize the overview is provided to allow the adjustment of the SSROD. This can be accomplished by dragging its borders to either enlarge or diminish its dimensions. As the viewfinder is resized in the same ratio, this does not influence the representation of the detail view.

4.5.2 Image streaming

In addition to the statements for DO-based techniques given in Section 4.3.3, specifics of the IDV regarding its spatial layout allow for further substantiation.

RoI/LoD partition The IDV uses only one overview. For image partition, this means only three RoIs are used – one for the WoI, one for the overview, and one for the background. Scaling factors for WoI ($x : y$) and overview ($x_o : y_o$) depend on the respective task. The resulting target-LoDs are shown in Table 4.2.

	IDV representation		
	WoI	**overview**	**background**
target-LoD:	$LoD(\frac{1}{x}, \frac{1}{y}, img_a, img_c)$	$LoD(\frac{1}{x_o}, \frac{1}{y_o}, img_a, img_c)$	$LoD(0, 0, 0, 0)$

Table 4.2: *RoI/LoD partition of an image represented by IDV.*

Applied streaming technology

Calculation of contributing elements: WoI as well as overview are represented by rectangular regions. Thus, the solution for the *calculation of RoI-elements for rectangular RoIs* is applicable. However, contents partially covered by the overview might not be transferred. As this leads to an irregular RoI partition, it is useful to apply the features of the proposed *synchronized signalization* strategy. *Limited Spatial Access* can be used to further reduce the transmitted data. *Subband-wise selection* is of minor interest to IDV.

Sequencing of calculated elements: Due to the reason that the IDV consists of two different views, with different purposes, *global prioritization* between the respective RoIs is meaningful. *R-D optimized local sequencing* might only be applied if the fast refinement of the WoI is crucial.

Signalization of sequenced elements: The IDV requires no specific guidelines for the signalization of elements.

Applied streaming strategy   At the beginning, it is reasonable to prioritize data belonging to the overview. Since parts of the data also refine the WoI, this leads to a simultaneous content transfer. After the target-LoD for the overview has been reached, only incremental data required to represent the WoI at its target-LoD is needed. This significantly increases the response rates if the WoI is changed during image exploration.

4.5.3   Discussion

Similar to GbZP, this section evaluates the proposed IDV regarding the introduced requirements for image browsing and the most limiting factors in mobile environments.

Providing information   The layout of the IDV provides most of the desired features regarding the communication of important browsing information. Thereby, the overview is of crucial interest. Its outline represents the proportions of the browsed image and also shows a low detailed version of its content. Compared to ZP-based techniques, this is a strong advantage. Due to its strongly scaled content and its property to hide parts of the WoI, however, it might happen that content displayed in viewfinder and WoI cannot be comprehended and matched. In such cases it makes no sense to display the downscaled content, and the overview should be hidden or more appropriate browsing techniques should be used. Another solution based on content reduction is proposed in the next chapter.

Valuable browsing information is also provided by the viewfinder. Similar to GbZP, this structure always ensures the determination of position and dimensions of the current WoI regarding the whole image. Thus, the user is well assisted in keeping orientation during browsing. However, switching between the views requires additional cognitive efforts.

Computing power   The spatial layout of the IDV is quite simple. Both provided views represent the content either uniformly scaled (WoI, overview) or unscaled (WoI). Thereby, the scaling of the overview has to be performed only once. This leads to a low complexity that is comparable to GbZP.

Intuitive Interactions The largeDetail-View provides powerful means for interaction and intuitive support for all common browsing tasks. Thereby the options for inputs are centered at overview and viewfinder. By manipulating size and position of the viewfinder, the user gets an immediate feedback of what he is doing. For generalized views, this concept is called *Linking and Brushing* and has proved to perform well in navigating within multiple views [NS997; Sch00].

Due to the fact, the overview hides some of the details, additional interactions are provided. They allow to replace or resize the overview. This requires more interactions, but significantly increases the usability of the approach.

The information seeking mantra is well supported by IDV. The determination of a new region is achieved by 3 interactions only: resizing the viewfinder for an overview, tapping on a relevant area, and resizing the viewfinder for details.

Bandwidth As target-LoDs for WoI and overview are different, the required bandwidth also varies for either view. As the WoI is presented in a similar manner as within GbZP, the given statements can be applied accordingly (cf. Equation 4.4) – *the required bandwidth strongly correlates with the ratio between WoI and image.*

Nevertheless, providing support for the overview takes additional bandwidth and requires the transfer of a low resolution image. This corresponds to the statements provided for scaling. However, in general higher scaling values are applied. Thus, bandwidth required for the overview is little compared to the WoI.

As some content is shown in WoI and overview, the save can be further increased if belonging data is not transmitted twice. The amount of bandwidth required to transmit these image parts can be formulated based on Equation 4.4 and the need for bandwidth to achieve the image resolution corresponding to scaling factors $x_o : y_o$ ($x_o, y_o = 2^r, x_o = y_o$) (Equation 4.5). It can be stated as:

$$\left(\frac{screen_1 \cdot screen_2}{s_1 \cdot s_2}\right) \cdot 2^{2(r_{max} - \log_2 x_o)} \tag{4.8}$$

As this amount is small compared to all available image data, however, this does not significantly improve the image transmission. Better results can be achieved by taking advantage of the spatial overlap between both views. Here, it is reasonable not to transmit the details covered by the overview. Overall, IDV requires more bandwidth than GbZP, but the difference is small.

4.6 The rectangular FishEye-View (rFEV)

In some applications the user is more interested in context information rather than a specific image detail. To satisfy this, the rectangular FishEye-View [Rau99a; Rau00] has been introduced. This technique integrates the WoI into the context, and therefore, belongs to the group of Focus&Context techniques. This representation substantially facilitates interactive exploration of large images and does not require a viewfinder as for GbZP and IDV. As only one lens view is used for the representation, cognitive switches between different views are avoided.

The global lens effect of the rFEV is achieved by a complex partition of the context into multiple belts and different detail levels. Thereby, the respective LoD is determined based on the reasonable assumption that the interest of the user decreases with the distance from the focus (cf. Figure 4.13). Overall, the rFEV provides the following beneficial features:

1. The focus indicates its position in relation to the whole image.

2. The context is appropriately represented by multiple belts.

3. Fast and intuitive navigation based on the lens metaphor.

To introduce the reader to the rFEV, the next section serves to review this tech-nique. The actual contribution of the author, however, is to provide detailed state-ments to the design of a sophisticated communication system. A discussion of the results serves to justify the proposed solutions.

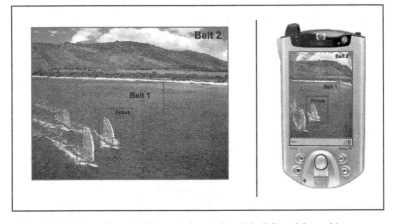

Figure 4.13: *Partition of the original image in focus and two belts (left), and the resulting represen-tation within the rectangular FishEye-View (right).*

4.6.1   Image browsing

4.6.1.1   Spatial image representation

In this section the spatial representation of the image content during browsing is briefly reviewed. More detailed statements to their calculation and to available interactions can be found in [Rau99a] or [Rau00]. In [Rau01a], the reader can also find information to different belt partition.

Crucial for the spatial representation of all FC-based techniques is the partition of the context into multiple belts. In opposition to the local lens technique introduced in Section 4.3.3, this leads to decreased visual discontinuities on the edges of the WoI. Contrary to the WoI usually shown in final-LoD, the detail of each belt de-creases towards the borders of the representation. Accordingly, varying degrees of distortion are applied to the different image regions starting with less distortion near the focus and progressing to strong distortion near the borders. These dis-tortions amount to selective scaling (compaction) of rectangular regions from the original image, as illustrated in Figure 4.13. To achieve a consistent representation of the whole image, specifically, the original image data is classified into separate RoIs each of which is assigned a pair of scaling factors. As seen in Figure 4.14/left, however, the choice of scaling factors is not completely arbitrary, since the overall transformation from original image to display must preserve continuity at the re-gion boundaries. Although other scaling values may also be chosen, RAUSCHEN-

BACH proposes to apply factors, which are powers of 2 [Rau99a].

4.6.1.2   Means for interaction

Like the spatial representation, provided means for interactions have already been discussed by RAUSCHENBACH. Due to their lacking relevance to image communication, they are not further reviewed. Summarizing it can be said that all basic interaction techniques are well supported by rFEV (cf. Figure 4.14/right). This has also been verified by experiments of the author [Kar03b]. For more information on this topic, the interested reader is referred to [Rau99a; Rau00] or [Kar03b].

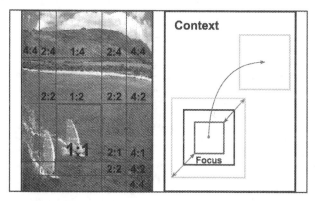

Figure 4.14: *Applied scaling values in accordance with Figure 4.13 (left) and supported interactions (right / roaming, zoom in, zoom out).*

4.6.2   Image streaming

In [Rau99a] an EZW-based transmission strategy for the rFEV is described. The proposed statements, however, do not provide details to the respectively applied techniques at the different transmission stages. This section serves to show the belonging statements for an appropriate streaming based on JPEG2000.

RoI/LoD partition   Of certain interest to the rFEV is the handling of context data. As RoI partition and the LoD assignment vary strongly with position and size of the focus and the number of belts, concrete statements cannot be given. The partition leads in either case to multiple RoIs. A general formulation of the respective detail levels can be formulated as follows:

If n determines the number of all belts and x_b represents the scaling value of a RoI belonging to belt b ($1 \leq b \leq n$, starting from the WoI) in x dimension (y dimension respectively), the particular detail values must be chosen conform to $1 \geq \frac{1}{x_1} \geq \frac{1}{x_2} \geq \cdots \geq \frac{1}{x_n} > 0$.

As most of the scaling values are supported by the LoD-hierarchy, the partition shown in Figure 4.14/left is a beneficial property for JPEG2000-based image streaming. Thus, the respective scaling values can be further specified as to be $x_b = 2^i$, $1 \leq i \leq n$, whereby a value of a region belonging to belt b is required to conform to $x_b \leq 2^b$ (y_b, respectively).

Applied streaming technology

Calculation of contributing elements: Due to many RoIs scaled by different values in each direction, it is obvious that the proposed *subband-wise selection* strategy can be suitably exploited. As each RoI has a rectangular shape, this also applies for the *calculation of elements belonging to rectangular RoIs. Limited Spatial Access* is of minor interest to rFEV.

Sequencing of calculated elements: The rFEV partition leads to many RoIs with different degrees of importance. To satisfy this, it is proposed to apply *global prioritization. R-D optimized local sequencing* can be applied to the WoI.

Signalization of sequenced elements: The rFEV does not require a certain signalization strategy.

Applied streaming strategy In order to maximize the perceived impact of progressive refinement, global prioritization might be accomplished by accuracy. This takes advantage of the fact that the perceived impact of any given quality layer on visual quality is generally lower in the context regions than the WoI. Equivalently, uniform perceived image quality generally involves a smaller number of layers for RoI-elements which contribute only to the context region than for elements which contribute to the focus region. One reason for this is simply that the WoI is by definition more important to the interactive user. Another reason is that context regions are scaled. Scaling an image region by factors $x : y$ reduces the impact of quantization on mean squared error in the rendered image by the factor xy. Although this value might be used for accommodating the later phenomenon through prioritization, it is less clear how the former aspect should be accommodated in a rigorous manner. To overcome this, it is proposed to always assign highest priority to the WoI and to lower this priority with increasing distance from focus. This applies the reasonable assumption that users interest decreases with increasing distance from the WoI and ensures that the WoI is presented first, followed by the adjacent belt and so forth. Thereby, prioritization values depend on the relative importance of the WoI and the number of belts.

4.6.3 Discussion

This section discusses the properties of rFEV regarding the respective requirements for *computing power* and *bandwidth*. Its abilities regarding image browsing have already been shown in [Rau00; Rau01a] and will be neglected.

Computing power Due to the complex partition in multiple RoIs with different scalings, it can be stated that much more computing power is required compared to ZP- or DO-based techniques. To achieve an acceptable quality of scaled contents, however, this consumption is even increased [Rau01a]. Experiments on mobile hardware conducted by the author and published in *"Pixels vs. Vectors: Presentation of large images on mobile devices"* [Ros03c] and *"Graphical Content on Mobile Devices"* [Ros06b] show, that sophisticated scaling techniques often require up to 10 times more computing power than simple methods. This decreases the response rates and the suitability of the rFEV for low power devices.

Bandwidth Generally valid statements regarding the need for bandwidth are difficult to give. Instead the author provides empirical results which might be seen as an example on creating an adapted communication strategy. They are based on imagery of dimensions of 1024×1024 and a compressed representation of length 727 kB consisting of 9 layers, with 2 levels of DWT decomposition. The cumulative bit-rate associated with each successive layer in the original bitstream is $\sqrt{2}$ times that of the previous layer. The focus region for the rFEV has been placed in the center of the image, having $\frac{1}{8}$ of the full image width and height. The context is partitioned as shown in Figure 4.14/left. *Global prioritization* ensures that data belonging to the WoI has a competitive edge of 2 layers before any data belonging to the context is handled. Data belonging to RoIs of the first context belt are prioritized by 1 layer regarding data belonging to RoIs of the second belt. Considered key elements are *precincts*.

Figures 4.15/left and right present numerical results which indicate the impact of the proposed adaptation on transmission efficiency. The upper curve, marked "naive" in each of the figures, corresponds to the transmission of all image data belonging to a single RoI up to its final-LoD. A second curve in each figure identifies the performance of an adapted transmission based on the respective LoD, whereby original data-containers are not sub-divided to accommodate differences in the horizontal and vertical scaling factors. The third, lowest curve, in each figure corresponds to the *subband-wise selection* to avoid the transmission of subbands which do not belong to the target-LoD of a RoI. As the applied *inherent signalization* is based on a dynamic assignment of data contributions to different layers, Figure 4.15/left identifies the size of each transmitted layer, and Figure 4.15/right the cumulative size of the layers. The resequenced data-stream contains 12 layers.

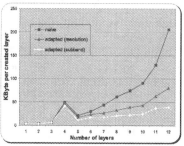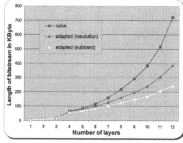

Figure 4.15: *Bandwidth required by 3 different data selection strategies for the rFEV at each individual layer (left) and their accumulated size (right).*

As shown in the Figures, the naive scheme produces the largest layers, and hence has the lowest transmission efficiency, because all subbands from all resolutions are included in both focus and context regions. The performance of the adapted transmission scheme is clearly superior, and most notably so when subband-wise selection is used. From Figure 4.15/left, it can be seen that the ratio between the most and least efficient transmission schemes can be as large as 4.5 : 1. This is because RoIs which have large scaling factors generally represent the largest portion of the original image, and these are the very RoIs which stand to benefit most from the proposed adapted transmission scheme.

Evidently, the effect of the adaptation is significant only in the later layers. This is because the prioritization scheme delays the scheduling of context information until later layers. The strong increment in transmitted length observed at layer 4 corresponds to the first appearance of packets from the second belt; these represent the largest region on the original image.

The cumulative layer sizes presented in Figure 4.15/right are perhaps more indicative of the overall impact of the proposed transmission scheme, revealing a maximum overall gain of approximately 3 : 1 in transmission efficiency relative to the naive approach. Thus, image transmission adapted to the respective requirements of the rFEV can greatly decrease the need for bandwidth.

4.7   Conclusion of the chapter

This chapter covered the appropriate representation and handling of raster imagery to achieve an appropriate mobile image browsing. After defining the aim of this task, requirements for the problems *spatial representation*, *means for interaction*, and *appropriate image streaming* have been derived.

Regarding *spatial representation*, an introduced hierarchical classification scheme able to categorize known and new browsing techniques served to review recent work in image and data exploration. Thereby, three basic approaches have been identified. Although each has its beneficial advantages, none is able to outperform in all conditions. Although *means for interaction* are an important part of a browsing technique, they are of minor interest to image communication, and thus, discussed by the fundamental actions *roaming*, *panning* and *scaling* only.

To satisfy the demand of an *appropriate image streaming*, again the introduced taxonomy is applied. It has been shown that based on the classification of a certain browsing technique, *general guidelines* for the adaptation of the streaming process can be derived. As the scheme is able to handle arbitrary techniques, this approach can be applied universally. Due to the fact the classification is founded on RoI partition and LoD assignment, furthermore, the given statements can be *easily implemented* by JPEG2000 and the streaming technology introduced in last chapter.

To accommodate the need for new and innovative concepts in image browsing, two new techniques, *Grid-based Zoom&Pan* and *largeDetail-View*, have been proposed. Both introduce new ideas for spatial representation and interaction to raster imagery. The coupling of image representation and streaming achieves massive savings in the consumed resources. This has also been shown for the *rectangular FishEye-View*. The provided results show that all techniques allow *appropriate mobile image browsing*.

Proposals and results presented in this chapter confirm the authors assertion that appropriate image representation and transmission adapted to the respective needs can greatly increase the performance in mobile environments. However, representations for image browsing always provide the content in the best possible detail. This might not be required to achieve viewer guidance. The consequences with regard to mobile environments are discussed in the next chapter.

Chapter **5**

Viewer guidance for raster imagery

To quickly extract relevant content from large information spaces is a difficult task [Kos01a]. The aim of viewer guidance is to intuitively direct the user's attention to this information. This is a significant difference to image browsing and opens up for a new distinct application field.

A general problem of viewer guidance within raster imagery is the processing power required to create the content representations during client-side filtering (cf. Figure 5.1). Due to this, only straightforward techniques have yet been applied. Furthermore, same bandwidth is used for interesting and uninteresting regions.

After deriving requirements for viewer guidance in mobile environments (Section 5.1) and discussing related work (Section 5.2), this chapter introduces two new approaches based on *blurring* (Section 5.3) and *content reduction* (Section 5.4). By exploiting the beneficial properties of JPEG2000, it will be shown how the limitations of mobile environments can be overcome during creation and streaming of the respective representations, and how the general idea is applied to enhanced image browsing. Conclusions close this chapter (Section 5.5).

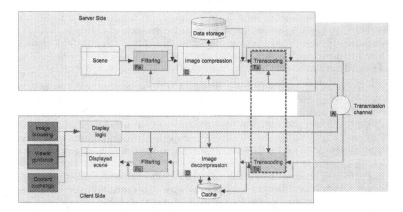

Figure 5.1: *The visual representations for viewer guidance are created by transcoders only. Due to this, the display logic may also adapt the cache management.*

5.1   Aims and requirements

To alert a user to a problem or to show matching objects in response to a query is a common feature of applications in data visualization [Bie94a]. Thereby, the user usually wants to quickly understand the information pointed out in the context and not just be shown the result items. *The aim of viewer guidance* within images is to intuitively direct the user's attention to a predefined region embedded in the context. Continuing the application of terms introduced for image browsing this is the *WoI* respectively the *background*. To allow a clear visual distinction between both types of regions, however, the difference must be strong enough and able to detract the attention of the viewer from background to WoI.

To accomplish this in mobile environments a number of problems must be solved. The highlighting of relevant objects is complex and might exceed the capabilities of the client regarding *computing power*. In case of large images this also applies for *bandwidth*. Thus, these sensible resources must be used properly. Additional problems not in focus of the proposed solutions are the limited screen space and the determination of relevant regions. Thus, the viewer guidance task requires the fulfilment of the following points:

Content representation: must achieve visual determination of focus and back-
    ground, must be able to direct the attention and simple to create

Image streaming: demand-driven non-redundant transmission of image data con-
    tributing to the current representation

This clearly leads to a *partition* of the image and a *different representation* of the regions belonging to WoI and background. Thereby, it is required that the rep-resentation still *represents desired features* of the belonging content. Although there might be more than one WoI, only one is assumed for the remainder of the chapter.

The following section will discuss existing approaches introduced for viewer guid-ance and review proposed implementations for raster imagery.

5.2   Discussion of related work

Although visual guidance can heavily increase the usability of a visualization task, not many approaches have been proposed in literature. This especially applies for techniques considering mobile environments. Only a few publications have addressed the limited computing power, none the narrow bandwidth.

Common to all techniques found in literature is the separation of the content in WoI and background. To make it more attractive, often a local operator is applied to the WoI. Thereby two main concepts have been proposed: *spatial transformation* or *highlighting by visual cues*. To achieve the first point, usually lenses similar to the FC approach discussed in the last chapter are applied [IDE05]. Most proposals for solutions, however, are founded on the second point. One of the mostly applied techniques is the introduction of external contents as colored or animated frames [Bau03; Mee05] or annotations [Imh62; McE95]. Although widely accepted, a sig-nificant drawback of this approach is the disregard of the image content. This can be overcome by an appropriate manipulation and representation of its properties.

"Representing information by images is so effective and useful because it utilizes one of the channels to our brain that have the most bandwidth: our eyes. But even this channel can be used more or less efficiently. It is therefore very important that we know about the different

properties of visual cues, and processing of visual information in the brain." (GOLDSTEIN [Gol80])

Effects of the HVS able to direct the attention within a graphical representation are color coding [Sch00; Kos02a; Mee05], the presentation of different data dimensions [Sto94; Bie94b; Lok95; IDE05], or the Depth of Field effect [Ada91; Kos02b; The05]. Although color coding has been proven to be rather successful for highlighting, a fundamental drawback in mobile environments is that some devices only support a limited number of colors. Here, it is more promising to display different data dimensions for WoI and background. Such an approach is called *tool glass* [Bie94b]. It achieves viewer guidance by introducing visual discontinuities within the representation. The *Depth of Field* effect (DoF) is founded on a different perception of visual information within the HVS. Objects not in focus appear as if they have been blurred (cf. Figure 5.2).

As one of the contributions of this chapter is the application of concepts from tool glasses and DoF to viewer guidance in raster imagery, in the following, both approaches are reviewed in detail. Thereby, the evaluation of related work to accomplish the belonging content representations serves to show the need for new ideas in mobile environments.

 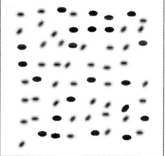

Figure 5.2: *The Depth of Field effect (left, src:[Bur03]) and its application in Information visualization (right, src:[Kos01a]).*

5.2.1   Depth of Field

5.2.1.1   General approaches

The difference between sharp and blurred content is a very effective means of guiding attention. Blur makes features harder to recognize and can hide information completely. As humans do not like to look at blurred objects, a sharply displayed WoI immediately attracts the attention of the viewer (cf. Figure 5.2). This effect is called *Depth of Field* [Ada91] and has already been successfully used in photography and cinematography [Kat91; Lee90] over years. For the purpose of Information visualization, KOSARA [Kos01a] enhanced the basic concept to *Semantic Depth of Field* (SDoF) and applied the principle to distract the attention of the user from irrelevant data. In his works he also provided extensive user tests to show the applicability of this principle [Kos02b; Kos02a]. He has evaluated that DoF makes very efficiently use of the bandwidth of the HVS to convey a lot of information in very little time. Interestingly, it has also been shown that to attract a viewer's attention blurring performs as well as highlighting using color or saturation [Kos02a]. Thereby, attraction increases with growing dimensions of the WoI. In case of multiple foci, it has been proposed not to exceed 3 or 4 distinct regions [Kos02b]. Due to limited abilities of the HVS to distinguish between the degree of blurring, the prioritization of certain foci is of little use.

The concept of DoF applied to graphical content is also used in the image browsing system *Macroscope* of LIEBERMAN (cf. Section 4.2.3). He applies blurring to the overviews so as to direct the viewer's attention to the detail view.

5.2.1.2 Approaches for raster imagery

Although it has its origin in 3D, DoF can also be successfully applied to 2D data (cf. Figure C.8). As single pixels are treated as independent data values and blurring does not distort their spatial relationship, KOSARA achieved quite good results on raster imagery [Kos01a]. Another research group [The05] applied the concept to moving imagery, e.g. to accentuate relevant information in a newscast. Due to the strong relation of DoF to the HVS, they labeled the technique *foveated imaging*. In any event blurring must be applied to the background.

Blur is characterized by two effects: (1) less high spatial frequencies and (2) reduced contrast. Thus, it causes a smoothing of edges and a general loss of detail [Kay96b; Kay96a; Eld98]. Consequentially, mainly low pass filters are used to introduce blurring. Almost all proposed techniques calculate new pixel values based on a matrix with $m = (n)(n)$ weight factors moving sequentially over the pixel array. For each pixel in center of the matrix a new value is calculated by summing up neighboring pixels. Both criteria of blurring are direct consequences of this procedure. There are two primary categories for blurring techniques in pixel domain: *Mean filters* and *Order filters*.

Mean filters: The simplest mean filter is a *arithmetic mean filter* [Kos01b; Gon01]. All weight factors are one and the sum is divided by the number of matrix coefficients m. However, pixels which have a greater distance from the center contribute in the same amount to the sum. A more sophisticated distribution of the weight factors in shape of a 2D Gaussian bell is used within the *Standard Gaussian filter* [Pra01]. It achieves quite good smoothing, but quality depends on the dimensions of the matrix. There are many variations, like the *harmonic mean* and *geometric mean filter* [Pra01], or the *adaptive median* [Pra01], or *adaptive Gaussian filter* [Gom02].

Order filters: Instead of replacing a pixel value with the weighted sum of neighboring pixel values, order filters sort these values into numerical order and the currently handled pixel value is replaced by an appropriate representant. This often preserves useful details in the image, and thus, achieves better results. Depending on the choice of the representant, different strategies such as the *minimum*[Pra01], *median* [Gon01], *maximum filter* [Pra01], or variations [Pra01] have been proposed.

"One of the reasons blur has been little used in computer graphics is that it is slow when done in software" (KOSARA ET AL. [Kos02a])

Although KOSARA applied DoF to raster imagery, he was not able to solve the problem of the high complexity. Thereby, computational needs as well as quality of the resulting image correlate with matrix dimensions. Some filters must even be applied multiple times to achieve reasonable results. As the described filters are applied in pixel domain, encoded imagery must also be decoded before to being processed. This even increases the demand for computing power. If the blurred image is to be encoded again, it has also been reported that artifacts might introduce high contrast in the blurred areas [Kos01b].

Interestingly, in image compression, blur is usually considered to be an imperfection [Ton04]. This especially applies for DWT-based image compression schemes, where low pass filtering is usually applied multiple times. If the filtered signals are afterwards subject to strong quantization, the reconstructed image appears as it has been blurred [Mar02; Mar04; Ton04]. This is an interesting feature and a foundation for techniques proposed in this chapter. For more information on the properties of the wavelet transformation regarding blurring, the interested reader is referred to [Mal89; Lai00].

 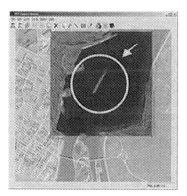

Figure 5.3: *A tool glass applied to explore map contents (src:[IDE05]).*

5.2.2   Tool glasses

5.2.2.1   General approaches

Tool glasses or *magic lenses*® have their origin in Information visualization [Sto94; Bie94b] and GIS [Lok95], where they have been successfully applied to the interactive exploration of large multi-dimensional data sets. The main idea is to show a different number of data dimensions within WoI and background. Thereby, the displayed data is aligned to the task at hand. Due to the fact that the layout is kept, and thus, the user's mental map is not destroyed [Mis95], it is possible to discover information not immediately visible within the original data. More precise, this approach shows more or less detail, but in terms of data not screen dimensions. This is a large difference to image browsing approaches. STONE ET AL. [Sto94; Bie94b] describe a tool glass as ... *a filter to read an underlying model of some data, create a new model based on the lens viewing operation, and format the new model to present a new view of the data within the lens boundary or viewing region.* As the resulting representation highly depends on such models, they are also called *semantic lenses*. In [Bie94a] the applicability of this approach has proved for many different application areas spreading from data exploration to enhanced editing (cf. Figure C.10). Tool glasses have also been applied in Non-Photorealistic Rendering (NPR) [Str02; Lu02] to emphasize important data regions (cf. Figure C.11/right).

A typical example for tool glasses has been proposed by LOKUGE AND ISHIZAKI [Lok95]. Based on a GIS, it enables a user to highlight crime data, certain cities, and hospitals to derive conclusions about possible correlations (cf. Figure C.11/left). The data is displayed in the same spatial context, but relevant items have other representations. This easily guides the viewer's attention to those objects.

5.2.2.2   Approaches for raster imagery

Applying tool glasses to arbitrary raster imagery is still problematic. The content is only described by single pixels, more exactly their respective color and spatial relationship. Thus, content extraction and manipulation is difficult. In fact, no adequate technique is known to the author. To bypass these problems two concepts have been proposed. The first idea is to spread single attributes over multiple layers of imagery, which are afterwards combined depending on current needs (cf. Figure 5.3). This, however, requires certain preparations and additional storage space. The second idea is founded on the content description by *meta information* (cf. Figure C.12). Although useful for small annotations, much additional bandwidth is required to transfer all valid attributes of an image. Thus, there is no reasonable solution for arbitrary imagery and mobile environments.

The remainder of this section focusses on the reduction of the content of an arbitrary raster image to its edges and details. A picture composed entirely of lines, without any narrative content, can be a strong and aesthetically satisfying image [Lat95]. As shown later on, this property can be exploited for viewer guidance.

Edge detection operators are based on the idea that edge information in an image is found by looking at the relationships between neighboring pixels. Almost all proposed techniques applied in pixel domain calculate new pixel values based on a matrix similar to that explained for blurring. The main difference is the assignment of the matrix. As usually not all orientations are considered within one matrix, often multiple matrices are applied to catch all types of edges. Two basic approaches can be extracted from literature: *differential detection* and *model fitting*.

Differential detection: The general idea of this approach is the creation of a differential image with accentuated spatial amplitude changes. In a subsequent step, a differential detection operation is performed to determine pixel locations of significant differentials – the actual detection. Depending on the kind of applied operation two sub classes can be identified: *first-* and *second-order derivatives*.

First-order derivatives perform a kind of a spatial first-order differentiation and compare the resulting edge gradient to a threshold value. An edge is found if the respective point exceeds the threshold value. Classical examples are the *Roberts* [Rob63], *Prewitt* [Pre70, p.108], or *Sobel operator* [Gon01]. As their performance depends on image content [Pra01], others techniques such as the *boxcar, truncated pyramid* or *FDOG operator* [Pra01] differing in dimension n and assignment of the matrix have been proposed. However, all those methods have been found heuristically. CANNY [Can86] has taken an analytic approach based on a specific mathematical model. However, it was too complex for a concrete implementation. This has been solved by DEMIGNY AND KAMIE [Dem97], who have developed a discrete version of Canny's criteria.

Although quite similar, second-order derivatives judge an edge to be present if there is a significant spatial change in the polarity of the resulting values. To achieve this, usually Laplacian derivatives are applied. Examples are the *Lapla-*

cian masks, *Kirsch compass masks*, and *Robinson compass masks* [Pra01]. Second-order derivatives are more sensitive to noise. To cope with that, MARR AND HILDRITH [Mar80] proposed the *Laplacian of Gaussian* edge detector in which gaussian shaped smoothing is performed prior to application of the Laplacian.

Model fitting: This approach is based on the assumption that edges may only have a limited number of appearances. Thus, a local region of pixel values is tried to fit to a certain basic model. If the fit is sufficiently close, an edge is said to exist, and is parameterized by the values of the respective model. Examples are the proposals by HUECKEL [Hue71] or NALWA AND BINFORD [Nal86].

However, all pixel-based techniques are costly in terms of computing power. Quality as well as computing costs increase with matrix dimensions or the complexity of the applied model. Moreover, in communications systems where images are often stored in compressed representation, content must be decoded before edges can be extracted. This can be overcome by processing the image in transformed representation, e.g. in DCT [She96a] or DWT domain [Mal92]. MALLAT AND ZHONG [Mal92] assayed the multiscale properties of wavelet theory and found that wavelet transform maxima strongly indicate edges. They have also shown that the dyadic DWT can be exploited for edge detection. If using extrema detection and a specific class of wavelets, this idea is even similar to Canny's approach. Thus, working in wavelet domain is of advantage for edge and detail extraction. Thereby, the quality of the edge representation depends strongly on the used wavelet transform and kernel, and the character of the transformed data [Sta02]. As shown later on this domain is also the foundation for own proposals.

5.2.3 Summary of related work

Due to the relevance of the topic, multiple approaches for viewer guidance have been published. Common to all of them is the partition of the image in WoI and background, and the enhancing or diminishing of selected visual attributes within the respective region. Of all proposed strategies, *tool glasses* and the exploitation of the *DoF* effect seem especially useful to achieve the strived goal.

However, no work has yet been done on how to apply these concepts to mobile environments. As shown, the creation of the respective content representations is complex and *requires strong computing power*. Furthermore, none of the proposals in related work addresses the required *bandwidth*. To cope with that, the following sections propose new ideas for an uncomplex creation of the content representations and efficient strategies for their transfer.

5.3 Depth of Field for JPEG2000-encoded imagery

Blurring for viewer guidance is effective and can be applied to decrease the visual relevance of image regions belonging to the background (cf. Figure 5.4). The creation of the belonging representation, however, is complex. This section focusses on the efficient creation of blurred image representations based on imagery encoded with JPEG2000. The shown solutions have been proposed by the author in *"JPEG2000-based Viewer Guidance for Mobile Image Browsing"* [Ros06a]. They save valuable computing power and are rather suited for mobile environments. The shown concept is also exploited for efficient image streaming.

Figure 5.4: *The Depth of Field effect applied to still imagery by a JPEG2000-based blurring of the background. This directs the viewer's attention to the unchanged WoI.*

5.3.1 Creation of the image representation

To overcome the high computational effort during the creation of DoF representations, the author proposes to take advantage of the features of the DWT domain. As images are usually stored in compressed representation, this does not require any additional operations for content transformation and even omits efforts needed to decompress the content for traditional pixel-based processing. The foundation for the proposed approach is JPEG2000. Image content encoded with JPEG2000 is scalable in a variety of dimensions and can be accessed by widely independent data containers. The creation of a DoF representation is achieved by an un-complex selection of data containers. After transcoding, selected data can simply be decoded and does not require further processing before to be displayed. The following list represents the requirements of DoF representations and their solution in JPEG2000 domain:

Selection of blurred content: DWT supports the inherent *separation of detail and approximation,* layer concept provides *reduction in quality*

Different representation of WoI and background: Limited Spatial Access to encoded image data enables *independent access* to disjoint image regions

The following statements provide further information to each of these points.

Separation of detail and approximation   The DWT is an integral part of JPEG2000. During the decomposition of the image, subsequently details are extracted and separated from a given approximation (cf. Section 2.2.3.2). As blurring is mainly characterized by a general loss of detail, this is exploited by neglecting these parts for blurred representations. Consequentially, only data belonging to the approximation LL_0 is used. This process and its consequences are depicted in Figure 5.5 for a grey-scale image.

As each successive decomposition stage extracts certain detail from the approximation, the number of wavelet decompositions d_{max} strongly influences the quality of the blur. The author conducted various subjective tests. It has been revealed that a value of $d_{max} \geq 6$ is appropriate for many contents. In case the image has to be encoded using less decomposition, at least 3 stages should be applied to introduce a noticeable blur.

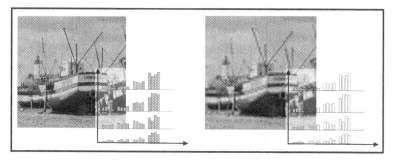

Figure 5.5: *Compared to the use of all available data (left), content reconstructed by using only data belonging to the lowest available resolution appears as it has been blurred (right).*

Reduction in quality   Nevertheless, decoding of this data only leads to a low resolution image shown in original spatial dimensions. Due to the fact that the approximation still contains details, the blurring effect might not be as strong as desired. To achieve a stronger blur, ideas from pixel domain are applied. As described, blur can be achieved by averaging adjacent pixel values to remove sharp variances and details. In JPEG2000 domain this can be accomplished by taking advantage of quality layers. By removing higher quality layers, the accuracy of the wavelet coefficients is reduced. As each coefficient contributes to multiple pixels, this leads to an averaging of the belonging values and in turn to similar values of adjacent pixels. This proceeding can heavily increase the strived blur effect. By continuing the given example, this is depicted in Figure 5.6.

Subjective tests have revealed that the best quality of the blur is achieved if approximately 8-12% of all available image data reside at the handled layers. Although this value also considers data from higher resolutions not used for the blur, this significantly simplifies the specification of belonging encoding parameters for traceable experiments. These values, however, can only be a rough guideline and vary depending on image content. Thereby, reducing quality has less impact on blurring than detail reduction. The influence further decreases with increasing d_{max}.

Quality also depends on the character of the transformed data [Sta02]. The author conducted a number of experiments and found that CDF 9/7 kernels achieve the best results. Due to the larger influence of the kernels, they produce smoother blurring than the 5/3 kernels.

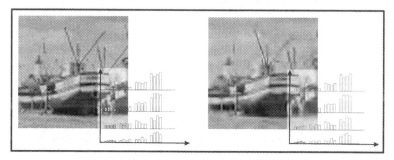

Figure 5.6: *Compared to the use of all data belonging to the approximation (left), further discarding data residing at higher layers intensifies the blurring effect (right).*

Independent access   An important part of the DoF effect is the embedded WoI. Thus, it is necessary to combine focus and background. To achieve this in JPEG2000 domain, it must be possible to access data contributing to either region independently. As the approximation is required for both type of region, this especially applies for data containing image details. To achieve this the belonging DWT subbands must be partitioned. As the WoI position is not required to be static, it is proposed to apply the flexible concept of *Limited Spatial Access*. Based on this, both types of regions can be simply combined by a selection or omission of respective data containers.

Decoding data selected as described will restore the content in the WoI with all details and blurs the background (cf. Figure 5.4).

5.3.2   Image streaming

As described for image browsing it is not always required to transmit all image data available at server side. A DoF representation can be achieved by a smart selection and omission of data containers in JPEG2000 domain. This can directly be applied for an efficient image streaming.

RoI/LoD partition   The DoF image representation is divided into WoI and background, whereby both are differently represented. Thus, it is reasonable to assign to either type a different RoI and respective LoD. As the WoI is required to represent the belonging content as detailed as possible, to this RoI is assigned the final-LoD. This is not surprising and corresponds to the representation of the WoI within image browsing techniques. The blurring of the background is achieved by a reduction in resolution and quality. This can be fully mapped to the respective LoD. If the encoded image contains $d_{max} + 1$ inherent resolutions, the LoD attributes *x*- and *y-resolution* are direct consequences of the scaling factors assigned to the approximation, which can be stated as $2^{d_{max}} : 2^{d_{max}}$. The LoD regarding quality depends on the number of layers used to achieve the blurring effect. If the encoded image consists of l layers, whereby the m lowest layers contribute to the blurring effect, the quality attribute for the LoD can be stated as *accuracy*= m. Based on this, LoDs for WoI and background can be specified as shown in Table 5.1.

	DoF representation	
	WoI	**background**
target-LoD:	$LoD(1, 1, img_a, img_c)$	$LoD(\frac{1}{2^{d_{max}}}, \frac{1}{2^{d_{max}}}, m, img_c)$

Table 5.1: *RoI/LoD partition of an image represented by DoF.*

Applied streaming technology

Calculation of contributing elements: In most cases the proposed strategy for *element selection for rectangular RoIs* can be applied. For more complex WoI shapes it is useful, to exploit the flexibility of the *synchronized signalization* strategy. While *Limited Spatial Access* is mandatory, *Subband-wise selection* is of minor interest to DoF representations.

Sequencing of calculated elements: As WoI as well as background are of different interest, *prioritization-based global sequencing* might serve to couch their relevance during streaming. To accomplish a fast refinement of the WoI, *R-D optimized local sequencing* can be also be applied.

Signalization of sequenced elements: There is no specific requirement to support the signalization of elements contributing to a DoF representation.

Applied streaming strategy   Depending on the respective task, two different options to stream relevant data are imaginable. In case the context is of high importance, it is proposed to transmit all data required for a blurred representation first. Once this data has been handled, the details of the WoI are transferred. This leads to a completely blurred image first and a progressive refinement of the WoI afterwards. Although this is the most reasonable strategy for many situations, the refinement of the background might also be postponed until all data belonging to the WoI has been handled. This leads to a exclusive refinement of the focus, but might impose longer response rates in case the WoI is moved in early transmission stages.

5.3.3 Discussion

In this section, the results achieved by the JPEG2000-based approach are discussed. Thereby, the degree of fulfillment of the derived requirements for viewer guidance in mobile environments is shown. For content representation, the focus is on the *quality of the representation*. The general ability of the DoF effect to achieve viewer guidance has already been proven in literature and is therefore neglected. Mobile environments are evaluated by the need for *computing power* and *bandwidth*.

Quality of the representation: To evaluate the quality of the blur effect, the proposed approach is compared to a 5×5 gaussian filter. It can be stated that the quality of the blur produced by transcoding JPEG2000-encoded image data is not as good as by applying a filter purely designed for this purpose. Here, it is noticeable that the JPEG2000-based blurring leads to coarser results than gaussian filtering. Although the shape of the WoI can only be approximated, contrary, transcoding leads to a smoother integration of the focus into the background. This is due to the slight overlap of wavelet kernels at element borders (precincts, code-blocks). Overall, the achieved results still allow appropriate and satisfying DoF representations. The reader can get an impression of the differences by comparing Figure 5.4 (JPEG2000-based) and Figure E.6 (Gaussian).

Computing power: Selection of data containers contributing to the DoF representation is accomplished via the RSA feature of JPEG2000. This is less demanding and only requires access (precincts, tiles) or partial decoding (code-blocks). Thus, it is much faster than gaussian filtering. Concrete results are shown in Figure 5.7. They refer to grey-scaled imagery and precincts as key elements. Thereby, the spatial influence of all precincts has been set to 32×32 (LSA). The results are obtained by measuring the time needed for transcoding or filtering only. For decoding the same time is assumed for both methods. It can be seen that transcoding is on average 3 times faster than filtering, which requires numerous operations to calculate each pixel value.

Bandwidth: The proposed approach only requires the transmission of those data containers contributing to the DoF representation. As this might be only a fraction

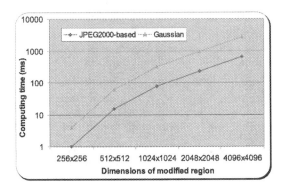

Figure 5.7: *Time required for blurring using the traditional* 5×5 *gaussian filter and the proposed transcoding approach based on JPEG2000.*

of all available data, much bandwidth can be saved. Due to the reason all data available for the focus are transferred, this especially applies for the large background region reconstructed by parts of the approximation only (cf. Figure E.7).

To give an estimation of the save of bandwidth, again the general assumption that the need for bandwidth increases exponentially with the enhancement in resolution is exploited. If $2^{2.0}$ represents the data required to restore the image in lowest provided resolution the data needed to reconstruct the whole image is $2^{2d_{max}}$. By assuming equally distributed image data and the focus region to cover $\frac{1}{f}$ of the image, the amount of bandwidth consumed to transmit data can be stated as:

$$Focus : \frac{1}{f} \cdot 2^{2d_{max}}$$
$$Background : \frac{f-1}{f}$$

For a typical value $d_{max} = 6$ and setting $f = 10$ this means that only 10.02% of all available image data is needed. In practice this value is even smaller as skipped data from higher quality layers is not considered. However, the additional gain is small. Figure 5.8 depicts the save of bandwidth by a real example considering multiple focus dimensions. The effect on economy is tremendous.

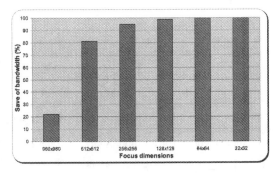

Figure 5.8: *The influence of the WoI dimension on the save of bandwidth (Image dimensions: 960x1240, decompositions stages: 6).*

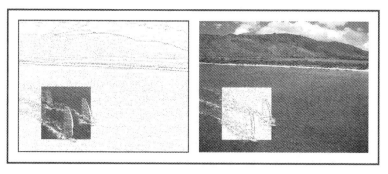

Figure 5.9: *A tool glass applied to still imagery by reducing the content within the background (left) or the WoI (right) to its details. This directs the viewer's attention to the embedded focus.*

5.4 Tool glasses for JPEG2000-encoded imagery

Tool glasses are an important metaphor to modify the importance of data attributes within WoI or background. This leads to a different representation for either type of region – a typical property of representations that are able to guide the viewer. Due to the resulting inconsistencies within the representation, the embedded WoI inherently attracts attention (cf. Figure 5.9). To achieve this, it is proposed to reduce the content belonging to WoI or background to its details and edges. The implementation of this idea is the topic of this section. Thereby, most of the proposed innovations have been published by the author in *"Transcoding JPEG2000-streams for modern image browsing techniques"* [Ros04c] and *"JPEG2000-based Viewer Guidance for Mobile Image Browsing"* [Ros06a].

The following part gives a deeper insight into the importance of image details and their application to viewer guidance. In the following paragraphs, a new low-complexity approach to create tool glass representations based on JPEG2000-encoded imagery is introduced and coupled to image streaming. A discussion of the achieved results serves to show the potential of this approach in mobile environments. Due to the potential of the idea, the last section is dedicated to show further application of content reduction to image browsing.

5.4.1 On the importance of image details for tool glasses

The reduction of the content to details and edges is the foundation of the proposed approach for raster image tool glasses. This section briefly explains why content represented by these important image primitives preserves much of its original information and might also serve to emphasize interesting properties. For more detail, the interested reader is referred to [Mow87; AG94].

Edges, which can be thought of as anomalies in the spatial domain, represent extremely important information despite the fact that they are represented in only a tiny fraction of the image samples. (SHAPIRO [Sha93])

The edge is a fundamental primitive in pictures. Natural scenes usually consist of objects with sharply defined surfaces. Therefore 2-dimensional projections of natural scenes often consist of domains of sharp variations in brightness separated by well-defined edges and contours. Although the visual cortex is the central proces-

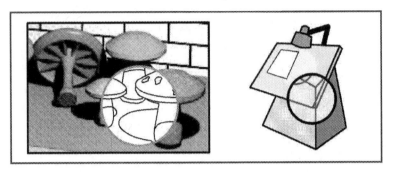

Figure 5.10: *Examples of tool glasses applied to multi-dimensional data based on the reduction to contours and details (src: [Bie97]).*

sor of the HVS, there is little spontaneous activity, and several stimulus features are needed to drive the cells. The most important of such features has proved to be the response of the brain to lines or edges [Mus05]. HUBEL AND WIESEL [Hub62] have even shown that the combination of the rods and cones provides color vision with high resolution and sensitivity to edges, and the retina may do the work of edge abstraction before the visual information is even presented to the brain (*intermediate illumination*). This shows the relevance of these primitives for the recognition of visual contents. Even if composed entirely of lines, without any narrative texture, such a representation is a strong, aesthetically satisfying picture [Lat95] conveying meaning almost as well as a photograph. This also explains the success of non-photorealistic images, as cartoons.

This principle has already been successfully applied to tool glasses. As shown in Figure 5.10, it is especially useful to get rid of information distracting the user from the comprehension of contents he is really interested in. These might be fine details hidden by texture and not visible in the original content. As stated by BIER ET AL. [Bie97], a suitable background color, where these reduced contents are projected onto, must be chosen. The respective color, however, depends on the task at hand and the image content (cf. Figure 5.10).

Two different configurations for tool glasses based on the concept of content reduction are possible (also cf. Figure 5.9).

- **Objective WoI:** WoI represents original, background reduced content
- **Subjective WoI:** WoI represents reduced, background original content

The first approach is similar to the spatial layout of the proposed DoF representation and applies the assumption that content belonging to the background serves only for orientation. It is related to tool glass techniques reducing the amount of information shown for the background, e.g. [Lok95] or [IDE05]. The second is a equivalent to the tool glass techniques shown in Figure 5.10. In order to enhance the comprehension of the belonging details, it applies content reduction to the WoI. Both approaches might have a rather different application field.

5.4.2 Creation of the image representation

In this section a fast technique for the creation of tool glass representations based on content reduction is introduced. Although the configuration of both possible layouts is different, the proposed method can be applied similarly.

Working in compression domain can be rather useful for mobile applications. This also applies for content reduction to edges and details. Thereby, the aim of the proposed ideas is not to develop a new method for edge detection based on wavelets, but to show how properties of JPEG2000 can be exploited to support the fast and efficient creation of tool glass representations. The proposed procedure does not violate the compliance of the encoded data and leads directly to the desired result without additional processing. The following points show the associated demands as well as their respective solution in JPEG2000 domain:

Separation of the details: DWT supports the inherent *separation of detail and approximation*

Different representation of WoI and background: Limited Spatial Access to encoded image data enables *independent access* to disjoint image regions

Each solution is now discussed in detail.

Separation of detail and approximation   The beneficial property of the DWT to inherently separate detail and approximation of an input signal has already been exploited for the creation of DoF representations. However, the approximation is of little use to represent details. Instead it is reasonable to focus on data from decomposition levels which have been filtered with a detail preserving high band filter. They mainly keep contours and sharpness information of the image. Within the transformed image this corresponds to the subbands HL_d, LH_d, HH_d (cf. Figure C.1). Due to the RSA feature of JPEG2000, access to the data is easy to accomplish for all types of key elements.

To display the details, however, the belonging data containers must be decoded. As synthesis starts with the missing approximation, this leads to problems. This can be easily overcome by the features of the JPEG2000 codec. As the decoder assumes average values for positions within the decomposition scheme belonging to missing parts of the data-stream, data from detail subbands can be decoded even if the belonging approximation is not provided. This is a beneficial property not available for all codecs and again shows the flexibility of the new standard. The visual outcome of the procedure is shown in Figure 5.11.

Although the result represents the details, a significant drawback of this approach is that fine details visually perish in the averaged energy and cannot be recognized.

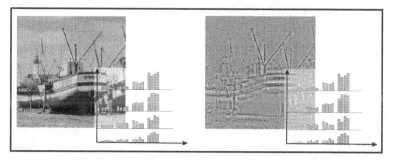

Figure 5.11: *If the approximation is not available during synthesis, the image content is represented by its details only.*

This is due to the fact of them having low altitude and variance and only slightly varying from the approximation. Thus further steps are necessary to enhance the quality of the representation. To keep the required computing power as small as possible, it is desirable to achieve this in compression domain also.

The approximation contains most of the information required to restore the texture of an image. Due to this, a uniform approximation can be basically seen as a single colored canvas on which the details are projected onto. To increase its difference to the details, it is proposed to substitute the original approximation by more appropriate data. Here it is reasonable to chose an approximation that is able to reconstruct the canvas by a color that enhances the contrast of the edges and that fits to the task at hand [Bie97]. While it is less clear how the second point should be accommodated in a rigorous manner, the first point can be achieved by using an approximation able to reconstruct a white colored canvas.

To achieve this in JPEG2000 domain, a new approximation must be created and included. Thereby, the format of the substituted data must by perfectly aligned with the remaining data to ensure it can be successfully restored. The format depends on a number of factors, but can be generally achieved by creating and encoding a second image with the same dimensions and identical encoding parameters as applied to the original image. Thereby, the content of the second image must represent the desired canvas color. The inclusion of the new approximation can be simply accomplished by replacing data containers belonging to the approximation of the original image by their pendant from the new stream. The result of this procedure is shown in Figure 5.12.

Similar to the creation of expressive DoF representations, the results achieved by content reduction depend on the parameters chosen during encoding time. Experiments have revealed that at least 5 decomposition stages must be applied to extract sufficient image details. Regarding the choice of wavelet kernels, best visual appearance is achieved by applying CDF 9/7 kernels. As shown in Figure E.8, details extracted by the 5/3 kernels are more accurate and unsteady.

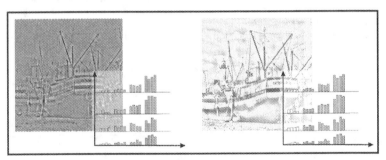

Figure 5.12: *If the original approximation is replaced, the representation of the details is improved.*

Independent access   To achieve different representations for WoI and background, concepts similar to the ones proposed for the creation of DoF representations are used. If the LSA feature is applied, all data containers can be either assigned to WoI or background. In case of tool glasses, however, details are required for WoI and background. Thus, partition of the belonging subbands is optional. This conclusion might lead to an appropriate partition of the approximation only and as a result to a slightly better compression performance (cf. Section 3.3.2.1).

In any event, only data containers belonging to the approximation are substituted by supplementary data. Decoding encoded content modified this way leads to the desired tool glass representation without further modifications (cf. Figure 5.9).

5.4.3 Image streaming

The partial use of image data also offers potential for an adapted streaming of data contributing to tool glass representations. Contrary to blurring, however, the LoD-model must be enhanced to fit to the proposed substitution of the approximation.

RoI/LoD partition   Due to the application of a single WoI, the partition is similar to a DoF representation and leads to two RoI – one shown in full and one with reduced content. The LoD-model introduced in Section 2.2.1, however, covers only cases for the regular refinement of image data up to a certain target-LoD. As the process starts with data belonging to the approximation of the image, this leads to problems for the proposed approach. Due to the fact that the approximation is not required for regions represented by details only, the transfer of the respective data can be omitted. To achieve this, an additional *start-LoD* is introduced and basically serves to signal that only the LoD-delta between start- and target-LoD is of interest for the belonging region. As the start-LoD does not violate the LoD-hierarchy, the respective communication components might react as if all data required to achieve the start-LoD has already been handled. To keep track of all already served data, however, relevant start-LoDs must be stored.

Based on this enhancement, the data required for a tool glass representation can be described as shown in Table 5.2. The encoded content used to substitute the original approximation is not considered for streaming and assumed to be created at client side. This requires only little computing power. Selected parts might also be stored for multiple use.

Tool glass representation		
	RoI (original)	**RoI (reduced)**
start-LoD:	–	$LoD(\frac{1}{2^{d_{max}}}, \frac{1}{2^{d_{max}}}, img_a, img_c)$
target-LoD:	$LoD(1, 1, img_a, img_c)$	$LoD(1, 1, img_a, img_c)$

Table 5.2: *RoI/LoD partition of an image represented by the proposed tool glass approach.*

Applied streaming technology

Calculation of contributing elements: Due to the completely different representation of WoI and background, the application of *Limited Spatial Access* ensures that each part of the content belongs to one RoI only. Depending on the shape of the RoI, either *element selection for rectangular RoIs* or the selection strategy inherent in *synchronized signalization* can be applied. *Subband-wise selection* is of minor interest to tool glasses.

Sequencing of calculated elements: As the WoI is of higher relevance than the background, *prioritization-based global sequencing* can be used to stream belonging elements earlier than others. *R-D optimized local sequencing* may be applied if the fast refinement of the WoI is crucial.

Signalization of sequenced elements: There is no specific requirement of the tool glass approach regarding the application of a certain signalization.

Applied streaming strategy   Suggestions for a reasonable streaming strategy depend on the chosen spatial representation and application field. In case of an objective WoI, it is reasonable to transfer its approximation first. This gives a first impression of the belonging content and is achieved by assigning a prioritization tuple of $prio(\frac{1}{2^{d_{max}}}, \frac{1}{2^{d_{max}}}, 0, 0)$. Later on, WoI data might be exclusively refined or interleaved with background data. In case of a subjective WoI, it is proposed to assign an even higher priority. This ensures many details are already available before first approximation data for the background is handled.

Specifics   The creation of DoF representations can be fully achieved by a selective transmission and subsequent decoding of contents available within the client cache. Due to the inclusion of a new approximation from a second stream, this concept must be enhanced for tool glass representations. The included data may overwrite some of the received data and lead to a redundant data-transfer in case the overwritten data is required a second time. To overcome this, it is proposed to use two cache structures – one for the incoming data and one for the data relevant for the current representation. Thereby, the display logic determines the relevant data, which is afterwards copied and merged with the supplementary data in the second cache. Decoding of all contents within the second cache immediately leads to the desired representation.

5.4.4 Discussion

In this section, the proposed approach to apply the concept of tool glasses to raster imagery and its implementation for mobile environments is discussed. Thereby, the same points as for DoF – *quality of the representation*, and need for *computing power* and *bandwidth* – are proven.

Quality of the representation: To compare the visual quality of content reduction based on JPEG2000, the well-known canny edge detector is used. The results achieved by the new approach are rather good. Although, the representation is not as rich in contrast as by applying the canny approach, much of the details are preserved (cf. Figure 5.13). This is of particular interest for the strived application field and has not been expected to be achieved by an image codec primarily designed for image compression. In case the image content mostly consists of texture, both approaches fail to extract meaningful details.

Computing power: Transcoding based on Random spatial access is fast. As this feature is also used to reduce content, a much faster execution speed compared to traditional approaches is achieved. Concrete results for the processing of a greyscale picture using precincts as key elements are shown in Figure 5.14. They are obtained by measuring the time needed for transcoding or edge detection only. The spatial influence of all precincts (LSA) has been set to 32×32. It can be seen that the proposed method is up to 20 times faster than the canny approach. This is due to the fact only fast selection and copy tasks are performed. Contrary, the canny approach applies multiple and complex matrix operations.

Figure 5.13: *Details extracted from a greyscale image applying canny edge detection (left) or the proposed JPEG2000-based approach (right).*

The proposed approach based on transcoding is also rather suited for progressive refinement. The desired details refine over time and subsequently increase in resolution and quality. This only requires a decoding of relevant data and is a great advantage compared to traditional approaches. As content reduction might be executed after each progression step, this further increases the differences regarding complexity. It is also questionable if traditional techniques deliver similar results if they are applied to content partially restored during early transmission stages.

Bandwidth: For tool glass representations, bandwidth can only be saved by adapting the transmission belonging to the RoI represented by reduced content. Unfortunately the neglected approximation is very small compared to the size of the data containing details (cf. Figure E.9). If $2^{2\cdot 0}$ represents the data required to restore the approximation, the full amount of data required to reconstruct the highest image resolution is $2^{2d_{max}}$. Consequentially, the amount of data containing details is $2^{2d_{max}} - 1$. This data must be transferred in any case. In addition, pieces of the approximation are required to fully restore one of the RoIs. If this region is considered as the focus and covers $\frac{1}{f}$ of the image, the required bandwidth can be stated as:

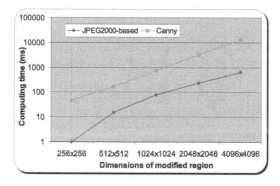

Figure 5.14: *Time needed to extract details using traditional Canny edge detection or the proposed transcoding approach based on JPEG2000.*

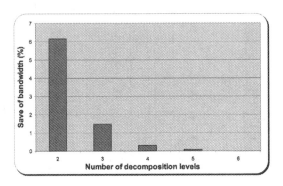

Figure 5.15: *The influence of the number of decomposition stages on the save of bandwidth for the proposed tool glass approach (Image dimensions:* 960×1240*, focus dimensions* 128×128*).*

$$Focus : \frac{1}{f} \cdot 2^{2d_{max}}$$
$$Background : \frac{f-1}{f} \cdot \left(2^{2d_{max}} - 1\right)$$

Thus, the overall save of bandwidth can be expressed by $\frac{\frac{f-1}{f} \cdot 100}{2^{2d_{max}}}\%$. The resulting value is mainly influenced by the number of decomposition stages d_{max} and depicted for different configurations in Figure 5.15. Obviously, the save is much less than for DoF representations. In case of multi-component imagery, however, this value can be increased by considering selected components only, e.g those containing the important luminance information. This data already contains most of the details required for the proposed content reduction and representation.

5.4.5   Application to image browsing

The idea to reduce negligible image content paired with an efficient image transmission also provides new options for other application fields. This section serves to show how to apply the principle to image browsing. As discussed in the last chapter, image browsing techniques also divide the image into regions with different importance. To save screen space, background regions are strongly scaled, and due to this, often difficult to comprehend. Content reduction to edges and details is able to solve this problem. This has been shown in *"Transcoding JPEG2000-streams for modern image browsing techniques"* [Ros04c], where the author has successfully applied this idea to the representation of the largeDetail-View (lDV, Section 4.5, p. 76). By describing appropriate content streaming, the later publication *"Remote raster image browsing based on fast content reduction for mobile environments"* [Ros04b] completes the given statements regarding image communication. The following sections explain the idea in detail.

Image representation   Within the lDV, the screen is split into detail and overview. The detail view is of major interest. The overview, provides means for interaction and communicates important image properties. The content displayed within the overview is a fundamental part of the representation and must be displayed. In literature, however, it has been stated that DO-based techniques are useful for Image/WoI ratios of 5-30 [Bau02]. This leads to a strong scaling and can render the displayed content incomprehensible.

To overcome this, it is proposed to reduce the content of the overview. As edges and details are important structures of an image, they are selected to represent its content. Texture does not contribute to orientation and navigation, and thus, will be removed. Such an adaptation basically corresponds to the concept of an *information mural* (cf. Section 4.2.3).

To achieve this, the described approach for content reduction based on JPEG2000-encoded imagery with all of its advantages can be applied. This neither changes the spatial layout of the IDV nor the dimensions of overview or viewfinder. Only the content within the overview is reduced. The image representation resulting from this process is depicted in Figure 5.16/left. As shown in Figure 5.16/right, content reduction can also be suitably applied to other browsing techniques.

Image streaming   As the spatial representation is not changed by content reduction, unsurprisingly, general statements proposed for the IDV and image streaming do not vary strongly. However, the enhancements introduced to handle the neglected approximation must be applied. To skip the approximation of the overview the start-LoD for the belonging RoI must be set to $LoD(\frac{1}{2^{d_{max}}}, \frac{1}{2^{d_{max}}}, img_a, img_c)$. The target-LoD remains the same and can be stated as $LoD(\frac{1}{x_o}, \frac{1}{y_o}, img_a, img_c)$ if the overview is scaled by factors $x_o : y_o$. It is worth noting, the handled data-stream must support a sufficient number of resolution levels to be able to apply the idea ($x_o, y_o \leq 2^{r_{max}}$).

Useful streaming technology to be applied to a modified IDV also remain the same as for the original IDV. To provide content for the most interesting region, a reasonable streaming strategy transfers the approximation of the detail view first. If finished, the details from the overview are transmitted. As both views profit from this data, they are refined simultaneously. Later on the remaining data from the detail view required to achieve the target-LoD are streamed.

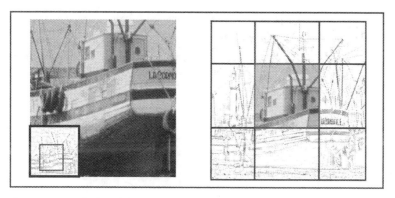

Figure 5.16: *Application of content reduction to image browsing: The reduction of the content within overview (IDV, left) or context belts (rFEV, right).*

Discussion   By applying content reduction to the highly scaled overview, its content is better to grasp. This leads to enhanced orientation and navigation. As the proposed content reduction fails for certain contents, this might not be valid for all images. In such cases, the content is mainly described by texture and the original IDV should be used.

The proposed content reduction does not increase the complexity to create the image representation. Due to the omission of the approximation, slightly less bandwidth is required. Equation 4.5 stating the amount of data required by the overview within the original IDV, may be adapted to content reduction as follows:

$$100 - \frac{100 \cdot \left(2^{2(d_{max} - \log_2 x_o)} - 1\right)}{2^{2d_{max}}} \tag{5.1}$$

Overall, applying content reduction to the IDV, usually increases the comprehension of the content within the overview and saves further bandwidth.

5.5   Conclusion of the chapter

Viewer guidance is applied such as to direct the attention of an image viewer to regions of importance. A review of related techniques, however, has revealed most of the *current approaches* for imagery are either *straightforward* or require many resources. Due to this, there is a need for new developments in mobile image communication.

To overcome the problem of viewer guidance, two different techniques from the field of Information visualization have been adapted to raster imagery: *Depth of Field* and *Tool glasses*. It has been shown that both techniques are *able to guide the attention of the viewer* to a desired image region. To be able to apply these techniques in mobile environments, however, new ideas for the creation of the respective content representation and image streaming were required.

This has been accomplished by a proposal based on *fast and efficient transcoding* of imagery encoded with JPEG2000. This strategy is *3 times faster for blurring* image content (DoF) and almost *20 times faster for content reduction* (Tool glass) compared to traditional techniques. This is of crucial importance for low power mobile gadgets. By omitting the transmission of data not contributing to the current content representation, the strategy also allows to *save much bandwidth*. This can be more than *98%* for image content that is shown in DoF. Although the save is not as high for content reduction, the general idea of content representation has *further potential* and can also be applied to other application areas. As shown for image browsing content reduction is able to increase usability and to further decrease bandwidth requirements.

As shown for image browsing and viewer guidance, static image contents can be appropriately represented and handled in mobile environments. The temporal dynamic of visual information, however, also requires the handling of changing contents. Belonging problems and solutions are discussed in the next chapter.

Chapter 6

Content exchange between images

The exchange of content between two or more images in consequence of modifications is a frequent task in modern image communication. This task is easy to accomplish in pixel domain, but requires much resources if the content has already been compressed. To overcome this, it is proposed to apply the introduced concepts for dynamic RoIs in order to exchange the content directly in compression domain. This is achieved by appropriate transcoding operations (cf. Figure 6.1).

Content exchange requires detailed statements to selection and replacement of the encoded contents. After formulating *aims and requirements* (Section 6.1) and reviewing *related work* (Section 6.2), a scheme for content exchange in JPEG2000 domain is introduced and discussed (Section 6.3). The proposed idea is also suited for image streaming and allows for sophisticated exchange procedures not available in pixel domain. All strategies are discussed and evaluated.

The potential of the basic approach is enormous. This is shown by a number of selected *applications* for still and moving imagery (Section 6.4). The chapter closes with conclusions (Section 6.5).

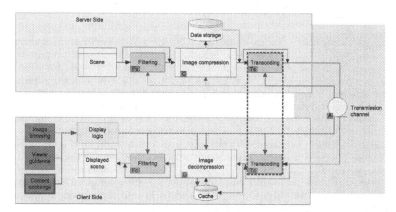

Figure 6.1: *Content exchange is fully accomplished by transcoders at server and client side. Due to the handling of contents from multiple images, the display logic is also involved in cache management.*

6.1 Aims and requirements

The aim of content exchange between imagery is the *region-wise* and *resource-saving* replacement of content belonging to a *destination image* by content from a *source image*. Although this process seems straightforward it is still challenging in image communication, where contents are usually stored in encoded form at server side.

The most obvious way to accomplish the modification is by replacing belonging pixel values. In image communication, however, they are only accessible at the filtering step at server (F_s) or client side (F_c). In case the exchange is done at server side, the communication pipeline must be fully passed by the new content. This is costly regarding *computing power* and *bandwidth* [LTI05] and can only be applied for occasional replacements or strongly constrained clients [Fox96; LTI05]. A flexible handling can be achieved by submitting both images and applying changes at client side. Such an approach, however, moves the additional needs of the replacement process to the client. This is especially disadvantageous in case additional operations, such as content scaling, must be applied before replacement. Furthermore, often not all content is required, but has to be transferred. Due to this, new ideas are required to solve the task. Thereby, a valuable contribution must ensure the fulfilment of the following points:

Content exchange: fast replacement of image regions at client side

Content streaming: non-redndant transmission of the image contents

As shown in the former sections, the new image coding standard JPEG2000 provides a number of beneficial features regarding the access and streaming of image data. They can also be exploited for appropriate content exchange. To achieve this, it is proposed to accomplish the exchange in compression instead of pixel domain. By *replacing encoded data*, this allows for fast processing and by a *reasonable selection* strategy the appropriate transmission of image data. To emphasize the innovation of the introduced concepts, related work for content manipulation in compression domain is reviewed in the following section.

6.2 Discussion of related work

Images transformed to a compressed representation are often understood as static and indivisible objects. However, approaches handling the image in compressed representation have been developed for a variety of application areas such as image retrieval [Sch96; Man99; The00], segmentation [Gon01; Fen03], or edge detection [She96b]. As reported such a strategy only requires selected pieces of the encoded image and needs far less computing power during processing [Jia02]. Thus, they seem rather suited for mobile environments. Those techniques, however, are based on the extraction of relevant features and do not replace information as required for content exchange. This task is much more difficult. Only a few publications cover the modification of content in DCT- [Smi93; Smi96; Jia02] or DWT domain [Dro00; JPG02a; Tau01; SI02; Dro03]. Due to the limitations imposed by compression domain, however, the described manipulations are rather limited. Beside a strategy for *Virtual Network Computing* (VNC) [Vir02], none of the reviewed techniques cover problems in remote communication.

SMITH AND ROWE [Smi93] address the issue of modifying JPEG-compressed images by performing coefficient-wise scalar addition and multiplication. Thus, they are able to solve the problem of transferring subtitles between two video sequences very efficiently. In a later paper [Smi96], their method is extended to single images of Motion-JPEG sequences.

In [Jia02], JIANG AND FENG describe the efficient extraction of a smaller version of a JPEG-image for browsing and indexing. Although no dynamic image content is mentioned, the extraction is done in compression domain. To achieve this, average values similar to the DC coefficient are calculated and used to create the downscaled image. The contribution is limited to this task only.

DRORI AND LISCHINSKI [Dro00; Dro03] exploit the advantages of the wavelet domain to implement a wide class of image processing operations directly in wavelet domain. The basic strategy is to apply operation matrices each designed for a certain task to wavelet coefficients. They show this can save much computational power and deliver great results. This is also stated in [SI02] for *image fusion*. Nevertheless, the authors do not address the application of the operations to an independent spatial region only. As coefficients interleave in their spatial contribution, this is a general problem in wavelet domain. An arbitrary modification leads to unpredictable results.

Beside the feature to access RoI contents directly within the data-stream, JPEG2000 inherently provides interesting properties for image processing and editing without decompression. Beside the support of different LoDs, even complex geometric manipulations such as *rotation*, *flipping*, or *mirroring* without fully decoding the content are possible [JPG02a]. Although *cropping* can also be applied in compression domain, additional processing is required at boundaries of the cropped region [Tau01]. Nevertheless, each task must be supported by the properties of the underlying data-stream. If this is not the case, the content must be fully decompressed.

A hybrid strategy adopting techniques proposed for pixel and transformation domain are applied within the image editing SDK *ePIC* [PEG05]. As each coefficient block of JPEG-encoded imagery contributes to an independent image region only, this technique separates and decodes all blocks related to regions which are going to be altered. As belonging content is now available in pixel representation applying image editing is straightforward. The result is again encoded and replaces the related original block values. A great advantage of this method is a single compliant bitstream including all modifications. By exploiting the properties of tiles as independent sub-images, a similar strategy is applied by the FlashPix-codec [FPX97], VNC [Vir02], and the JPEG2000 standard [JPG02a].

Summary of related work   Only a few publications address the problem of manipulating image contents in compression domain. Thereby, most of the approaches have been designed to solve specific tasks. The exchange of content is often only briefly mentioned. This also applies for the manipulation of JPEG2000-encoded imagery, where proposals are usually limited to geometric manipulations. Only a few publications mention the options to apply tiles for content exchange [JPG02a]. However, tiles are limited by a number of unpleasant properties and should only be used where required. In literature no proposals to cope with remote editing of JPEG2000-encoded contents have been published so far. Thus, there is a strong requirement for new ideas on this topic.

The following section serves to provide detailed statements to all key elements suitable to accomplish the content exchange in JPEG2000 domain, their appropriate selection, and streaming.

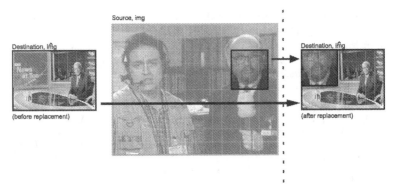

Figure 6.2: *A region of the destination image (left) is replaced by a region from a source image (middle) to combine contents (right). The exchange is organized by an access grid.*

6.3   A new approach for content exchange in JPEG2000 domain

This section introduces new ideas for fast content exchange between imagery encoded with JPEG2000 and their appropriate handling in remote environments. After showing the main idea of the basic approach, different strategies for the content replacement are introduced and explained. Based on these techniques, strategies for an appropriate image streaming are described. A provided discussion shows the eligibility of the proposed ideas for mobile environments. Many of the proposed ideas have been published by the author in *"Merging images in JPEG2000 domain"* [Ros03a] and adapted to remote tasks in *"Limited spatial access in JPEG2000 for remote image editing"* [Ros04a].

6.3.1   The main idea

The RSA property of JPEG2000-encoded data has already been successfully used for image browsing and viewer guidance. By a reasonable selection strategy for data containers, it was possible to separate the encoded contents belonging to certain image regions and to adapt the streaming process accordingly. For tool glasses, it has also been shown that certain data can be replaced directly in JPEG2000 domain. This led to strongly decreased requirements regarding computing power and bandwidth.

This chapter continues these ideas by proposing strategies able to replace all content belonging to a certain image region by new content of a second image. This is accomplished by substituting all data containers contributing to the reconstruction of the region by their respective counterparts. Data containers are represented by a selected type of *key element*. Due to their coarse spatial influence (cf. Section 2.3.1, p. 22ff), the exchange is organized by an *access grid*. The main idea of the replacement strategy is illustrated in Figure 6.2.

To achieve content exchange in JPEG2000 domain, these problems must be solved:

1. Due to the *multiresolution representation* of the content, multiple elements contribute to a single grid cell (cf. Figure 6.3).

2. The dimensions of the *spatial contribution* of elements residing at different

levels within the DWT hierarchy may be different. To suitably replace the content, all elements must be aligned with the access grid.

3. In case source and destination image have been encoded by different *transformation parameters*, e.g. the applied wavelet kernels, decoding leads to a unpredictable reconstruction of the content.

This can be overcome by exploiting the properties of JPEG2000 as follows:

Multiresolution representation: All elements contributing to the reconstruction of an affected cell within the destination image must be identified and replaced by an appropriate counterpart from the source image.

Spatial influence: The spatial influence of elements can be suitably selected during encoding time. To achieve the correspondence of elements with the access grid, *Limited Spatial Access* (LSA) (cf. Section 2.3.4, p. 27ff) is applied.

Transformation parameters: To ensure synthesis corresponds with analysis, it is proposed to encode source and destination with an identical parameter set.

While the last two problems can easily be overcome by applying appropriate parameter sets during the encoding of both images, the first point requires more detailed statements to selection and assignment of elements. This will be shown in the next section. For simplicity, each replaced region is required to be of rectangular shape. Complex shapes may be approximated by multiple rectangular regions if required.

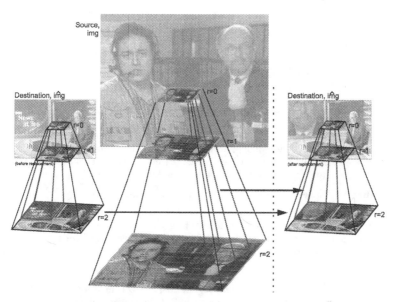

Figure 6.3: *The basic exchange scheme substitutes certain key elements (pyramids) from a source image for elements of a destination image considering the multiresolution property of JPEG2000.*

6.3.2   Content exchange

Due to the capabilities of the standard, content exchange in JPEG2000 domain can be accomplished by different strategies and key elements. Founded on the basic exchange scheme described in the next section, more sophisticated techniques exploiting the multiresolution representation of the content are introduced later on.

6.3.2.1   Basic exchange scheme

The goal of the basic exchange strategy is the replacement of all image content belonging to a region within the destination image $\hat{img}$ by content from a source image img. This is accomplished by *selecting relevant elements* within both images and *forming pairs of associated elements*. Replacing a single element within the destination image by its counterpart from the source image leads to the strived content exchange without leaving JPEG2000 domain (cf. Figure 6.3). Thereby, either *code-blocks*, *precincts*, or *tiles* may be chosen as key element for the exchange procedure. To simplify belonging descriptions and to show similarities between these elements, they are represented by the introduced *generic key element*. For better readability, the notation of elements is consistent with the notations used in former chapters. This also applies for set-based element determination and selection.

General proceeding   The formation of corresponding element-pairs basically consists of 4 main steps:

1. **Requirements check**

2. **Element selection**

3. **Verification of the RoI elements**

4. **Formation of element pairs**

The **requirements check** serves to ensure that all involved elements are either tiles, precincts, or code-blocks. If this cannot be ensured, it might happen that some elements are replaced by elements of a different type. This would lead to unpredictable results. As they cannot be arbitrarily replaced or inserted, the process also detects elements truncated by image borders. Detailed statements to the implementation of the requirements check can be found in Appendix F.1.

Result: All valid elements of a chosen type are determined.

Element selection serves to determine all RoI elements contributing to the reconstruction of the respective pixel regions to be exchanged. Applied to each image independently it is equal to the described procedure for *element selection for rectangular RoIs* introduced in Section 3.3.1, p. 38, for image streaming.

Result: All RoI elements for both regions are determined.

Due to the option to chose different region offsets and dimensions within both images, it might happen that the number of RoI elements is different. Since the proposed exchange scheme is based on the creation of pairs, this must be avoided. A **verification step** ensures that to each element a corresponding partner is found. How to accomplish this is described in Appendix F.2.

Result: The number of determined elements is equal for both images.

The final step is the **formation of element pairs** from both images. This is accomplished by exploiting the relative element position within the respective region. Elements from corresponding decomposition levels that are assigned equal relative positions form a single pair. This is shown in Appendix F.3.

Result: The final step leads to pairs of RoI elements which must be replaced to accomplish content exchange. Thereby, all determined pairs must be considered to fully replace belonging data.

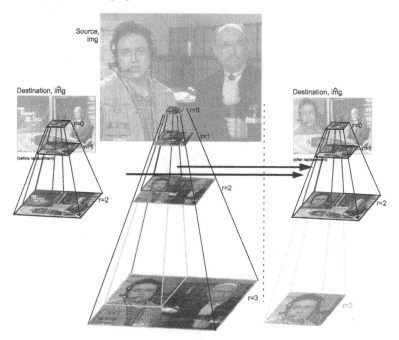

Figure 6.4: *Content belonging to higher resolutions within the source image are skipped to scale and fit the new content into the provided space within the destination.*

6.3.2.2   Content exchange joint with simultaneous scaling

In certain cases, it might happen that the selected source contents are too large to be included into the belonging space within the destination ($reg_i \approx r\hat{e}g_i \cdot 2^g$, $i = 1, 2$). To overcome this, the source contents are downscaled by a factor 2^g. This, however, imposes additional complexity if accomplished in pixel domain. Here, the multiresolution property of contents encoded with JPEG2000 may be exploited to replace and scale contents simultaneously. The proposed enhancement is still based on the exchange of certain key elements and does not strongly vary from the introduced basic scheme. The main idea is shown in Figure 6.4.

Downscaling in DWT-schemes is accomplished by decoding image content up to a certain image resolution only. Due to a dyadic decomposition applied by JPEG2000, only scaling factors which are powers of 2 and equal in both directions are supported. If the image is to be downscaled by a factor of 2^g, only data belonging to resolution levels r, $0 \leq r \leq r_{max} - g$, must be considered. If for all elements

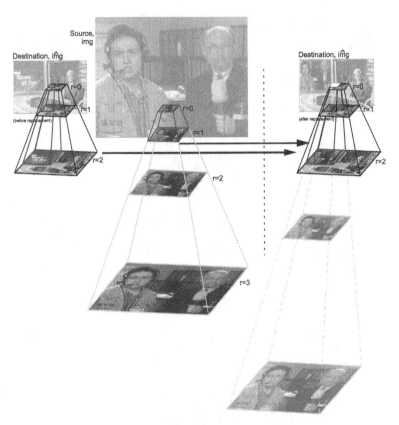

Figure 6.5: *Areas associated with different tiles may provide a different number of resolution levels. In the given example this leads to less inherent resolutions for the replaced region within the destination.*

within the reduced source image corresponding elements within the destination and vice versa can be found, they may simply be exchanged as described. After replacement, they represent the belonging content reduced in its spatial extent by a factor of 2^g in both dimensions.

Such a doing requires the adaptation of the statements provided for the *requirements* and *element selection* step. Other stages do not consider the particular resolution assigned to an element, and thus, do not differ from the described basic exchange scheme. How to accomplish the adaptation is described in Appendix F.4.

Nevertheless, this enhancement still requires adequate and corresponding resolution levels for source and destination image. This cannot always be taken for granted. In Appendix F.5 the interested reader is provided with a third scheme overcoming this limitation by exploiting the properties of tiles. This scheme provides means to exchange regions even if the number of image resolutions does not match. The main idea is drafted in Figure 6.5. Although still constrained by certain limitations, this further enhances the applicability of the approach. A general solution able to handle all possible configurations between source and destination is the image editing framework introduced in Section 6.4.1.

6.3.3   Content streaming

Within the proposed communication scheme content exchange is mostly accomplished by the transcoding units. Thereby, the unit at server side (T_s) serves to select relevant data containers required for the current modification. The transcoder at client side (T_c) applies the literal replacement by assigning received contents to the respective positions within the cache. Decoding cache data leads to the modified image content in pixel representation. No additional processing is required. Statements given in this section assume a scenario where the destination image is currently sent to the client and is to be updated by a certain image region of the source image. The viewer at client side profits from the updates without further interaction.

RoI/LoD partition   Similar to image browsing and viewer guidance, during content exchange every involved image is partitioned into two different types of regions. For content exchange they are labeled *exchanged* and *remaining*. If a region is used for a current image representation, it is shown in final-LoD. This applies for the region which has been included from the source image and the region not affected by the replacement within the destination. All other regions are not of interest. This leads to the following LoD configuration for either type of image (Table 6.1).

| | Content exchange | |
	Exchanged region	Remaining region
Source:	$LoD(1, 1, img_a, img_c)$	$LoD(0, 0, 0, 0)$
Destination:	$LoD(0, 0, 0, 0)$	$LoD(1, 1, img_a, img_c)$

Table 6.1: *RoI/LoD partition of source and destination image for content exchange.*

Applied streaming technology

Calculation of contributing elements: As described *element selection for rectangular RoIs* and *Limited Spatial Access* are of crucial interest to determine and trim contributing elements within source and destination. For more complex shapes, the element selection strategy inherent in *synchronized signalization* can also be applied. *Subband-wise selection* is of minor interest for content exchange.

Sequencing of calculated elements: As there is only one relevant image region within a single image, there is no suggestion for appropriate sequencing.

Signalization of sequenced elements: Of certain benefit for content exchange are the flexible *synchronized* and *external signalization*. *Inherent signalization* is strongly aligned to the structure of a single encoded image and cannot handle multiple images.

Applied streaming strategy   Contrary to the previously discussed applications, content exchange requires the transmission of data from multiple images. Thus, proposed statements are slightly different. The streaming process starts with the destination image. As soon as a modification appears, the server arranges the modified data containers corresponding to containers already sent for streaming. This ensures modified contents arrive early at client side and can update the original content. All remaining original data chunks are replaced by their modified counterparts at server side. This avoids the redundant transfer of containers which will be overwritten anyway. Depending on the task at hand the modified data may be interleaved with the remaining original data or exclusively handled until both regions have achieved an identic state-LoD.

Specifics   Similar to data streaming for tool glasses, combining content from different images requires additional statements to cache the data. The problem is the handling of multiple elements assigned to equal positions of the cache. However, content exchange does not require keeping the original data that has been replaced, and already filled positions are overwritten. So basically only a single cache is required. In case of a JPIP-based transmission, however, such doing violates the requirements of the protocol [Tau03a; JPG04]. In case compliance is of importance, it is proposed to use a second cache structure. Together with still valid portions of the original content collected in the first cache, modified parts are directly transferred to a second structure. After the transfer, this cache contains all data valid to represent the updated image content, which now may be decoded and displayed. The first cache is obsolete and may be removed.

6.3.4   Discussion

In this section the results of the proposed content exchange in JPEG2000 domain are discussed. The limitations of mobile environments – *computing power* and *bandwidth* – are of exceptional interest. Content modification, however, also requires the consideration of the resulting *image quality* and the *granularity of spatial access*.

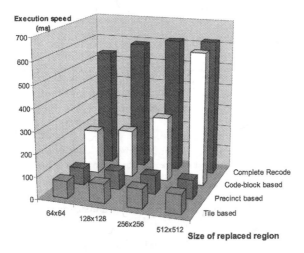

Figure 6.6: *Comparison of execution speed between 4 different key elements.*

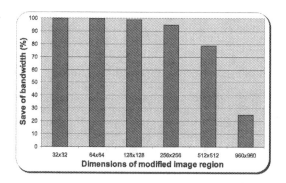

Figure 6.7: *Save of bandwidth for modified regions of different dimensions.*

Computing power   Working in compression domain strongly decreases the complexity of content exchange. Due to the reason that only transcoders are involved, former steps of the communication pipeline are skipped.

Figure 6.6 reveals the computation time required by each of the element types able to accomplish the content exchange. The measurements refer to the exchange between 2 grey-scaled images each of size 1024×1024 pixels. The spatial influence (LSA) of all elements is set to 32×32 so as to meaningfully compare the results. Unsurprisingly, tile- and precinct-based exchange requires much less processing time than a traditional approach which fully decompresses each image, exchanges pixel regions, and re-compresses the result. For both, tile and precinct-based exchange, it is only necessary to replace data containers from one data-stream with containers from another. This is almost *9 times faster* than the ordinary approach. Due to the need to undo parts of the codec, the code-block-based approach is slower than using tiles and precincts. The effort increases with bigger regions, but the proposed strategy is still faster than the traditional approach. The differences regarding the need for computing power are even bigger if additional scaling must be applied. Contrary to the exchange in compression domain, which requires even less data containers to be handled, the traditional approach is further burdened with downscaling operations.

Bandwidth   The fact that encoded content is piece-wise accessed and transmitted offers high potential for the save of bandwidth. Instead of retransmitting the modified image completely, only data containers which differ from the original data are sent. Obviously, the performance gain of such a strategy varies depending on the ratio between modified and remaining data. This is depicted in Figure 6.7 for modified image regions of different dimensions. If $[reg_1, reg_2]$ denote the dimensions of the modified region and $[s_1, s_2]$ the dimensions of the whole image, the save of bandwidth can be approximated by

$$100 - \frac{reg_1 \cdot reg_2 \cdot 100}{s_1 \cdot s_2}\%$$

(6.1)

Of course, this equation is only a rough estimation, but clearly shows the correlation between the influencing factors – *the larger the image and the smaller the modified region, the bigger the performance gain.* In the given example this leads to a save of more than 99% for a small region of 32×32 pixels.

Image quality   Although content exchange in JPEG2000 domain can achieve good results regarding complexity and bandwidth, the quality of the resulting image must also be considered. As the combined contents are encoded in two different contexts, there are interferences at the borders between new and remaining image regions. This especially applies for code-blocks and precincts which only group wavelet coefficients, and thus, do not prevent their overlapping during DWT analysis and synthesis. Due to this, the transition between both regions becomes blurred somewhat by the wavelet synthesis operators. In practice, however, this softening of the boundaries does not appear to adversely affect the visual impression of the merged image (cf. Figure 6.8). Further on, this effect does not appear if there is sufficient space between modified wavelet coefficients and the boundaries. Tiles are not concerned by this drawback.

Figure 6.8: *By content exchange founded on code-blocks or precincts, the transition between new and remaining regions becomes blurred. Due to coarse spatial granularity of the access grid more content than desired might be replaced.*

Granularity of spatial access   A general drawback of image composition in JPEG2000 domain is the alignment restraint imposed by the spatial access to the encoded data. For this reason, spatial access granularity is significantly reduced, relative to pixel-based exchange (cf. Figure 6.8). This can be reducing the sizes of the structural elements, but not without significant loss in compression efficiency (cf. Section 2.5.2). Thus, spatial access granularity always depends on the respective task. A size of 32×32, however, offers a good trade-off for many applications.

The proposed method cannot provide pixel-accuracy. An examination of the problem, however, revealed that this might not always be required and can be overcome by a hybrid approach exploiting the advantages of pixel and compression domain. This is one of the possible applications of content exchange in JPEG2000 domain and will be considered in detail in the next section of this chapter.

6.4   Applications

As shown, exchanging contents in compression domain offers many advantages.
In this section it will be shown how to apply the proposed strategies to increase the
performance of selected tasks. Two different approaches are discussed: **content
composition** and **content updates**. *Content composition* refers to the combination
of imagery with completely different contents. Here, the general task consists of
the merging of different contents to design new content. As this task often requires
the pixel-accurate replacement of exchanged regions, the proposed basis technique
must be enhanced. This will be shown by an image editing framework combining
the advantages of working in pixel and compression domain. *Content updates* appear if the content of a single image has been changed. As changes often appear in
local regions only, there are many redundancies between the old and new image.
This property can be exploited by applying the proposed exchange strategy and
will be shown by an enhancement of the efficiency of Motion-JPEG2000-encoded
pictures. The capacity of the proposed approach is further emphasized by briefly
describing other valuable applications for both content manipulations.

6.4.1   An image editing framework

As shown for the basic approach, a number of requirements must be met before
content can be exchanged between imagery encoded with JPEG2000. This is not a
problem of the proposed strategy, but a general drawback if working in compression domain. However, it limits the application of the efficient exchange procedure
as the proposed strategy cannot be arbitrarily applied. Main limitations affecting
the applicability are:

1. **Coarse spatial granularity:** Content exchange must comply with the respective access grid. No pixel-accuracy between regions selected in source and
   destination can be granted.

2. **Accordance of parameter sets:** Exchanged elements must have been encoded
   with adequate parameter sets to ensure proper content decoding.

This section introduces an image editing framework to overcome these limitations
and to satisfy all possible demands appearing through image editing. Similar to
the statements given for the basic exchange scheme, it is assumed there are two
images - source and destination. The *aim* is to accomplish an arbitrary region-wise
content transfer as fast as possible. This is achieved by data exchange in compression domain whenever possible. By keeping the number of modified elements as
small as possible, the framework may also be effectively applied in remote environments.

6.4.1.1   Achieving spatial granularity

Content exchange can be accomplished in a variety of ways. All strategies, however, achieve different results regarding the spatial granularity and complexity of
the procedure. Thereby, it can be stated: *The exchange of elements providing highest
spatial accuracy also leads to highest complexity and vice versa.* This leads to the significant drawback that fast content exchange can only be applied to certain use cases.
Although for environments where content exchange is a frequent issue, the underlying data-streams can be trimmed to allow fast replacement, this is not the case
for arbitrary imagery.

Figure 6.9: *Not all source contents covered by cells involved in the exchange process (left) are desired to be included in the destination (right).*

To overcome this, the proposed framework is designed as a wrapper managing the exchange procedure. It basically consists of the following 2 main stages:

1. Recursive subdivision of the regions to handle
2. Transcoding of elements which cannot be replaced without limitations

Recursive subdivision   As shown in Figure 6.9, high spatial accuracy is not always required for all elements. It can be seen that the contribution of elements belonging to cells 5/6 and 8/9 does not exceed the respective area and are perfectly aligned to the access grid of the destination. Thus, the exchange procedure is applied as described, even if other cells (1-4 and 7) required further consideration. For all remaining cells, it is reasonable to apply a *recursive subdivision* into sub-cells. Cells which can be replaced without limitations are immediately handled and neglected during further subdivisions.

Transcoding of elements   Elements which cannot be replaced immediately are *transcoded* in order to increase the spatial granularity and the chance that replacement can be accomplished by the next element type available within the pipeline. The transcoding starts with precincts and tiles requiring only little efforts for access and modification and ends with pixels (cf. Figure 6.10 and E.10).

As *tiles* and *precincts* are structural elements of the encoded data-stream, no transcoding is required for access and replacement. As they are included in precinct structures, *code-blocks* require an undo of the data-stream organization. Replacement of *pixels* requires full decoding. It is worth mentioning that the content of source and destination image must always be available at the same transcoding stage. To create a compliant result it is also required to redo the undone steps of the compression pipeline after replacement.

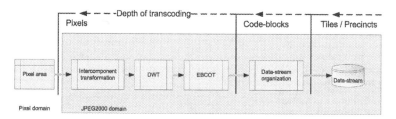

Figure 6.10: *The encoding pipeline of JPEG2000 and the transcoding steps required to access a certain type of element to accomplish the exchange process.*

6.4.1.2 Achieving accordance of parameter sets

The handling of images encoded with different parameter sets requires more distinct considerations of the respective parameters. As a variety of different parameters can be applied, general statement seem difficult to give. Considered in detail, however, most of the parameters influence a certain step of the encoding pipeline only and can be adapted by redoing the respective step with corresponding values for both images. Similar to the statements given for spatial adaptation, this requires the transcoding of affected contents. Contrary, it must be applied to one of the images only. The following list shows the respective codec steps which must be adapted to solve the corresponding differences in parametrization:

Data-stream organization: Different tile or precinct partition[1]

Arithmetic encoding: Different code-block partition

DWT: Different parameters of the applied DWT[2]

Color transformation: Remaining differences

In case an exchange task imposes issues regarding spatial granularity and parametrization, solutions provided for both problem fields may also be combined.

6.4.1.3 Content streaming

The image editing framework may also be applied in remote environments. Thereby basically the same statements regarding content streaming as given for the basic exchange scheme apply. This is obvious as the main difference between framework and proposed basic strategy is the subdivision of the exchanged region and an additional transcoding of certain codec steps. *Subdivision* is just a logic step to separate elements which can be immediately replaced and others requiring additional handling. Thus, it does not influence the streaming process. Although affected elements are decoded into their constituent parts by *transcoding*, this process is undone after replacement. This again leads to compliant elements which may be streamed as described. In case there have been conflicts in *parametrization*, however, the modified content is required to be recoded with identical parameters regarding the content which has already been sent.

---

[1] As this may also influence the underlying code-block partition, certain adjustments also include the undoing of the arithmetic encoding.

[2] Not required for different number of decomposition levels in case of simultaneous scaling.

6.4.1.4   Discussion

Similar to the discussion of the results achieved by the basic exchange scheme, this section examines the performance of the introduced editing framework. The *main advantage*, in any case, is its meaningful applicability to all tasks requiring content exchange between multiple images.

Computing power   Depending on the respective task and the structure of the used data-streams, the complexity of the replacement is usually higher than that of the basic exchange scheme. This is due to the additional efforts required to apply transcoding operations. Due to many possible configurations of the exchange task, complexity can only be estimated. The lowest border is the performance achieved if all elements are exchanged without additional transcoding. Contrary, highest complexity is required by exchanging the whole region pixel-wise. This corresponds to an ordinary pixel-based approach and ensures the proposed scheme is always at least as fast as the traditional scheme.

Figure 6.11 introduces an example involving typical operations during the exchange of an arbitrarily selected region. It can be seen that the whole region (90×80 pixels) is divided into sub-regions whereby the belonging content is exchanged at different levels of transcoding. The resulting complexity is depicted on the right-hand side, and shows that content exchange using the proposed framework is more than 3 times faster than applying a full pixel-wise exchange. Thereby, the region is exactly replaced by its selected dimensions. This is not the case for pure precinct-based replacement, which has only been regarded to show the small difference to the proposed framework.

 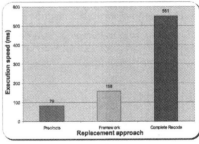

Figure 6.11: *Comparison of complexity in case of a complex exchange task (left) involving precincts, code-blocks, and pixels. The depicted execution time (right) shows that the proposed framework is much faster than the traditional approach.*

Bandwidth   The proposed framework is designed to undo the applied transcoding steps after the replacement procedure. The result are modified data-containers, which are of the same structure as before partial decoding. Thus, there is no significant difference in the consumed bandwidth as stated for the basic exchange scheme. The redundant transfer of contents that have already been sent but which again are part of transcoded data-containers may be neglected if the substantially facilitated data handling is considered.

Image quality In case content at regions boundaries is replaced by precincts or code-blocks, interferences at element borders might still impose the described blurring. The exact replacement of a region usually requires a pixel-wise handling at its borders. Although, interferences do not appear, this increases complexity.

Granularity of spatial access A strong gain regarding the basic exchange scheme is the provided granularity of the spatial access. Due to the cascaded spatial access, it is even possible to exchange content on pixel level. Although, this leads to a certain degree of independence from the spatial influence of the elements, it is still reasonable to inherently support a small spatial access. This increases the possibility that elements are replaced on high transcoding levels, and thus, significantly reduces the complexity of the procedure.

6.4.2 Encoding image sequences with spatial coherence

Nowadays, research interests move more and more from the handling of single imagery to image sequences. Due to recent developments in mobile hardware it is often possible to provide the required computing power. Unfortunately, this does not apply for transmission bandwidth. Recorded image sequences, however, are subject to many redundancies. This is due to the fact that the content between two adjacent *frames* does usually not fully change. In some application areas, such as news casts, teleconferences, or surveillance, the content of some image regions (background) is even identical. In this case a reasonable strategy for encoding and representation is to *update changing contents* only.

The relevance of describing the appropriate handling of image sequences has been addressed in Part III [JPG02c] of the JPEG2000 standard. This part is commonly called *Motion-JPEG2000* (M-JPEG2000) to stress its application to temporally changing contents. However, M-JPEG2000 does not exploit *inter-frame redundancies*. After a brief introduction to Motion-JPEG2000, it will be shown how to increase its performance by applying the proposed strategies for content exchange. Contrary to the introduced editing framework, where modified regions are known before the exchange, the given statements assume that no prior knowledge about a given Motion-JPEG2000 data-stream is available. To apply the proposed content exchange, this also requires the *detection of modified regions*. To avoid heavy computations, detection as well as *encoding* is accomplished in JPEG2000 domain. Thereby, the proposed strategy may also be applied to content streaming in remote environments.

6.4.2.1 Motion-JPEG2000

M-JPEG2000 is the successor of a variety of non-standard Motion-JPEG (M-JPEG) methods used to create and access consecutive JPEG frames at reasonable quality [Shi99]. Each frame (*sample*) within a M-JPEG2000 *movie* has been individually compressed using JPEG2000. All frames are usually *intra-frame* encoded with equal parameter sets. All frames are collected in a standardized data format, which may also include audio data and means to time these media. There may be multiple *tracks* each consisting of multiple frames. The resulting encoded image sequence of each track has the structure as depicted in Figure 6.12/left. For more details on M-JPEG2000 the interested reader is referred to [JPG02c].

This is usually not the case for many video codecs, such as the widely accepted

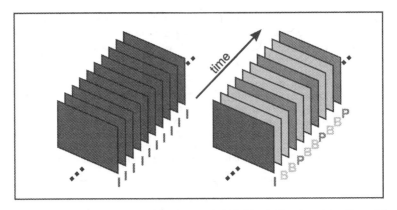

Figure 6.12: *Within a M-JPEG2000 data-stream, each single frame has been intra-frame (I) encoded with JPEG2000 (left). Codecs based on motion compensation use additional frame types to apply uni- (P) or bidirectional prediction (B) (right).*

MPEG family [MPE93; MPE95; MPE02] providing less accurate temporal access, but much better compression performance. The performance gain is mostly founded on the removal of existing inter-frame redundancies. A common strategy is the use of *motion compensation* (cf. Figure 6.12/right). It is based on the fact that many contents do not substantially change but only move their spatial positions. By appropriate detection and description of this movement, the belonging region can be efficiently encoded and reconstructed. This, however, requires different frame types, which describe all contents (*I-frames*) or for which content is predicted by using knowledge from prior frames (*P-frames*), or prior and later frames (*B-frames*). The repeating sequence of *I-*, *P-*, and *B-frames* is fixed and pre-determined.

Motion compensation cannot be applied to M-JPEG2000 without violating compliance. Thus, new ideas to remove inter-frame redundancies between frames are required. The next sections introduce such ideas founded on the proposed approach for a fast content exchange in JPEG2000 domain.

6.4.2.2 Detection of modified regions in JPEG2000 domain

In case no a-priori knowledge of the differences between frames is provided, it is required to detect those image regions where content has changed. This is straightforward in pixel domain, but requires additional consideration in case the sequence has already been encoded. To avoid the strong computing power required to decode each single frame, this section proposes a strategy to accomplish this task by examining single key elements directly in JPEG2000 domain. The main problem here is the prevention of *false positives* (elements considered as modified, but they are not) and *false negatives* (elements considered as identical, but they contain different content).

Main idea The main idea of the detection is a comparison regarding the length of the encoded data available for corresponding elements within source and destination. As the length of the encoded data strongly depends on the content, it can be assumed that elements contributing to image regions which are subject to temporal changes have a different length than their counterparts. By comparing all corresponding elements within source and destination, this clearly reveals the modified content and ensures that no false negatives appear.

Due to the reason of there being a spatial overlap between adjacent code-blocks and precincts, their encoded representation may slightly vary if new content is introduced in adjacent elements. As these elements might not belong to the modified region defined in pixel domain, the proposed strategy is vulnerable to false positives. The detection of such elements, however, can be a beneficial advantage to avoid artifacts (cf. Figure E.11/regions adjacent to black rectangle).

Detection strategies   Working in mobile environments requires the detection of modified elements with *little complexity*. Although access to elements can be accomplished quickly, the comparison of all elements for every frame pair is costly. To overcome this, different strategies are proposed. They take advantage of the multiresolution property to derive information to related elements contributing to the same region. Although this reduces complexity, its might also lead to wrong decisions, and thus, to a reduction in *quality*.

The following modi of comparison are proposed:

Mode 0 All elements of a resolution are compared. If one element differs from its counterpart, all elements contributing to the same region are replaced.

This mode achieves the best visual quality, but also has highest complexity.

Mode 1 Starting at highest resolution, all elements are compared. If one differs from its counterpart, only this and belonging elements contributing to lower image resolutions are replaced.

This mode is based on the fact that the spatial overlap of elements increases with decreasing resolution and is considered to achieve the best trade-off between the number of compared and replaced elements and resulting quality.

Mode 2 Only elements belonging to the highest resolution are compared. If one element differs from its counterpart, all elements contributing to the same spatial region are replaced.

As for these elements spatial influence is smallest, the number of false positives can be reduced. This, however, also leads to more false negatives. Due to the fact, only a small number of elements is compared, complexity is little.

In case differences between two elements are very small, they might also be negligible. To handle such events, all introduced modes may be combined with a *threshold* regarding their relative difference. As this difference is founded on the length of the encoded data, reasonable values vary depending on the respective image contents, and thus, cannot be applied generally. High values might lead to the addressed artifacts or false negatives (cf. Figure E.11/white square).

6.4.2.3   Description of the encoding

The goal of the proposed enhancement is to achieve higher compression ratios by removing inter-frame redundancies and keeping the simple content access and high quality of each frame at the same time. The proposed strategies for content exchange in JPEG2000 domain are key technologies to achieve this. The most important fact for their successful application is the property that two adjacent frames have been independently encoded with JPEG2000 and the individual datastreams are easily accessible and modifiable. Although, not all frames within the

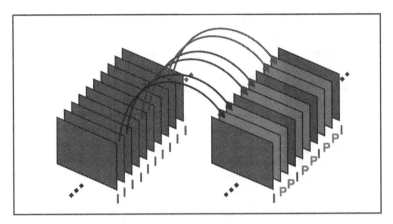

Figure 6.13: *The new structure of the M-JPEG2000 data-stream: After the proposed enhancement some of the original I-frames (left) serve as P-frames (right).*

enhanced data-stream contain the original content, an uncomplex transcoding can easily transfer the result back to the original streams.

The proposed enhancement is mainly based on two points:

- An adapted structure of the data-stream
- An encoding of changed regions only

In the following a deeper insight in the implementation of these points is given.

Adapted structure   To achieve a better compression performance for M-JPEG2000, a new frame type is introduced. Similar to the approaches founded on motion compensation, *P-frames* are used to contain content predicted from the last ordinary *I-frame* or P-frame that comes (temporally) immediately before it (cf. Figure 6.13/right). Thus, a reasonable sequence starts with an I-frame followed by a certain number of P-frames. The number of subsequent P-frames influences granularity of the frame access and the resulting compression performance. The total number of frames within both sequences is identical.

Encoding of changed regions   The main idea of the enhancement is the creation of a *compliant P-frame* containing only contents which have changed from the last frame (cf. Figure 6.14). All other positions are represented by elements without attached content. This ensures valid contents can easily be identified.

A significant drawback of encoding strategies based on motion compensation is the complex determination of regions, their movement, and the belonging descriptions to allow unequivocal decoding. In the proposed encoding strategy, this is overcome by neglecting any movement and considering corresponding spatial image regions only. The foundation are initial P-frames containing only empty element contributions. In case a modification between two regions has been detected, the described *basic exchange scheme* is applied to transfer the belonging content from the corresponding I-frame (*source*) within the original sequence to the currently handled P-frame (*destination*) within the enhanced sequence (cf. Figure 6.13).

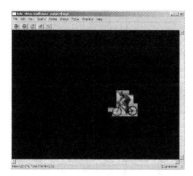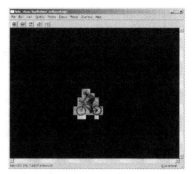

Figure 6.14: *Two examples of P-frames. Each is compliant to the JPEG2000 baseline standard and contains only contents from image regions that have changed to the previous frame.*

Before decoding, the content of an original I-frame can easily be restored by transferring the static contents from the prior frame to the P-frame applying the same principle. This leads to the original M-JPEG2000 sequence.

6.4.2.4 Content streaming

The handling of image sequences requires the consideration of multiple instead of single imagery. However, all frames are sorted regarding their temporal order and the streaming is accomplished frame-wise. Thus, for each frame the statements given for the general exchange strategy can be applied. The fact that the transcoder creates compliant P-frames to ensure the unequivocal assignment of the included image content strongly corresponds to the proposed *inherent signalization* strategy (cf. Section 3.5.1, p. 49).

If the file is not to be stored at client side, there is no need to reconstruct the original M-JPEG2000 data-stream; the transcoder at client side just assigns relevant content to its corresponding position within the client cache. A possibly existing entry at this position is deleted. As this is done for each frame, decoding always restores the content of the current frame.

6.4.2.5 Discussion

This section discusses the results achieved by applying the content exchange in JPEG2000 domain to decrease the size of M-JPEG2000-encoded image sequences. Consequentially, the focus is on the save of bandwidth.

Computing power   The proposed enhancement mostly consists of two stages: *detection* and *exchange*. Statements to the requirements of the first point have already been given and depend on the respectively applied mode. Generally applies – *the smaller the amount of elements to compare, the faster the procedure*. Due to the reason that content exchange must be applied for multiple P-frames, the efforts already stated for the basic exchange procedure between two images multiply.

A revoke of the enhancement does not require any detection and only consists of the exchange procedure.

Bandwidth   The proposed enhancement is based on the omission of belonging content in case two corresponding regions have been detected as identical. During the creation of the P-frame, belonging elements are replaced by empty element contributions. Thus, the transmission of sequences enhanced by the proposed strategy always requires equal or less bandwidth than the original sequence. This is a beneficial property and shows the potential of the idea. In the ideal case, two adjacent frames are identical. Consequently, the belonging P-frame is rather small.

The degree of enhancement strongly depends on the correlations between the compared frames, and thus, varies for each sequence. Beside the stated boundaries, the measures depicted in Figure 6.15 allow comparison between the performance achieved with and without applying the proposed enhancement. They refer to two sequences with a distinct characteristic. Within the first sequence, most of the image regions are *static* and do not vary between adjacent frames. Contrary, most of the content within the second sequence is *dynamic*. To give the reader an impression of the respective contents, selected screen shots of both sequences are shown in Figure E.12 and E.13. The ratio between P- and I-frames within the enhanced data-stream is 4 : 1.

From Figure 6.15 it can be clearly seen that best performance has been achieved if the enhancement is applied to the static sequence. As much of the content is neglected within P-frames, the stream is approximately *6 times smaller*, and thus, requires only 16% of the bandwidth needed by the original data-stream. As the proposed approach does not apply motion compensation, the performance gain is much smaller for the dynamic sequence. The resulting stream is only 1% smaller than the original. In such cases, the performance can be further enhanced by applying a reasonable threshold during element detection. By this threshold more regions are considered as identical (cf. Figure E.14) and the performance increases. This, however, might lead to a decrease in quality.

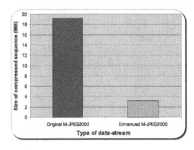 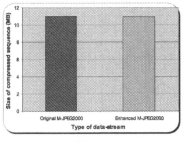

Figure 6.15: *Applied to mostly static contents, the proposed approach can heavily increase compression efficiency (left). For dynamic scenes the increment is small (right).*

Quality   The quality of the reconstructed image sequence depends on the detection strategy only. Depending on the chosen mode, the result is restored losslessly (Mode 0, no threshold) or at some decrease in quality (Mode 2, high threshold). *Quality correlates with the need for bandwidth and computing power.* Quality in lossy schemes can be increased by applying the cascaded element selection strategy proposed within the editing framework. Elements with little variations are further divided to separate modified elements.

Granularity of spatial access   This point is of minor interest for the encoding of image sequences. However, small spatial access increases the probability that identical elements can be detected. Dimensions of 32×32 have proved to perform well for the majority of the tested sequences.

Overall, the proposed enhancement is rather suited for storage and transmission of image sequences in high quality. The access to content stored in P-frames, however, is slightly more complex compared to M-JPEG2000. For dynamic sceneries and applications where frame-wise access is negligible, techniques applying motion compensation are more appropriate.

6.4.3   Further applications

As already shown, the applicability of the proposed content exchange strategy in JPEG2000 domain is manifold and spreads over all areas dealing with frequently changing contents. This section serves to briefly introduce 3 further applications applying concepts of content composition or update.

Location-based services (content update)   Location-based services (LBS) are the most obvious applications in mobile environments. Via a mobile device equipped with a position tracker, a user is able to request information on its current local surrounding. In case this information is associated with spatial details, it is useful to provide a map showing the respective points of interest in relation to the position of the user [The06; Map06]. Map and additional information usually require transmission. They are often combined to a single content to avoid the use of a second transmission channel. If the user requests more or other data concerning the same position, however, this imposes the transmission of an updated image and a redundant handling of some map contents. This can be overcome by applying the proposed *basic exchange scheme* as described. Only regions which differ regarding their shown contents are transmitted.

Creation of thumbnail gallery files (content composition)   In the era of digital photography often hundreds of images are taken and grouped. To get a quick overview over the respective contents often a thumbnail gallery is provided to the viewer [Dig06; Cen06]. As contents from all files are usually stored in compressed representation, the creation of such a gallery takes quite long [Khe04]. The solution might be the creation of a JPEG2000 gallery file combining the contents from all files in a single data-stream. As only thumbnail images are desired, this just requires the inclusion of low resolution data. To achieve this, the described *content exchange joint with simultaneous scaling* may be applied. Due to the fact images of a single gallery usually provide identical or similar parameters and resolutions, the replacement procedure and the spatial alignment of the thumbnails within the gallery file are quite easy to achieve. The only difference is the creation of a new destination file depending on current needs.

Application to image browsing (content composition)   Image content may be represented in a variety of ways. This, however, requires the fast creation of the respective representation. As this is accomplished by the filtering step at client side, this might exceed the capabilities of a mobile device. To overcome this, the proposed content exchange can be applied. This seems especially useful for the largeDetail-View consisting of a large WoI and an embedded overview (cf. Figure 4.11, p. 77).

Here, the representation might be created by including the scaled overview apply-ing the proposed scheme for *content exchange joint with simultaneous scaling*. The whole image might also be cropped to the WoI by applying the shown principles for data selection.

6.5   Conclusion of the chapter

As the content must usually be decoded to be handled in pixel representation, ex-changing contents available in compressed representation is complex. If the con-tent is to be stored or transmitted, such a procedure further requires an additional encoding of the manipulated result. The non-redundant handling of the data after modification is another unsolved issue in mobile environments.

These problems can be overcome by *accomplishing the exchange task in JPEG2000 do-main*. This approach is even capable to handle contents which require a downscal-ing of the new content for presentation. To achieve this, a *scheme allowing exact de-termination of corresponding elements* within two data-streams has been introduced. The achieved results are excellent. As working in compression domain only re-quires the fast determination and replacement of data containers, the *complexity* of the proposed approach is *9 times less* than that of a pixel-based approach. By transferring modified parts only, the belonging transmission strategy also achieves *heavy improvements regarding bandwidth*. For a modified region covering 25% of the whole image, the save of bandwidth is approximately 75%.

However, working in compression domain is afflicted with a number of restric-tions preventing the application of the idea to arbitrary tasks and data-streams. To overcome this, an *image editing framework* has been introduced. This framework is based on the reasonable assumption that spatial granularity and applicability increases with the subsequent undo of the encoding pipeline. Although this also increases complexity, it has been shown that content exchange using the frame-work is *usually faster and never slower* than the traditional pixel-based approach.

The basic idea may also be applied to increase the compression efficiency of Motion-JPEG2000-encoded image sequences. This is achieved by exploiting inter-frame redundancies. Instead of completely storing each frame, some frames only contain the content of regions which have changed. *Best results can be achieved for mostly sta-tic contents.* As shown by an example, the size of the whole data-stream is reduced by the factor 6. This corresponds to 84% less bandwidth in case the sequence is to be transmitted. The approach is not efficient for dynamic contents.

Beside the discussed enhancements in complexity and bandwidth, the general ad-vantage of the proposed exchange strategies is the rather simple data handling. Most of the complexity is moved to the server to unburden the highly limited client. The potential of the idea has been further emphasized by introducing other applications for the proposed approach.

The results achieved in this chapter underly the beneficial options which emerge from taking advantage of capabilities of the JPEG2000 standard:

Appropriate selection, streaming, and restoration of relevant image content can heavily decrease the effects imposed by the most limiting factors in mobile environments.

This is the general conclusion of this thesis summarized in the next chapter.

Chapter 7

Summary and future work

Summary of the thesis

Mobile image communication is still constrained by a number of restrictions. Although there is a continuous development, limitations regarding *computing power*, *bandwidth*, and *screen size* will still exist in the near future. This thesis has proposed new ideas to overcome or heavily reduce the drawbacks imposed by these restrictions. Thereby, the whole process from image encoding at server side to representation at client side is considered to appropriately design mobile communication strategies.

Many of the proposed ideas are founded on JPEG2000-encoded imagery. Beside a superior compression performance, the new image compression standard provides numerous useful features. However, *Regions of Interest* and *Levels of Detail* are barely supported by the standard. As these paradigms have been adopted for the description of the demands at application side, new ideas were required. As a foundation for *dynamic RoIs*, which are even able to react to frequently changing demands, a *formal model for random spatial access within JPEG2000-encoded imagery* has been introduced. It has been shown that the LoD-hierarchy provided by applying this idea is rather flexible.

Mobile environments require the *transmission* of remote contents. It has been shown that a reasonable transmission strategy consists of the 3 subsequent steps: *calculation, sequencing*, and *signalization*. As there is no general solution for all possible tasks, new strategies for each of theses communication steps have been proposed. Thereby, the introduced ideas consequentially make use of the suggested RoI/LoD-model. Provided results show that much *bandwidth* can be saved during transmission if the proposed ideas are suitably applied. The suggested sequencing strategies also lead to additional *functionality*.

An important part of an image communication system is the presentation of the content to the viewer. Here, the small displays of mobile clients, however, inherently lead to problems. To overcome this, many different *image browsing* techniques have been proposed in literature. To derive common properties and basic approaches, a *classification scheme* has been developed. As the scheme is consequentially founded on the introduced RoI/LoD model, it also serves to derive meaningful statements regarding image transmission for all currently existing browsing approaches. However, most of the proposed techniques lack two different factors:

(1) they are not designed to be supported by JPEG2000 or (2) their provided content representation is insufficient. To show options to overcome the first point, the applicability of the proposed statements to the implementation of an appropriate JPEG2000-based image communication strategy has been shown for an existing technique – the rectangular FishEye-View. As expected, a strong decrease in the required transmission *bandwidth* has been achieved. To cope with the second point, *2 new techniques for image browsing* on small screens have been introduced. They apply the reasonable assumption that at a single browsing step only a certain region, the *Window of Interest*, is of main importance. Limiting the displayed content to this region only, however, leads to massive problems regarding orientation and navigation. Thus, both proposed techniques provide intuitive support to simplify the browsing task. For both techniques statements for the design of an appropriate image communication systems have been provided.

Even in case there is sufficient screen space, not all content of an image might be of equal importance. To intuitively direct the attention of the viewer to important regions is the aim of *viewer guidance*. Existing techniques are still insufficient or too complex. To overcome this, *2 new techniques* founded on accepted approaches from Information visualization have been proposed. Beside their adaptation to raster imagery, the novelty of the proposals mainly consists of the utilization of properties of JPEG2000-encoded imagery to create the respective content representations. As shown by provided results the adaptation of the content requires *3 to 20 times less computing power* than traditional techniques. Both ideas may also be coupled to an image communication system and are able to reduce requirements regarding *bandwidth*.

Frequently changing contents are a common property of modern image communication. In case an original image is stored in encoded form, *content exchange* is quite complex. Pixel-based techniques require decoding before manipulation and a new encoding before transmission. To cope with that, it has been proposed to apply changes directly in JPEG2000 domain. Exact statements on the determination of relevant image parts within the original and modified data-stream have been provided. They are founded on a set-based approach to ease the application within concrete implementations. The general applicability of the idea is shown by conducted measures. The proposed strategy is up to *9 times faster* than the traditional approach. Based on the reasonable assumption that only contents that have changed are transmitted, the *save of bandwidth is enormous* if the modified region is small. The potential of the approach has been shown for different tasks enhancing its applicability (editing framework) or application area (image sequences, thumbnail file, LBS, image browsing).

Proposals presented in this thesis have been implemented in different applications for stationary and mobile environments. The achieved results confirm the authors assertion that appropriate image communication adapted to the respective needs can greatly increase the performance in mobile environments; the introduced ideas and strategies heavily outperform traditional techniques regarding the most limiting factors. Thus, this thesis is a reasonable contribution to the development of appropriate mobile image communication systems and applications.

Future work

Solutions designed to decrease the influence of the most limiting factors in mobile environments – *low computing power, small bandwidth, and small screen space* –
can significantly increase the performance of applications. This has been shown in
the thesis at hand for different application scenarios. Three major improvements
of the proposed ideas are imaginable: (1) the *enhancement of the content handling,*
(2) the *enhancement of existing applications,* and (3) the *development of new applications*. Future work might lead to the application of these ideas on other content
descriptions, such as vector data. Due to the potential of a progressive data handling, appropriate communication strategies might also be developed for arbitrary
instead of image data. These ideas are now explained in detail.

Enhancement of the content handling   In the proposed solutions the image content
has always been assumed to be stored in a single data-stream. By spreading the
content over multiple data-streams, it is possible to apply the idea of *information
layers* as used in GIS. This introduces an additional dimension to the LoD model,
and thus, enables further options for data transfer and handling. The applicability
of this concept has proved within a commercial system [IDE05], which, however,
does not cope with the multiple problems imposed by the support for dynamic
RoIs.

The solutions proposed within this thesis only assume ordinary raster imagery to
describe single image or video contents. As this may be the best choice for the
majority of tasks, there are application areas, where a different content description
achieves better results. Examples are vector graphics or hyperspectral imagery.
Here, the provided solutions can also be applied, but must be suitably adapted to
the completely different characteristic of the data. This applies for all stages of the
communication pipeline, and has already been proved by the author for selected
problems and *vector data* [Ros03c; Ros04d]. New standards, such as *Scalable Vector
Graphics* (SVG), provide flexible data structures to access the data and offer higher
potential for demand-driven data handling and transmission.

Enhancement of existing applications   Although the introduced ideas for appropriate
content representations designed to solve a task at hand have led to large improvements, there are is still space for enhancements. This especially applies for *image
browsing*. In preliminary works [Kar03a], the author figured out, that there is great
potential in 3D which has yet not been fully discovered. Here, it might also be interesting to consider *hyperspectral imagery*. With the development of sophisticated
recording hardware, this kind of imagery currently becomes more important. Due
to the fact that no current output device can deal with the inherent high preci-
sion, there is a particular need for an appropriate data representation. Enhanced
communication features of mobile devices [Wan02c] may also be utilized to allow
content exploration on multiple screens.

The applicability of the introduced approaches for content handling in JPEG2000
domain is enormous and might be applied in the future to solve quite different
tasks. Exemplary, the proposed idea to replace image data in compression domain
may be stated. With the goal to enable smooth transitions during the browsing
of multiple images, the author has already finished preliminary works exploiting
the ability of replacing all data belonging to a certain decomposition level between
JPEG2000-encoded data-streams. The quite promising results have already been
published in [Ros07b].

Development of new applications   The idea of examining the whole communication process to design appropriate mobile applications might also be applied to other contents. Probably the most challenging problem is the communication of arbitrary data as available in Information visualization. Here, the potential of *progression* has yet not been exploited. There is only little research on how to compress and stream the data, and to couple these processes with one of the numerous approaches from visualization. Due to the tendency to mobile and distributed working, this might change soon. However, the achievement of a reasonable solution requires a much broader view than needed for raster imagery. Data compression and visualization techniques must be examined and classified to be able selecting the most appropriate approach for a particular task. New compression techniques may also be developed or derived from existing strategies. Distributed data storage also allows for keeping of data at multiple points within a network. This makes data handling even more challenging. However, results gained from early experiments encourage to carry on with the researches.

Appendix A

Image communication systems supporting dynamic streaming

Internet Imaging Protocol (IIP) [Hew97]:

Pipeline	Support for RoI	Signalization	Application area
$(Fs)C+TsTcD+$	Resolution, Component	External	Image browsing, printing, and manipulation
Fs: Pre-processing, e.g. affine transforms, contrast adjustments, rotations, etc.			
$C+/D+$: Multiresolution Gauss-Pyramid, tiling, optional DCT/JPEG-coding per tile			
Ts: Transmission of requested data chunks			
Tc: Determination of relevant samples and identification after receiving			

Network-conscious Image Compression and Transmission System [Ire98; Ire99]:

Pipeline	Support for RoI	Signalization	Application area
$[C+Ts]TcD+$	Quality	External	Error-resilient image browsing
$C+/D+$: DWT, *network-conscious* SPIHT			
Ts: Wrapping of relevant SPIHT-structures in *Application Data Units* (ADUs)			
Tc: Identification of received data samples based on ADU			

Rauschenbach [Rau00]:

Pipeline	Support for RoI	Signalization	Application area
$CTsTcDFc$	Resolution, Quality	Synchronous	Image browsing
C/D: DWT, EZW			
Ts: Determination of relevant samples			
Tc: Identification of received samples			
$Fc+$: Spatial adaptation of image regions to achieve FishEye-View			

Owen et al. [Owe01]:

Pipeline	Support for RoI	Signalization	Application area
$FsCTsTcD$	Resolution, Quality	External	Image browsing
Fs: Tiling into independent sub images			
C/D: DWT, SPIHT			
Ts: Determination of relevant samples from each tile			
Tc: Identification of received samples			

Deshpande and Zheng [Des01] and Ortiz et al. [JO04]:

Pipeline	Support for RoI	Signalization	Application area
$CTsTcDFc$	Resolution, Quality	Synchronous	Image browsing
C/D: DWT, JPEG2000			
Ts: Transmission of requested data chunks			
Tc: Determination of relevant samples and identification after receiving			
Fc: Spatial adaptation to Zoom&Pan			

KAKADU [Tau02a; KAK05; Mee05]:

Pipeline	Support for RoI	Signalization	Application area
$(Fs)CTsTcDFc$	Resolution, Quality, Component	External	Image browsing
Fs: Pre-processing, Tiling into independent sub images			
C/D: DWT, JPEG2000			
Ts: Determination of relevant samples			
Tc: Identification of received samples			
Fc: Spatial adaptation to Zoom&Pan [Tau02a; KAK05] or highlighting of RoIs [Mee05]			

Appendix B

Relevant properties of current mobile devices

Devices	Display	Resolution	Colors	Processing power	RAM
Mobiles:					
Siemens SXG75	2.2"	240x320	18bit	-	128MB
Hagenuk S200	2.2"	160x220	16bit	TI OMAP 310	32MB
Samsung i600	-	176x220	16bit	PXA250 200MHz	32MB
	-	128x32	-		
Palm Treo 650	2.5"	320x320	16bit	PXA270 312MHz	32MB
Asus MyPal P505	2.8"	240x320	16bit	PXA272 520MHz	64MB
Qtek 9090	3.5"	240x320	16bit	PXA263 400MHz	128MB
Palmsize:					
Palm Zire 72	2.5"	320x320	16bit	PXA270 312MHz	32MB
BlackBerry 7750	3.0"	240x240	16bit	-	16MB
Palm Tungsten-T5	3.7"	320x480	16bit	PXA272 416MHz	256MB
Sony Clie PEG-UX50	4.0"	320x480	16bit	CXD2230GA 123MHz	64MB
Handheld:					
Gizmondo Force	2.8"	240x320	-	ARM9 400MHz + GPU Goforce 4500	64MB
Fujitsu Siemens LOOX 720	3.6"	480x640	16bit	PXA272 520MHz	128MB
Sharp Zaurus SL-6000	4.0"	480x640	16bit	PXA255 400MHz	128MB
Toshiba Pocket PC e830	4.0"	480x640	16bit	PXA272 520MHz	128MB

Handheld (cont.):					
Dell Axim X50v	3.7"	480x640	16bit	PXA270 624MHz + GPU 2700G - 16MB	196MB
HP iPAQ HX4700	4.0"	480x640	16bit	PXA270 624MHz	128MB
Sony VAIO U71	5"	800x600	24bit	Pentium® 1100MHz + GPU 855GME - 64MB	512MB
Stationary PC:					
generic	21"	2048x1536	32bit	P4-570J 3800MHz + GPU GeForce 6800	1 GB

Table B.1: *Specifications of different mobile devices and a stationary PC (01/2006).*

Appendix **C**

Additional figures and information to related work

C.1 An implementation of the DCT

Implementation of the DCT to transform a 8×8 pixel block (p_{xy}) into a related block of DCT-coefficients (g_{ij}) (Equation C.1) and the inverse operation (Equation C.2, src: [Sal00, p. 170f]).

$$g_{ij} = \frac{1}{4} c_i c_j \sum_{x=0}^{7} \sum_{y=0}^{7} p_{xy} t(x, y, i, j) \tag{C.1}$$

$$p_{xy} = \frac{1}{4} \sum_{i=0}^{7} \sum_{j=0}^{7} c_i c_j g_{ij} t(x, y, u, v), \tag{C.2}$$

$$\text{where } t(x, y, i, j) = \cos\left(\frac{(2x+1)i\pi}{16}\right) \cos\left(\frac{(2y+1)j\pi}{16}\right),$$

$$\text{and } c_f = \begin{cases} \frac{1}{\sqrt{2}} & : \quad f = 0 \\ 1 & : \quad f > 0 \end{cases}$$

C.2   The DWT multiresolution pyramid

The subsequent decomposition d_i of the LL-subband leads to a multiresolution pyramid representation of the image. A certain inherent resolution r is reconstructed based on lower resolutions and additional details.

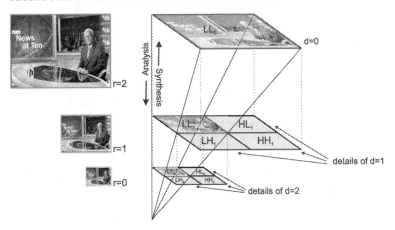

Figure C.1: *DWT-decomposition scheme and the resulting multiresolution pyramid.*

C.3   The progressive and hierarchical mode of JPEG

The JPEG - progressive mode   is an enhancement of the baseline mode to enable progressive refinement regarding quality, and is basically just a rearrangement of the same data into a more complicated order.

Level of Detail (progressive mode)				
X	Y	Accuracy	Component	**Orthogonality**
1	1	number of groups of bit-planes	usually Y, C_r, C_b	all

A baseline JPEG-encoded image is stored as a top-to-bottom *scan* of the image. Progressive JPEG divides the image into a series of scans. Each scan adds to the data already provided, so that the total storage requirement is roughly the same as for baseline JPEG. A scan is represented by one or multiple coefficients (spectral selection) or bit-planes (successive approximation).

Spectral selection describes a modified traversing scheme and assigns *spectral bands* into different scans (cf. Figure 2.4). As in baseline, DCs are handled independently. Typically scans are set up to code from low to high frequencies. Thus, each successive spectral band adds higher spatial frequency information. Although this might be viewed as a method to progressively refining resolution, it does not agree with commonly accepted notions of resolution [Tau02b], and is therefore not considered as a valid approach to refine the LoD.

Successive approximation scans the coefficient values based on their bit-planes. One or more bit-planes may be handled within one scan. Starting from the most significant bit, each successive scan refines image quality by a certain amount.

Successive approximation is often assumed to be the better approach. Contrary to spectral selection, where the image is more slowly becoming clearer and may still appear a little "blocky", the image is nicely diffused out uniformly in each block. This is depicted in Figure C.2. However, combinations of both approaches are also possible and provide finer progressive refinement.

Support for LoD: An image encoded in progressive mode is a data-stream consisting of separate sequences of DC and AC coefficients for each color component. Thereby AC-coefficients are further divided into individual sequences for each group of spectral bands or bit-planes. Thus, this mode supports constitutive quality levels, and thus, is scalable regarding accuracy and color.

Scan 1 (DC only)   Scan 4   Scan 7 (last)

Figure C.2: *The quality of an image restored using different numbers of spectral bands.*

The JPEG - hierarchical mode   is another enhancement of the basic proceeding [Pen93]. Due to its increased complexity and decreased performance [Pen93; Han96], however, it has only been of little interest so far.

Level of Detail (hierarchical mode)				
X	Y	Accuracy	Component	Orthogonality
$(1, ..., 2^n)$	$(1, ..., 2^n)$	1	usually Y, C_r, C_b	$Y = X$

In this mode the image content is encoded at multiple resolutions, each differing from its adjacent level by a factor of 2 in the horizontal and vertical direction. To provide the content in the lowest supported resolution, the image is sub-sampled by the desired number of multiples of 2. Afterwards the new reduced dimension image, a *frame* in JPEG terminology, is encoded using the baseline mode or any combination of the progressive modes[1]. To achieve the next higher resolution, this image is decoded, upsampled by a factor of 2 and used as a prediction of the original image at this resolution. Thus, only a *differential frame* must be computed, encoded and stored. The last two steps are repeated until the original image has been restored. As this mode is based on differential images, decoding must start from the low resolution frame. Higher resolution levels are restored by consecutively decoding and adding the according differential frames.

Support for LoD: The result of an image processed in hierarchical mode is a data-stream consisting of separate sequences of DC and AC coefficients for each color

---

[1] As only a few if any applications have exploited this option, it is not considered for LoD support.

component, frame and differential frame. It supports different resolutions and colors. Due to the decomposition scheme no arbitrary combinations of x- and y-resolution are possible.

C.4   Examples of Detail&Overview techniques

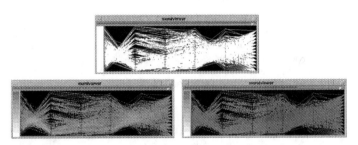

Figure C.3: *Information visualization with (bottom) and without (top) applying the information mural (src:[Jer98]).*

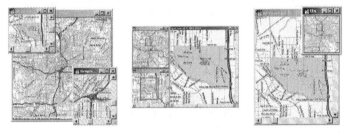

Figure C.4: *Different spatial configurations belonging to the Detail&Overview approach (src:[Sta03]).*

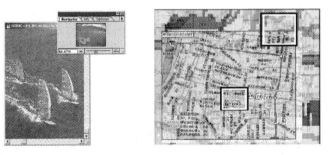

Figure C.5: *Application of the Detail&Overview approach within Adobe Photoshop (left) and Macroscope (right, src:[Lie97]).*

C.5   Examples of Focus&Context techniques

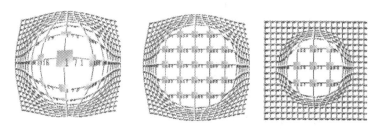

Figure C.6: *Different distortions of WoI and background (src:[Car97a]).*

Figure C.7: *Different configurations of the background distortion function applied to images: uniform (left), belt-based (middle), and exponential distortion (right).*

C.6   Examples of the application of Depth of Field

Figure C.8: *Depth of Field applied to 2D (left) and 3D data (right, src:[Kos01a]).*

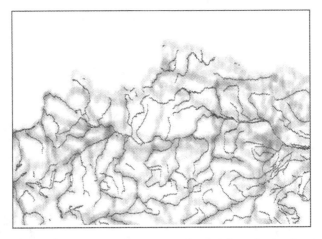

Figure C.9: *Application of Depth of Field to visualize spatially overlapping data structures (src:[Kos01a]).*

C.7   Examples of tool glass techniques

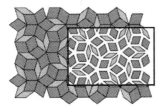 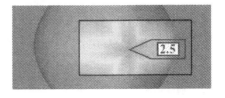

Figure C.10: *The general principle of a tool glass (left) and its application in Scientific visualization (right, src:[Bie94b]).*

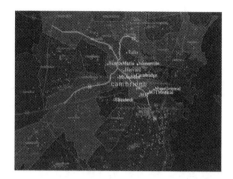 

Figure C.11: *Application of a tool glass to visualize crime (left, src:[Lok95]) or medical data (right, src:[Roe00]).*

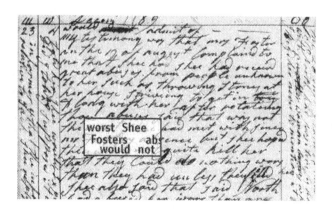

Figure C.12: *Application of a tool glass to raster imagery using additional meta-data (src:[DoH06]).*

Appendix D

Additional information to JPEG2000 and its key elements

D.1 The JPEG2000 intercomponent transform

If multiple image components are present, JPEG2000 provides options to transform them into *comp* image components. Part 1 of the standard requires this value to be *comp* = 3, which is basically a standard RGB/YUV-transform. Associated with each image component, c, $1 \le c \le comp$, are vertical and horizontal subsampling factors $sub_{1,c}$, $sub_{2,c}$, $1 \le sub_{1,c}$, $sub_{2,c} \le 255$. These factors decrease the dimensions of the canvas attributes e_1, e_2 and f_1, f_2 to component-specific values, e_i^c and f_i^c, and are calculated as follows

$$e_i = \left\lceil \frac{e_i}{sub_{i,c}} \right\rceil \quad and \quad f_i^c = \left\lceil \frac{f_i}{sub_{i,c}} \right\rceil, \; i = 1, 2 \tag{D.1}$$

D.2 Valid attribute values for code-block triples

To partition a certain subband into multiple code-blocks a regular grid anchored at the origin of the canvas is used. The standard demands that grid cell dimensions are conform to certain restrictions. If $[cbs_1, cbs_2]$ are the nominal cell dimensions, their values must be exact powers of 2, and $2^2 \le cbs_1, cbs_2 \le 2^{10}$, $cbs_1 \times cbs_2 \le 2^{12}$ must be fulfilled. For a given resolution, the number of code-block triples $cbt_{col,row,r}$ is equal to the number of code-blocks of an arbitrary subband residing at decomposition level $d = d_{max} - r + 1$ for $r > 0$ or $d = d_{max}$ for $r = 0$. It can be calculated based on dimensions of the canvas, the code-block grid and the respective decomposition level d as follows

$$cn_r = \left\lceil \left\lceil \frac{\left\lceil \frac{f_1}{2^d} \right\rceil}{cbs_1} \right\rceil - \left\lfloor \frac{\left\lfloor \frac{e_1}{2^d} \right\rfloor}{cbs_1} \right\rfloor \right\rceil \quad and \quad cm_r = \left\lceil \left\lceil \frac{\left\lceil \frac{f_2}{2^d} \right\rceil}{cbs_2} \right\rceil - \left\lfloor \frac{\left\lfloor \frac{e_2}{2^d} \right\rfloor}{cbs_2} \right\rfloor \right\rceil$$

As defined in the standard, the dimensions in terms of included samples for each code-block must be the same for every decomposition stage. Thus, attributes

a_3 and a_4 of a code-block triple $cbt_{col,row,r}$ correspond to the introduced terms cbs_1, cbs_2 for all r, whereby $a_3 = cbs_1, a_4 = cbs_2$ applies. Nevertheless, it might happen, that certain code-blocks are truncated at image boundaries. Thus, it is likely that attributes values of a_3 and a_4 are not equal for all code-block structures. In case all code-blocks have a non-empty intersection with the image, these are all elements with attribute values $a_1 = 0$, $a_1 = (cn_r - 1)$, $a_2 = 0$, or $a_2 = (cm_r - 1)$. The belonging attribute values a_3 and a_4 can be calculated depending on the respective d as follows:

$$a_3 = \begin{cases} \left\lceil \frac{\left\lceil \frac{e_1}{2^d} \right\rceil}{cbs_1} \right\rceil cbs_1 - \left\lceil \frac{e_1}{2^d} \right\rceil & : \quad \text{if } a_1 = 0 \\[2ex] \left\lceil \frac{f_1}{2^d} \right\rceil - \left\lfloor \frac{\left\lceil \frac{f_1}{2^d} \right\rceil}{cbs_1} \right\rfloor cbs_1 & : \quad \text{if } a_1 = (cn_r - 1) \end{cases}$$

$$a_4 = \begin{cases} \left\lceil \frac{\left\lceil \frac{e_2}{2^d} \right\rceil}{cbs_2} \right\rceil cbs_2 - \left\lceil \frac{e_2}{2^d} \right\rceil & : \quad \text{if } a_2 = 0 \\[2ex] \left\lceil \frac{f_2}{2^d} \right\rceil - \left\lfloor \frac{\left\lceil \frac{f_2}{2^d} \right\rceil}{cbs_2} \right\rfloor cbs_2 & : \quad \text{if } a_2 = (cm_r - 1) \end{cases} \tag{D.2}$$

Domains A_1, A_2 defining the possible amount of disjunct image regions in r are determined by the possible number of code-blocks per subband. They can be specified by considering extreme code-block and image dimensions.

$A_1 = A_2 = \{i | 0 \leq i < 2^{30}, i \in \mathbb{N}\}$.

Because attributes a_3 and a_4 correspond to cbs_1 and cbs_2, the belonging domains can be easily derived. The values are the same, except for lower boundaries, which must be extended to handle the special case of very small code-blocks.

$A_3 = A_4 = \{i | 2^0 \leq i \leq 2^{10}, i \in \mathbb{N}\}$.

The domains A_5, A_6 specifying possible values for spatial contribution also depend on valid code-block dimensions. Since the spatial influence of structures increases with decreasing r, a single structure may contribute to the whole image.

$A_5 = A_6 = \{i | 2^1 \leq i < 2^{32}, i \in \mathbb{N}\}$.

By using code-blocks and multiple components it is worth noting, that these domains may vary from component to component.

D.3   Valid attribute values for precincts

Although precincts organize code-blocks, and thus, mainly inherit their properties, the JPEG2000 standard specifies additional properties not available for code-blocks. Maybe the most important difference is the ability to select appropriate dimensions $[ps_{1,r}, ps_{2,r}]$ for each resolution level r independently, and thus, to steer their spatial influence. Furthermore, there are more lax demands regarding the amount of included samples $(1 \leq ps_{1,r}, ps_{2,r} \leq 2^{15})$. However, precinct partition does not significantly differ from code-block partition. This ensures that associated code-blocks exactly fit into a precinct. In case the code-blocks are larger than the precincts, the code-block dimensions are adjusted.

Because at every image resolution different precinct dimensions may be defined, the number of precinct structures $p_{col,row,r}$ depends on r and can be calculated by

$$pn_r = \left\lceil \frac{\left\lceil \frac{\left\lceil \frac{f_1}{2^{d_{max}-r}} \right\rceil}{ps_{1,r}} \right\rceil - \left\lceil \frac{\left\lfloor \frac{e_1}{2^{d_{max}-r}} \right\rfloor}{ps_{1,r}} \right\rfloor}{} \right\rceil$$

$$pm_r = \left\lceil \frac{\left\lceil \frac{\left\lceil \frac{f_2}{2^{d_{max}-r}} \right\rceil}{ps_{2,r}} \right\rceil - \left\lceil \frac{\left\lfloor \frac{e_2}{2^{d_{max}-r}} \right\rfloor}{ps_{2,r}} \right\rfloor}{} \right\rceil$$

Wavelet coefficients directly contributing to the reconstruction of a precinct defined in resolution level r, reside at decomposition level $d = d_{max} - r + 1$ for $r > 0$ or $d = d_{max}$ for $r = 0$. Thus, belonging attribute values a_3 and a_4 can easily be calculated by $a_3 = ps_{1,0}, a_4 = ps_{2,0}$ for $r = 0$, or otherwise $a_3 = \lceil \frac{ps_{1,r}}{2} \rceil, a_4 = \lceil \frac{ps_{2,r}}{2} \rceil$. Nevertheless, it might happen that precincts are truncated at image boundaries. In case all precincts have a non-empty intersection with the image, these are all elements with attribute values $a_1 = 0, a_1 = (pn_r - 1), a_2 = 0,$ or $a_2 = (pm_r - 1)$. Their attribute values a_3, a_4 can be calculated by considering the decomposition level d at which their contributing wavelet coefficients are located.

$$a_3 = \begin{cases} \left\lceil \frac{\left\lfloor \frac{e_1}{2^{d_{max}}} \right\rfloor}{ps_{1,r}} \right\rceil ps_{1,r} - \left\lceil \frac{e_1}{2^{d_{max}}} \right\rceil & : \text{ if } a_1 = 0, r = 0 \\ \left\lceil \frac{\left\lfloor \frac{e_1}{2^{d_{max}-r+1}} \right\rfloor}{\lceil \frac{ps_{1,r}}{2} \rceil} \right\rceil \lceil \frac{ps_{1,r}}{2} \rceil - \lceil \frac{e_1}{2^{d_{max}-r+1}} \rceil & : \text{ if } a_1 = 0, r > 0 \\ \left\lceil \frac{f_1}{2^{d_{max}}} \right\rceil - \left\lfloor \frac{\left\lceil \frac{f_1}{2^{d_{max}}} \right\rceil}{ps_{1,r}} \right\rfloor ps_{1,r} & : \text{ if } a_1 = (pn_r - 1), r = 0 \\ \left\lceil \frac{f_1}{2^{d_{max}-r+1}} \right\rceil - \left\lfloor \frac{\left\lceil \frac{f_1}{2^{d_{max}-r+1}} \right\rceil}{\lceil \frac{ps_{1,r}}{2} \rceil} \right\rfloor \lceil \frac{ps_{1,r}}{2} \rceil & : \text{ if } a_1 = (pn_r - 1), r > 0 \end{cases}$$

$$(D.3)$$

$$a_4 = \begin{cases} \left\lceil \frac{\left\lfloor \frac{e_2}{2^{d_{max}}} \right\rfloor}{ps_{2,r}} \right\rceil ps_{2,r} - \left\lceil \frac{e_2}{2^{d_{max}}} \right\rceil & : \text{ if } a_2 = 0, r = 0 \\ \left\lceil \frac{\left\lfloor \frac{e_2}{2^{d_{max}-r+1}} \right\rfloor}{\lceil \frac{ps_{2,r}}{2} \rceil} \right\rceil \lceil \frac{ps_{2,r}}{2} \rceil - \lceil \frac{e_2}{2^{d_{max}-r+1}} \rceil & : \text{ if } a_2 = 0, r > 0 \\ \left\lceil \frac{f_2}{2^{d_{max}}} \right\rceil - \left\lfloor \frac{\left\lceil \frac{f_2}{2^{d_{max}}} \right\rceil}{ps_{2,r}} \right\rfloor ps_{2,r} & : \text{ if } a_2 = (pm_r - 1), r = 0 \\ \left\lceil \frac{f_2}{2^{d_{max}-r+1}} \right\rceil - \left\lfloor \frac{\left\lceil \frac{f_2}{2^{d_{max}-r+1}} \right\rceil}{\lceil \frac{ps_{2,r}}{2} \rceil} \right\rfloor \lceil \frac{ps_{2,r}}{2} \rceil & : \text{ if } a_2 = (pm_r - 1), r > 0 \end{cases}$$

Since precinct dimensions may be smaller than code-block dimensions the maximal possible number of precincts at a given resolution is bigger. There may even be one precinct per sample. On the other hand, precincts may contain multiple code-blocks from each subband. Thus, domains A_1 and A_2 as well as A_3 and A_4 are different from those of code-blocks and can be stated as

$$A_1 = A_2 = \{i | 0 \le i < 2^{31}, i \in \mathbb{N}\}.$$

$$A_3 = A_4 = \{i | 2^0 \le i \le 2^{15}, i \in \mathbb{N}\}.$$

Nevertheless, domains A_5, A_5 specifying possible values for the spatial contribution of a single precinct structure are equal to those of code-blocks.

$$A_5 = A_6 = \{i | 2^1 \le i < 2^{32}, i \in \mathbb{N}\}.$$

Similar to code-blocks, only cells contributing to the image are considered to specify these domains.

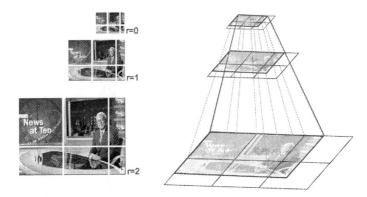

Figure D.1: *An image divided in multiple tiles (left) and the belonging multiresolution representation (right).*

D.4   Valid attribute values of tiles

Because a single tile describes a pixel region completely, tile partition is applied in spatial domain (cf. Figure D.1). Unlike code-block and precinct definition, the standard does not demand that the origin of the tile grid coincides with the origin of the canvas. Thus, it may have a certain offset, $[\Omega_1, \Omega_2]$. If ts_1, ts_2 are the dimensions of a tile grid cell in spatial domain, with $1 \leq ts_1, ts_2 < 2^{32}$, the tile offset is required to be $0 \leq \Omega_1, \Omega_2 < 2^{32} - 1$. Further on, the offset is demanded to conform to $0 \leq e_1 - \Omega_1 < ts_1$ and $0 \leq e_2 - \Omega_2 < ts_2$ to ensure that each tile contributes at least partially to the reconstruction of the image. Based on this, the number of tiles, $tn_r \times tm_r$, in pixel domain is determined by

$$ tn_{r_{max}} = \left\lceil \frac{f_1 - \Omega_1}{ts_1} \right\rceil \text{ and } tm_{r_{max}} = \left\lceil \frac{f_2 - \Omega_2}{ts_2} \right\rceil $$

To extract all tile contributions $t_{col,row,r}$ for each r, the tile grid is propagated to the different resolution levels. Obviously, the number of columns and rows of tile contributions tn_r and tm_r are equal for each r: $\forall r, tn_r = tn_{r_{max}}, tm_r = tm_{r_{max}}$.

Due to the reason, the number of wavelet coefficients contributing to a certain region decreases with each successive decomposition stage, the values for a_3 and a_4 depend on the resolution of the respective element. They can be stated as $a_3 = ts_{1,0}, a_4 = ts_{2,0}$ for $r = d_{r_{max}}$, or otherwise $a_3 = \lceil \frac{ts_1}{2^{d_{max}-r+1}} \rceil, a_4 = \lceil \frac{ts_2}{2^{d_{max}-r+1}} \rceil$. Similar to the other key elements, certain tiles may be smaller than others. The calculation of belonging values for a_3 and a_4 depends on grid offset, cell and image dimensions, element position, and the respective resolution level.

$$a_3 = \begin{cases} \left\lceil \frac{\Omega_1 + ts_1 - e_1}{2^{d_{max}}} \right\rceil & : \quad \textit{if } a_1 = 0, r = 0 \\[2mm] \left\lceil \frac{\Omega_1 + ts_1 - e_1}{2^{d_{max} - r + 1}} \right\rceil & : \quad \textit{if } a_1 = 0, r > 0 \\[2mm] \left\lceil \frac{f_1 - (\Omega_1 + ts_1(tn_r - 1))}{2^{d_{max}}} \right\rceil & : \quad \textit{if } a_1 = (tn_r - 1), r = 0 \\[2mm] \left\lceil \frac{f_1 - (\Omega_1 + ts_1(tn_r - 1))}{2^{d_{max} - r + 1}} \right\rceil & : \quad \textit{if } a_1 = (tn_r - 1), r > 0 \end{cases}$$

(D.4)

$$a_4 = \begin{cases} \left\lceil \frac{\Omega_2 + ts_2 - e_2}{2^{d_{max}}} \right\rceil & : \quad \textit{if } a_2 = 0, r = 0 \\[2mm] \left\lceil \frac{\Omega_2 + ts_2 - e_2}{2^{d_{max} - r + 1}} \right\rceil & : \quad \textit{if } a_2 = 0, r > 0 \\[2mm] \left\lceil \frac{f_2 - (\Omega_2 + ts_2(tm_r - 1))}{2^{d_{max}}} \right\rceil & : \quad \textit{if } a_2 = (tm_r - 1), r = 0 \\[2mm] \left\lceil \frac{f_2 - (\Omega_2 + ts_2(tm_r - 1))}{2^{d_{max} - r + 1}} \right\rceil & : \quad \textit{if } a_2 = (tm_r - 1), r > 0 \end{cases}$$

Domains for offset values a_1, a_2 are determined in pixel domain. If the first tile contribution has an offset value of 0, the extrem case of one tile for each pixel of an image with maximal dimensions $2^{32} - 1$ results in the offset $2^{32} - 2$. Thus, the respective domains can be stated as

$$A_1 = A_2 = \{i | 0 \le i < 2^{32} - 1, i \in \mathbb{N}\}.$$

Due to the fact that with increasing d the tile grid cell dimensions shrink in both directions, the biggest possible value for a_3 and a_4 can only be found in the first decomposition level $d = 1$. They appear if an image has maximal dimensions and one tile covers the whole image. Contrary, the smallest non-empty contribution of a tile is 1 sample.

$$A_3 = A_4 = \{i | 2^0 \le i < 2^{30}, i \in \mathbb{N}\}$$

Based on this, the range of possible pixel contributions can be derived.

$$A_5 = A_6 = \{i | 2^1 \le i < 2^{32}, i \in \mathbb{N}\}$$

Appendix **E**

Additional figures to own proposals

E.1 Measures on the impact of scalability

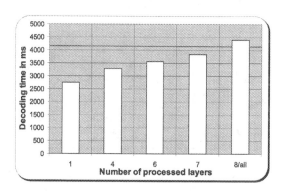

Figure E.1: *Comparison of the complexity of the JPEG2000 decoding process considering scalability regarding accuracy. The solid line marks the constant performance of JPEG.*

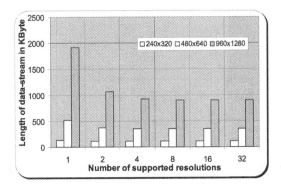

Figure E.2: *Compression performance of JPEG2000 depending on the number of inherent resolution levels for different dimensions of the original image.*

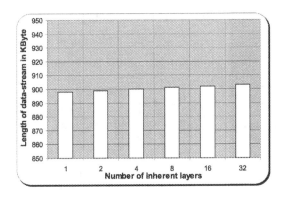

Figure E.3: *Compression performance of JPEG2000 depending on the number of inherent quality layers.*

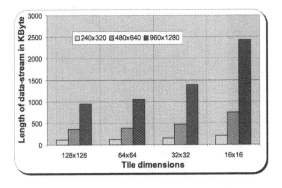

Figure E.4: *Compression performance of JPEG2000 depending on the dimensions of tiles.*

E.2   Measures on the performance of the proposed browsing techniques

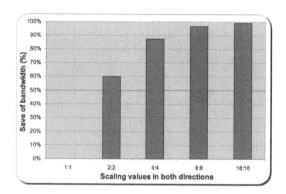

Figure E.5: *The influence of different scaling factors* $x : y$ *on the save of bandwidth. The source is an image of dimensions* 1024×1024 *encoded with 5 inherent resolution levels.*

E.3   Additional figures on the Depth of Field effect

Figure E.6: *The image representation after blurring the background with a* 5×5 *Gaussian filter.*

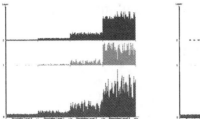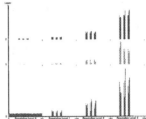

Figure E.7: *Illustration of the encoded image data: While traditional techniques often transmit all data (left), the JPEG2000-based approach requires only a fraction to support a DoF representation (right).*

E.4   Additional figures on Tool glasses

Figure E.8: *The application of 5/3 (left) or CDF 9/7 kernels (right) delivers different results.*

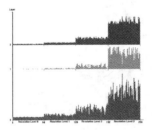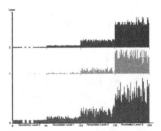

Figure E.9: *Illustration of the encoded image data: The difference between the amount of all encoded image data (left) and the data required to implement the proposed tool glass is insignificant (right).*

E.5   Measures on the complexity of transcoding

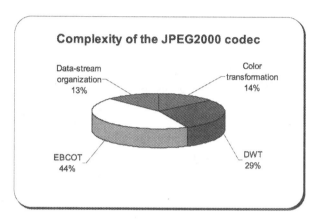

Figure E.10: *The complexity of the respective compression stages during the encoding of an image with JPEG2000 (src: [Che01]).*

E.6   Additional figures on the encoding of image sequences

Figure E.11: *The application of a high threshold value (shown example: 10%) can impose artifacts or even lead to the neglect of elements containing modified contents (src: [Sch03a]).*

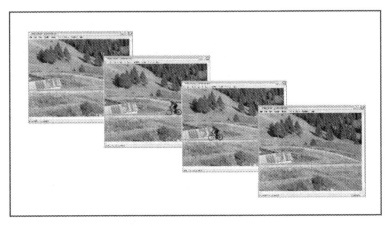

Figure E.12: *Selected screenshots from the static sequence used to measure the save of bandwidth (src: [See04]).*

Figure E.13: *Selected screenshots from the dynamic sequence used to measure the save of bandwidth (src: [See04]).*

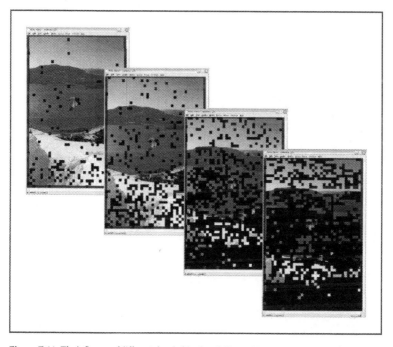

Figure E.14: *The influence of different threshold values (0%, < 1%, < 5%, < 10%) on the detection of modified elements (src: [See04]).*

Appendix F

Additional information to content exchange between images

F.1 The requirements check

Description   The exchange procedure is based on the substitution of data containers of a single type. Thus, all exchanged items must be either tiles, precincts, or code-blocks. As already shown through Equation 3.1, p. 38, this leads to sets KEY and $K\hat{E}Y$ for either type of image. To ensure a proper replacement it is important that all involved elements of both images are of the same type (Equation F.1).

Arbitrary imagery requires the handling of elements truncated at image borders. As they are smaller than other elements, they cannot be arbitrarily replaced. Thus, it must be ensured that all relevant elements at a certain resolution r are of equal dimensions (Equation F.2). The basic scheme also demands the number of resolution levels to be equal for both images (Equation F.3).

The procedure does not vary for both images and is shown for the source only.

Implementation   Based on sets KEY and $K\hat{E}Y$ determined for source and destination, the requirement that both sets contain elements of the same type is validated via attribute a_0. To be able to accomplish the aspired exchange via element pairs it must be equal for all involved elements.

$$\forall k \in KEY, \forall \hat{k} \in K\hat{E}Y : a_0 = \hat{a_0} \tag{F.1}$$

Furthermore, it must be ensured that both elements of a single pair cover the same number of coefficients ($a_3 = \hat{a_3}, a_4 = \hat{a_4}$) to perfectly substitute a certain position. Since these values may vary for each resolution level r, all levels must be tested independently. Here, it is useful to divide the whole set of key elements into subsets containing only elements belonging to a certain resolution level. To achieve this Equation 3.2, p. 38, may be used. Based on this, the requirement can be stated as

$$\forall \hat{r} \geq 0, \forall \hat{k} \in \hat{KEY}_{\hat{r}}, \forall k \in KEY_{\hat{r}} : \tag{F.2}$$
$$a_3 = \hat{a}_3 \cap a_4 = \hat{a}_4$$

The last limitation demands the number of resolution levels to be the same for source and destination.

$$r_{max} = \hat{r}_{max} \tag{F.3}$$

F.2   The verification of the selected elements

Description   Although all elements contributing to the involved image regions have been determined, it is possible that the number of elements associated with a certain resolution level is different for both sets. This is due the choice of different offsets and dimensions of the pixel regions selected in img and $\hat{img}$. To ensure all elements can be assigned in pairs, the numbers of elements must correspond to each other. The verification is accomplished via the determination of the top left (Equation F.5) and bottom right (Equation F.7) element for each resolution r and image. Based on the element offset values, a_1, a_2, it is easy to check if the number of elements do correspond. If the verification fails, different offsets or dimensions for one or both regions must be chosen.

The determination of the top left and bottom right elements does not vary for source and destination and is shown for the source image only.

Implementation   To check if the number of elements collected in $VALID$ and $\hat{VALID}$ is equal, two new sets are created. They contain only attribute tuples which identify the top left ($ATTF \subseteq ATTV$) and bottom right ($ATTL \subseteq ATTV$) RoI element at each resolution level r. They are used to extract their elements into element sets $FIRST$ and $LAST$. Thereby, possible grid offsets $goff_1, goff_2$ must be considered.

$$ATTF = \{attrib(k) | \forall k \in VALID : \tag{F.4}$$
$$a_1 a_5 - goff_1 \leq o_1 \cap a_2 a_6 - goff_2 \leq o_2\}$$

$$FIRST = retrieve(VALID, ATTF) \tag{F.5}$$

$$ATTL = \{attrib(k) | \forall k \in VALID : \tag{F.6}$$
$$(a_1 + 1)a_5 - goff_1 > o_1 + reg_1 \cap$$
$$(a_2 + 1)a_6 - goff_2 > o_2 + reg_2\}$$

$$LAST = retrieve(VALID, ATTL) \tag{F.7}$$

Based on the column and row offset of elements belonging to a single resolution r and the belonging top left (kf) respectively bottom right (kl) element, the number of all valid key elements for each resolution can be determined. It is required to be identical for $VALID$ and $V\hat{A}LID$. To increase readability, lone attributes of tuples collected in $ATTF$ are denoted as af and attributes from $ATTL$ as al.

$$\forall \hat{r}, kf \in FIRST \cap KEY_{\hat{r}}, kl \in LAST \cap KEY_{\hat{r}},$$
$$\hat{kf} \in FI\hat{R}ST \cap K\hat{E}Y_{\hat{r}}, \hat{kl} \in L\hat{A}ST \cap K\hat{E}Y_{\hat{r}} : \qquad \text{(F.8)}$$
$$al_1 - af_1 = \hat{al}_1 - \hat{af}_1 \cap al_2 - af_2 = \hat{al}_2 - \hat{af}_2$$

F.3   The formation of element pairs

Description   The final step forms element pairs by selecting corresponding elements from the verified sets $VALID$ and $V\hat{A}LID$. This is accomplished by considering each image resolution independently using a relative instead of an absolute element offset (attributes: a_1, a_2). To calculate them, the top left element of the region serves as a reference (Equation F.9). This process does not vary for source and destination and is shown for the source image only.

By considering the respective differences to the top left element deriving relative positions for the remaining elements is straightforward. To find matching elements from $VALID$ and $V\hat{A}LID$ only their relative positions must correspond (Equation F.10).

Implementation   Based on the calculated set $FIRST$ (Equation F.5) containing all top left elements, it is possible to extract the required element for each resolution r.

$$kf_r = FIRST \cap KEY_r \qquad \text{(F.9)}$$

The absolute offset values $off_{1,r} = a_1$, $off_{2,r} = a_2$ of these elements are the foundation to determine the relative position of all others. This is used within the following determination of element pairs from $VALID$ and $V\hat{A}LID$.

$$PAIRS = \{(k, \hat{k}) | \forall \hat{r}, \forall \hat{k} \in V\hat{A}LID \cap K\hat{E}Y_{\hat{r}}, k \in VALID \cap KEY_{\hat{r}} : \qquad \text{(F.10)}$$
$$a_1 - off_{1,\hat{r}} = \hat{a}_1 - \hat{off}_{1,\hat{r}} \cap$$
$$a_2 - off_{2,\hat{r}} = \hat{a}_2 - \hat{off}_{2,\hat{r}} \}$$

F.4   Content exchange joint with simultaneous scaling

Replacement with simultaneous downscaling by factors $2^g : 2^g$ can be accomplished by the selection of corresponding elements which belong to different resolution levels. This, however, requires the adaptation of the statements provided for the *requirements* and *element selection* step within the basic exchange scheme.

Requirements   Within the enhancement, it is no longer necessary for the number of inherent resolution to be equal within both data-streams (Equation F.3). The highest resolution r_{max} supported within the source image must only be sufficiently large ($r_{max} - g \geq \hat{r}_{max}$) so as to be able to skip at least g higher resolutions. However, elements of a single pair are still required to have the same properties and spatial extent.

Element selection   The main difference is in element selection. As corresponding elements now belong to different resolution levels, their determination differs for source and destination. While Equation 3.3 can still be applied for the destination, only a subset of all RoI elements within the source is required. Thus, it is necessary to limit the calculation of belonging attribute tuples to valid resolutions $r \leq r_{max} - g$ only.

$$
\begin{aligned}
ATTV = \ \{ attrib(k) | \forall k &\in KEY_0 \cup KEY_1 \cup \cdots \cup KEY_{r_{max}-g} : \\
o_1 &< (a_1 + 1)a_5 - goff_1 \cap a_1 a_5 - goff_1 \leq o_1 + reg_1 \cap \\
o_2 &< (a_2 + 1)a_6 - goff_2 \cap a_2 a_6 - goff_2 \leq o_2 + reg_2 \}
\end{aligned}
\tag{F.11}
$$

F.5 Tile-based content exchange joint with simultaneous scaling

F.5.1 Idea and description

As described in Section 6.3.2.2, it is possible to exchange and scale image content simultaneously. The proposed scheme, however, requires the inherent resolutions of both images to correspond. The overcoming of this limitation is the topic of this section. To achieve this, the properties of tiles are exploited. Tiles are basically sub-images and offer the opportunity to chose the number of image resolutions for each tile independently. Thus, they can be easily adapted to the required numbers. For simplicity, the given descriptions assume neither image nor grid offsets. Here, the belonging statements given for the basic exchange scheme can be applied if required.

By applying tiles for content exchange two different configurations are possible:

- The replaced region covers only a part of one or multiple tiles
- The updated region covers one or multiple tiles completely.

The first point requires partial modification of content available for a certain tile. Since remaining content does not allow taking advantage of adjustments in the number of resolution levels, the resulting exchange scheme may be derived from the scheme described in Section 6.3.2.2 – Exchange in pairs.

The more interesting problem, however, is the exchange of the whole tile content. Here, it is possible to modify the number of resolution levels depending on current needs (cf. Figure 6.5). As a change in the number of resolutions imposes differences on the number of involved elements between source and destination, *exchange in pairs is not applicable*. Instead it is assumed removing all content of the destination tile and including all belonging elements from the source image. This process consists of the four steps:

1. Determination of source elements
2. Determination of destination tiles

3. Assignment of source elements to destination tiles

4. Compliance check

These steps differ from the other schemes and are now explained in detail.

F.5.2   Implementation

Determination of source elements   Contrary to the basic exchange scheme, within the proposal for tile-based exchange only code-blocks or precincts are used as key elements. This is due to the fact that a lone tile cannot be substituted by multiple tiles without violating compliance. Thus, the determination of the initial set of key elements must be adapted.

$$KEY = \begin{cases} P_0 \ \cup \ P_1 \ \cup \dots \cup \ P_{r_{max}} & : \quad \text{if using precincts} \\ CB_0 \cup CB_1 \cup \dots \cup CB_{r_{max}} & : \quad \text{if using code-blocks} \end{cases} \tag{F.12}$$

The determination of RoI elements does not vary from the already described proceeding. Equation F.11 is applied as a foundation to create the belonging element set $VALID$.

Determination of destination tiles   As all content associated with an affected destination tile is completely displaced by source content, it is only required to determine these tiles. In the following procedure this is achieved by referring to the tile contributions $\hat{T}_{\hat{r}_{max}}$ associated to the spatial domain only.

Based on $\hat{T}_{\hat{r}_{max}}$, all tiles involved in the exchange process can be identified. They are collected into a set $VT\hat{I}LES$. The set of associated attribute tuples, $A\hat{T}TT$, identifying these tiles can be created by considering position and dimensions of the region within the destination image and belonging tile properties.

$$\begin{aligned} A\hat{T}TT = \ & \{attrib(\hat{k}) | \forall \hat{k} \in \hat{T}_{\hat{r}_{max}} : \\ & \hat{o}_1 < (\hat{a}_1 + 1)\hat{a}_5 \cap \hat{a}_1\hat{a}_5 \leq \hat{o}_1 + r\hat{e}g_1 \cap \\ & \hat{o}_2 < (\hat{a}_2 + 1)\hat{a}_6 \cap \hat{a}_2\hat{a}_6 \leq \hat{o}_2 + r\hat{e}g_2\} \end{aligned} \tag{F.13}$$

$$VT\hat{I}LES = retrieve(TI\hat{L}ES, A\hat{T}TT) \tag{F.14}$$

As shown for the basic exchange scheme, it is useful to exclude smaller elements truncated at image boundaries. Thus, the created tile set must be validated so as to contain only elements of identical dimensions.

$$\begin{aligned} & \forall \hat{k} \in VT\hat{I}LES, \nexists \hat{k}' \in VT\hat{I}LES : \\ & \hat{a}_5 \neq \hat{a}_5' \cap \hat{a}_6 \neq \hat{a}_6' \end{aligned} \tag{F.15}$$

Similar to the basic scheme, it is useful to determine top left and bottom right elements in order to control the access to all RoI elements. Based on the verified set

$VT\hat{I}LES$, such tile contributions are stored in sets $TF\hat{I}RST$ and $TL\hat{A}ST$ respectively.

$$TA\hat{T}TF = \{attrib(\hat{k})|\forall \hat{k} \in VT\hat{I}LES : \hat{a}_1\hat{a}_5 \leq \hat{o}_1 \cap \hat{a}_2\hat{a}_6 \leq \hat{o}_2\} \tag{F.16}$$

$$TF\hat{I}RST = retrieve(VT\hat{I}LES, TA\hat{T}TF) \tag{F.17}$$

$$TA\hat{T}TL = \{attrib(\hat{k})|\forall \hat{k} \in VT\hat{I}LES : \tag{F.18}$$
$$(\hat{a}_1 + 1)\hat{a}_5 > \hat{o}_1 + r\hat{e}g_1 \cap (\hat{a}_2 + 1)\hat{a}_6 > \hat{o}_2 + r\hat{e}g_2\}$$

$$TL\hat{A}ST = retrieve(VT\hat{I}LES, TA\hat{T}TL) \tag{F.19}$$

With the creation of these tile sets, the determination of involved destination tiles is finished. To be able to include the new source elements from $VALID$, all contents associated to tiles collected in $VT\hat{I}LES$ are removed. As multiple destination tiles might be involved, it will now be shown how to assign source elements to the respective destination tiles.

Assignment of source elements to destination tiles   To associate new source elements to a certain destination tile, for each tile a single element set $T\hat{I}LES_{\hat{i},\hat{j}}$ is created. Thereby, $\hat{i}$ and $\hat{j}$ are indices for all involved tiles: $\hat{af}_1 \leq \hat{i} \leq \hat{al}_1, \hat{af}_2 \leq \hat{j} \leq \hat{al}_2$, and $\hat{af}$ and $\hat{al}$ denote single attributes of the tuples belonging to tile contributions $\hat{kf} \in TF\hat{I}RST$ and $\hat{kl} \in TL\hat{A}ST$.

Similar to the determination of element pairs (Equation F.9 and F.10), the relative offset of elements in $VALID$ is used to achieve the assignment of an element to a certain tile. Thereby, the top left elements of the source region serve as an anchor with offset values, $off_{1,r}$ and $off_{2,r}$. The spatial contribution of a source element expressed in attributes a_5, a_6 refers to the original image resolution. To be able assigning the scaled region to the respective tile via these attributes, their values must be adapted accordingly. This leads to values $\tilde{a}_5 = \frac{a_5}{2^g}$ and $\tilde{a}_6 = \frac{a_6}{2^g}$.

$$\forall \hat{i}, \hat{j} : T\hat{I}LE_{\hat{i},\hat{j}} = \{attrib(k)|\forall r, \forall k \in VALID \cap KEY_r, \hat{kf} \in TF\hat{I}RST : \tag{F.20}$$
$$(\hat{i} - \hat{af}_1)\hat{af}_5 \leq (a_1 - off_{1,r})\tilde{a}_5 \cap$$
$$(\hat{i} - \hat{af}_1 + 1)\hat{af}_5 > (a_1 - off_{1,r})\tilde{a}_5 \cap$$
$$(\hat{j} - \hat{af}_2)\hat{af}_6 \leq (a_2 - off_{2,r})\tilde{a}_6 \cap$$
$$(\hat{j} - \hat{af}_2 + 1)\hat{al}_6 > (a_2 - off_{2,r})\tilde{a}_6\}$$

Compliance check   After all source elements have been assigned to a certain destination tile, it is reasonable to check if these elements can be included without violating compliance. Since a tile fully describes belonging image content, it is necessary that the new precinct or code-block structures also fulfill this requirement for each provided image resolution. The validation is based on the formation of sets $F\hat{TILE}_{\hat{i},\hat{j},r} \subseteq \hat{TILE}_{\hat{i},\hat{j}}$ and $L\hat{TILE}_{\hat{i},\hat{j},r} \subseteq \hat{TILE}_{\hat{i},\hat{j}}$ containing the top left respectively bottom right element for each tile and resolution.

$$\forall r, \hat{i}, \hat{j} : F\hat{TILE}_{\hat{i},\hat{j},r} = \{k | \forall k' \in \hat{TILE}_{\hat{i},\hat{j}} \cap KEY_r, \qquad \text{(F.21)}$$
$$\exists k \in \hat{TILE}_{\hat{i},\hat{j}} \cap KEY_r : a_1 \leq a_1' \cap a_2 \leq a_2'\}$$

$$\forall r, \hat{i}, \hat{j} : L\hat{TILE}_{\hat{i},\hat{j},r} = \{k | \forall k' \in \hat{TILE}_{\hat{i},\hat{j}} \cap KEY_r, \qquad \text{(F.22)}$$
$$\exists k \in \hat{TILE}_{\hat{i},\hat{j}} \cap KEY_r : a_1 \geq a_1' \cap a_2 \geq a_2'\}$$

Since all tiles have proved to be of equal dimensions, attributes $\hat{a}_5, \hat{a}_6$ from an arbitrary tile contribution $\hat{t} \in V\hat{TILES}$ are used as references. Thereby, single attributes denoted as af and al belong to elements $kf \in F\hat{TILE}_{\hat{i},\hat{j},r}$ or $kl \in L\hat{TILE}_{\hat{i},\hat{j},r}$ respectively.

$$\forall \hat{i}, \hat{j}, r, kf \in F\hat{TILE}_{\hat{i},\hat{j},r}, kl \in L\hat{TILE}_{\hat{i},\hat{j},r}, \hat{t} \in V\hat{TILES} :$$
$$(al_1 - af_1 + 1)a\tilde{f}_5 = \hat{a}_5 \cap (al_2 - af_2 + 1)a\tilde{f}_6 = \hat{a}_6 \qquad \text{(F.23)}$$

If this requirement is fulfilled, all source elements collected in $\hat{TILE}_{\hat{i},\hat{j}}$ can be included at positions associated to the destination tile $[i, j]$. Nevertheless, it is mandatory to keep the original order of the inserted elements within the destination data-stream.

Bibliography

[Ada91] A. Adams. *The Camera*. Little Brown & Company, 1991.

[Ado05] Adobe. Photoshop CS2. <http://www.adobe.de/products/photoshop/main.html>, 2005.

[AG94] R. Alter-Gartenberg, F. Huck, and R. Narayanswamy. Compact image representation by edge primitives. *GMIP*, vol. 56(1):pp. 1–7, January 1994.

[Ahm74] N. Ahmed, T. Natarajan, , and K. R. Rao. Discrete cosine transform. In *IEEE Transactions on Computers*, vol. C–23, pp. 90–93. 1974.

[Ahr01] J. Ahrens, K. Brislawn, K. Martin, B. Geveci, C. C. Law, and M. Papka. Large-scale data visualization using parallel data streaming. *IEEE Computer Graphics and Applications*, vol. 21(4):pp. 34–41, 2001.

[Alb00] M. G. Albanesi, M. Ferretti, and F. Guerrini. Adaptive image compression based on regions of interest and a modified contrast sensitivity function. In *ICPR*, pp. 3219–3222. 2000.

[App01] S. Appadwedula, M. Goel, N. R. Shanbhag, D. L. Jones, and K. Ramchandran. Total system energy minimization for wireless image transmission. *J VLSI Signal Processing Systems*, vol. 27(1-2):pp. 99–117, 2001.

[Ask02] J. Askelof, M. L. Carlander, and C.Christopoulos. Region of interest coding in jpeg 2000. In *Signal Processing: Image Compression*, vol. 17, pp. 105–111. 2002.

[Ats98] E. Atsumi and N. Farvardin. Lossy/lossless region-of-interest image coding based on set partitioning in hierarchical trees. In *Proceedings of ICIP98*, pp. 87–91. 1998.

[Azu05] H. Azuma, Y. Yuhki, N. Urano, and I. Nakaue. 5ghz band wireless video transmission chipset dc2z series. *Sharp Technical Journal*, vol. 23, 2005.

[Bar93] M. Barnsley and L. Hurd. *Fractal Image Compression*. AK Peters, Wellesley, 1993.

[Bar01] F. Bartolini, C. Pasquini, and A. Piva. Evaluating the effectiveness of SW-only video coding for real-time video transmission over low-rate wireless networks. In *Proceedings of SPIE – Real-Time Imaging V*. April 2001.

[Bau01] G. N. Baudisch, Patrick and P. Stewart. Focus plus context screens: Combining display technology with visualization techniques. In *Proceedings of the 14th annual ACM symposium on UIST*. 2001.

[Bau02] G. N. B. V. Baudisch, Patrick and S. P. Keeping things in context: a comparative evaluation of focus plus context screens. In *Proceedings of CHI02*. 2002.

[Bau03] P. Baudisch and R. Rosenholtz. Halo: a technique for visualizing off-screen locations. *Proceedings of CHI*, pp. 481–488, 2003.

[Bau04] P. Baudisch, X. Xie, C. Wang, and W.-Y. Ma. Collapse-to-zoom: viewing web
pages on small screen devices by interactively removing irrelevant content. In
*Proceedings of the 17th annual ACM symposium on User interface software and technol-
ogy*, pp. 91–94. ACM Press, New York, NY, USA, 2004.

[Bea90] D. V. Beard and J. Q. W. II. Navigational techniques to improve the display of
large two-dimensional spaces. In *Behaviour and Information Technology*. 1990.

[Bed94] B. B. Bederson and J. D. Hollan. Pad++: A zooming graphical interface for exploring alternate interface physicss. *Proceedings of ACM User Interface Software
and Technology*, pp. 17–26, 1994.

[Bed00a] B. B. Bederson. Fisheye menus. In *Proceedings of the 13th annual ACM symposium
on User interface software and technology*, pp. 217–225. ACM Press, New York, NY,
USA, 2000.

[Bed00b] B. B. Bederson, J. Meyer, and L. Good. Jazz: an extensible zoomable user interface
graphics toolkit in java. In *Proceedings of UIST*, pp. 171–180. 2000.

[Bed02] B. B. Bederson, B. Shneiderman, and M. Wattenberg. Ordered and quantum
treemaps: Making effective use of 2d space to display hierarchies. *ACM Transactions on Graphics*, vol. 21(4):pp. 833–854, 2002.

[Bed04] B. B. Bederson, A. Clamage, M. P. Czerwinski, and G. G. Robertson. Datelens:
A fisheye calendar interface for pdas. *ACM Transactions Computer-Human Interaction*, vol. 11(1):pp. 90–119, 2004.

[Bie94a] E. Bier, M. Stone, K. Fishkin, W. Buxton, and T. Baudel. A Taxonomy of See-
Through Tools. In *BIBCHI*, pp. 358–364. Addison-Wesley, April 1994.

[Bie94b] E. A. Bier, M. C. Stone, K. Pier, K. Fishkin, T. Baudel, M. Conway, W. Buxton, and
T. DeRose. Toolglass and magic lenses: the see-through interface. In *Conference
companion on Human factors in computing systems at CHI*, pp. 445–446. ACM Press,
New York, NY, USA, 1994.

[Bie97] E. Bier, M. Stone, and K. Pier. Enhanced illustration using magic lens filters. *IEEE
Computer Graphics and Applications*, vol. 17(6):pp. 62–70, 1997.

[Bjö98] S. Björk and L. Holmquist. The digital variants browser: An explorative tool for
literature studies. In *Proceedings of Computers, Literature and Philology*. 1998.

[Bjo00] S. Bjoerk and J. Redstroem. Redefining the focus and context of focus+context
visualizations. In *Proceedings of the IEEE Symposium on Information Visualization*.
Salt Lake City, Utah, USA, 2000.

[Bra02] A. P. Bradley. Jpeg 2000 and region of interest coding. In *Digital Image Computing
Techniques and Applications*. Melbourne, Australia, January 2002.

[Bra03a] A. P. Bradley. Can region of interest coding improve overall perceived image
quality? In *APRS Workshop on Digital Image Computing (WDICŠ03)*. Brisbane,
Australia, February 2003.

[Bra03b] A. P. Bradley and F. W. M. Stentiford. Visual attention for region of interest coding
in jpeg 2000. In *Journal of Visual Communication and Image Representation*, vol. 14,
pp. 232–250. 2003.

[Buc00] R. Buckley and G. Beretta. Color imaging on the internet. *Course scripts: SPIE
Electronic Imaging*, 2000.

[Bur03] S. Burkard. depth of field. <http://www.fotolia.com/id/45205>, 2003.

[Can86] J. Canny. A computational approach to edge detection. *IEEE Transactions on Pattern Analysis and Machine Intelligence*, 1986.

[Car97a] M. S. T. Carpendale, D. Cowperthwaite, M.-A. D. Storey, and F. D. Fracchia. Exploring distinct aspects of the distortion viewing paradigm. *Technical Report CMPT1997-08*, March 1997.

[Car97b] M. S. T. Carpendale, D. J. Cowperthwaite, and F. D. Fracchia. Extending distortion viewing from 2D to 3D. *IEEE Computer Graphics and Applications: Special Issue on Information Visualization*, vol. 17(4):pp. 42–51, 1997.

[Car99]   M. J. D. Card, S. K. and B. Shneiderman. *Readings in Information Visualization - Using Vision to Think.* Morgan Kaufman, San Francisco, 1999.

[CC000]   Visual evaluation of jpeg 2000 color image compression performance. Tech. rep., ISO/IEC JTC 1/SC 29/WG 1, N1583, Troy Chinen and Alan Chien, March 2000.

[Cen06]   T. D. M. Center. Ohiolink - library systems. <http://dmc.ohiolink.edu/>, 2006.

[Che01]   L.-G. Chen, C.-J. Lian, K.-F. Chen, and H.-H. Chen. Analysis and architecture design of jpeg2000. In *Proceedings of the 2001 IEEE International Conference on Multimedia and Expo.* IEEE Computer Society, 2001.

[Che03]   L.-Q. Chen, X. Xie, X. Fan, W.-Y. Ma, H. Zhang, and H.-Q. Zhou. A visual attention model for adapting images on small displays. *ACM Multimedia Systems Journal*, vol. 9(4):pp. 353–364, 2003.

[Chi00]   E. H. Chi. A taxonomy of visualization techniques using the data state reference model. In *Proceedings of the IEEE Symposium on Information Vizualization 2000*, p. 69. IEEE Computer Society, 2000.

[Chi01]   I. Chisalita and N. Shahmehri. Issues in image utilization within mobile e-services. In *Proceedings of the 10th IEEE International Workshops on Enabling Technologies*, pp. 62–67. IEEE Computer Society, Washington, DC, USA, 2001.

[Chr00]   E. Christopoulou, A. Skodras, T. Reed, and C. Christopoulos. On the jpeg2000 implementation on different computer platforms. In *Proceedings of the SPIE International Symposium, Special Session on JPEG2000*, pp. 561–569. August 2000.

[Chu95]   N. Churcher. Applications of distortionoriented presentation techniques in gis. In *Proceedings of the New Zealand Conference on Geographical Information Systems and Spatial Information System Research*, pp. 323–336. 1995.

[Clu00]   D. A. Clunie. Lossless compression of grayscale medical images - effectiveness of traditional and state of the art approaches. In *Proceedings of SPIE Medical Imaging.* 2000.

[Com99]   T. T. A. Combs and B. B. Bederson. Does zooming improve image browsing? In *Proceedings of the fourth ACM conference on digital libraries*, pp. 130–137. ACM Press, 1999.

[Cot98]   G. Cote, B. Erol, M. Gallant, and F. Kossentini. H.263+: video coding at low bit rates. *IEEE Transactions on Circuits and Systems for Video Technology*, vol. 8(7):pp. 849–866, 1998.

[Dan03]   H. Danyali and A. Mertins. Fully spatial and snr scalable, spiht-based image coding for transmission over heterogenous networks. *Journal of Telecommunications and Information Technology*, vol. 2:pp. 92Ű–98, 2003.

[Dan04]   H. Danyali and A. Mertins. Flexible, highly scalable, object-based wavelet image compression algorithm for network applications. *IEEE Proceedings Vision, Image and Signal Processing*, vol. 151:pp. 498–510, December 2004.

[Dar04]   E. Darling, C. Newbern, N. Kalghatgi, A. Burgman, and K. Recktenwald. An experimental investigation of magnification lens offset and its impact on imagery analysis. In *Proceedings of the IEEE Symposium on Information Visualization.* 2004.

[Day83]   J. D. Day and H. Zimmermann. The osi reference model. In *Proceedings of IEEE*, vol. 71, pp. 1334–1340. IEEE Press, December 1983.

[DeB00] V. E. DeBrunner, L. DeBrunner, L. Wang, and S. Radhakrishnan. Error control and concealment for image transmission. *IEEE Communications Surveys and Tutorials*, vol. 3(1), 2000.

[Dem97] D. Demigny and T. Kamle. A discrete expression of canny's criteria for step edge detector performances evaluation. *IEEE Transactions on Pattern Analysis and Machine Intelligence*, vol. 19(11):pp. 1199–1211, 1997.

[Des01] S. Deshpande and W. Zeng. Scalable streaming of jpeg2000 images using hypertext transfer protocol. In *Proceedings of the ninth ACM international conference on Multimedia*, pp. 372–381. ACM Press, 2001.

[DeV88] R. L. DeValois and K. K. DeValois. *Spatial Vision*. Oxford University Press, New York, 1988.

[DIO03] DICOM - Digital Imaging and Communications in Medicine, Base Standard PS 3.1, 2003.

[Dig06] Digital Photo Professional. Canon. <http://www.dpreview.com/reviews/canoneos5d/page19.asp>, 2006.

[DMM82] J. David M. Mckeown and J. L. Denlinger. Graphical tools for interactive image interpretation. In *Proceedings of the 9th annual conference on Computer graphics and interactive techniques*, pp. 189–198. ACM Press, New York, NY, USA, 1982.

[DoH06] DoHistory:. Martha ballards diary online. <http://www.dohistory.org/diary/exercises/lens/>, 2006.

[Dol01] S. Dolinar, A. Kiely, M. Klimesh, R. Manduchi, A. Ortega, S. Lee, P. Sagetong, H. Xie, G. Chinn, J. Harel, S. Shambayati, and M. Vida. Region-of-interest data compression with prioritized buffer management. *Earth Science Technology Conference (ESTC 2001)*, August 2001.

[DR04] R. S. Daniel Robbins, Edward Cutrell and E. Horvitz. Zonezoom: Map navigation for smartphones with recursive view segmentation. In *Proceedings of AVI*. 2004.

[Dro00] I. Drori and D. Lischinski. Wavelet warping. In *Proceedings of the 11th Eurographics Workshop on Rendering*. 2000.

[Dro03] I. Drori and D. Lischinski. Fast multi-resolution image operations in the wavelet domain. In *IEEE Transactions on Visualization and Computer Graphics*, vol. 9. 2003.

[Dür91] M. Dürst and T. Kunii. Progressive transmission increasing both spatial and gray scale resolution. In *Proceedings of the International Conference on Multimedia Information Systems*, pp. 175–186. McGraw-Hill, Singapore, 1991.

[Ebr00] T. Ebrahimi and C. Horne. Mpeg-4 natural video coding – an overview. In *Signal Processing, Image Communication*, vol. 15, pp. 365–385. 2000.

[Ebr03] T. Ebrahimi, J. Vesin, and G. Garcia. Brain-computer interface in multimedia communication. *IEEE Signal Processing Magazine*, pp. 14–24, January 2003.

[Eis96] M. Eisenberg. The thin glass line: designing interfaces to algorithms. In *Proceedings of the SIGCHI conference on Human factors in computing systems*, pp. 181–188. ACM Press, New York, NY, USA, 1996.

[Eld98] J. H. Elder and S. W. Zucker. Local scale control for edge detection and blur estimation. *IEEE Transactions on Pattern Analysis and Machine Intelligence*, vol. 20(7):pp. 699–716, 1998.

[EM02] N. S. E. Metois, P. Yarin and J. R. Smith. Fiberfingerprint identification. *Third Workshop on Automatic Identification*, March 2002.

[ER05] Image web server 7.0. <http://www.ermapper.com>, 2005.

[Fel55] P. B. Fellgett and E. H. Linfoot. On the accessment of optical images. In *Philosophical Transactions of the Royal Society London 247*, vol. 247, pp. 369–407. 1955.

[Fen03] G. Feng and J. Jiang. Image segmentation in compressed domain. *SPIE Journal of Electronic Imaging*, vol. 12(3):pp. 390–397, 2003.

[FIR05] FIRAXIS GAMES. Civilization III. <http://www.civ3.com>, 2005.

[Fol90] J. D. Foley, A. van Dam, S. K. Feiner, and J. F. Hughes. *Computer Graphics – Principles and Practice, Second Edition*. Addison-Wesley, 1990. ISBN 0-201-12110-7.

[Foo00] D. Foos, E. Muka, and e. a. Slone. Jpeg 2000 compression of medical imagery. In *Medical Imaging 2000*, vol. 3980, pp. 85–96. 2000.

[Fox96] A. Fox and E. Brewer. Reducing WWW latency and bandwidth requirements by real-time distillation. In *Proceedings of the 5th International World Wide Web Conference*. Paris, France, May 6-10 1996.

[FPX97] FlashPix format specification, Version 1.0.1. Eastman Kodak Company, 1997.

[Fra97] T. Frajka, P. Sherwood, and K. Zeger. Progressive image coding with spatially variable resolution. In *Proceedings of the IEEE International Conference on Image Processing*, vol. 1, p. 53ff. Santa Barbara, California, October 1997.

[Fro03] P. Frossard, P. Vandergheynst, and R. F. i Ventura. High flexibility scalable image coding. In *Proceedings of VCIP*. 2003.

[Fuc01] G. Fuchs. *Datenstrom-Transcoder für den neuen Bildkodierungsstandard JPEG2000 - Teil II*. FYP, University of Rostock, October 2001.

[Fur81] G. W. Furnas. The FISHEYE view: A new look at structured files. Tech. Rep. #81-11221-9, Murray Hill, New Jersey 07974, U.S.A., 12 1981.

[Fur86] G. W. Furnas. Generalized fisheye views. In *Proceedings of the SIGCHI conference on Human factors in computing systems*, pp. 16–23. ACM Press, New York, NY, USA, 1986.

[Fur95] G. W. Furnas and B. B. Bederson. Space-scale diagrams: understanding multi-scale interfaces. In *Proceedings of the SIGCHI conference on Human factors in computing systems*, pp. 234–241. ACM Press/Addison-Wesley Publishing Co., New York, NY, USA, 1995.

[Gar06] R. Gartner. Research in motion lifts pda market to 6.6 percent growth in 1q06. May 2006.

[GDA05] GDAL. Geospatial data abstraction library. <http://www.gdal.org/>, 2005.

[Gho99] P. Ghosh and B. Shneiderman. Zoom-only vs. overview-detail pair: A study in browsing techniques as applied to patient histories. Tech. rep., University of Maryland, Technical Report CS-TR-4028, 1999.

[GIF89] GIF89a - Graphics Interchange Format (tm). A standard defining a mechanism for the storage and transmission of raster-based graphics information. 1989.

[GIMP05] G. the GNU Image Manipulation Program. < http://www.gimp.org/>, 2005.

[Gol80] E. B. Goldstein. *Sensation and perception*. Wadsworth Publishing Co., Belmont, California, 1980.

[Gom02] G. Gomez. Estimating local variance for gaussian filtering. In R. Fisher, editor, *Contribution to CV-Online: On-Line Compendium of Computer Vision*. February 2002.

[Gon01] R. C. Gonzalez and R. E. Woods. *Digital Image Processing*. Addison-Wesley Longman Publishing Co., Inc., Boston, MA, USA, 2001.

[Grg04] S. Grgic, M. Grgic, and M. Mrak. Reliability of objective picture quality measures. In *Journal of Electrical Engineering*, vol. 55, pp. 3–10. 2004.

[Gro01] R. Grosbois, D. Santa Cruz, and T. Ebrahimi. New approach to jpeg2000 compliant region of interest coding. In *SPIE 46th annual meeting, Applications of Digital Image Processing*. July 2001.

[Gut04] C. Gutwin and C. Fedak. Interacting with big interfaces on small screens: a comparison of fisheye, zoom, and panning techniques. In *Proceedings of the 2004 conference on Graphics interface*, pp. 145–152. Canadian Human-Computer Communications Society, 2004.

[GVS05] GeoVista Studio, Version 1.2.   <http://www.geovistastudio.psu.edu/jsp/index.jsp>, 2005.

[Haa10] A. Haar. Zur Theorie der orthogonalen Funktionensysteme. *Mathematische Annalen*, vol. 69:pp. 331–371, 1910.

[Han96] J. Han and G. Polyzos. Networking applications of the hierarchical mode of the jpeg standard. In *Proceedings of the IEEE International Phoenix Conference on Computers and Communications*. Phoenix, AZ, March 1996.

[Han01] R. J. Hanisch, A. Farris, E. W. Greisen, W. D. Pence, B. M. Schlesinger, P. J. Teuben, R. W. Thompson, and A. W. III. Definition of the flexible image transport system (fits). *Astronomy & Astrophysics*, pp. 359–376, 2001.

[Hew97] Hewlett Packard, Live Picture and Eastman Kodak. *IIP - Internet Imaging Protocol*, 1997.

[Hoi03] K. K. Hoi, D. L. Lee, and J. Xu. Document visualization on small displays. In *Proceedings of the 4th International Conference on Mobile Data Management*, pp. 262–278. Springer-Verlag, London, UK, 2003.

[Hor01] K. Hornbaek and E. Frokjaer. Reading of electronic documents: the usability of linear, fisheye, and overview+detail interfaces. In *Proceedings of the SIGCHI conference on Human factors in computing systems*, pp. 293–300. ACM Press, 2001.

[Hor02] K. Hornbaek, B. B. Bederson, and C. Plaisant. Navigation patterns and usability of zoomable user interfaces with and without an overview. *ACM Transactions on Computer-Human Interaction*, vol. 9(4):pp. 362–389, 2002.

[Hu04] Y. Hu, X. Xie, Z. Chen, and W.-Y. Ma. Attention model based progressive image transmission. In *Proceedings of the IEEE International Conference on Multimedia and Expo*. Taipei/Taiwan, June 2004.

[Hub62] D. Hubel and T. Wiesel. Receptive fields, binocular interaction, and functional architecture in the cat's visual cortex. *Journal of Physiology*, vol. 160:pp. 106–154, 1962.

[Hue71] M. H. Hueckel. An operator which locates edges in digitized pictures. *Journal of the ACM*, vol. 18(1):pp. 113–125, 1971.

[IDE05] IDELIX. Pliable display technology SDK. <http://www.idelix.com>, 2005.

[Ima05] Image Viewer. Microsoft ® windows mobile 5.0, 2005.

[Imh62] E. Imhoff. Die Anordnung der Namen in der Karte. *Internationales Jahrbuch fuer Kartographie II*, 1962.

[Imi96] T. Imielinski and H. Korth, editors. *Mobile Computing*. Kluwer Academic Publishers, Boston, 1996.

[IQW98] Intel quickweb technology. Whitepaper, Intel Corporation, 1998.

[Ire98] S. Iren, P. D. Amer, and P. T. Conrad. NETCICATS: Network-conscious image compression and transmission system. vol. 1508 of *Lecture Notes in Computer Science*, pp. 57+. 1998.

[Ire99] S. Iren. *Network-conscious Image Compression*. Ph.D. thesis, University of Delaware, 1999.

[Jer98] D. F. Jerding and J. T. Stasko. The information mural: A technique for displaying and navigating large information spaces. *IEEE Transactions on Visualization and Computer Graphics*, vol. 4(3):pp. 257–271, 1998.

[Jia02] J. Jiang, A. Armstrong, and G. Feng. Direct content access and extraction from jpeg compressed images. In *ELSEVIER journal - Pattern Recognition*. 2002.

[JO04] I. G. J.P. Ortiz, V.G. Ruiz. Remote browsing of jpeg 2000 images on the web: Evaluation of existing techniques and a new proposal. In *Proceedings of VIIP*. September 2004.

[Joh01] B. Johanson, S. Ponnekanti, C. Sengupta, and A. Fox. Multibrowsing: Moving web content across multiple displays. In *Proceedings of the 3rd international conference on Ubiquitous Computing*, pp. 346–353. Springer-Verlag, London, UK, 2001.

[JPG94] Information technology - JPEG - digital compression and coding of continuous tone still images - part 1: Requirements and guidelines. Tech. rep., ISO/IEC 10918-1 and ITU Recommandation T.81, 1994.

[JPG96] Information technology - JPEG - digital compression and coding of continuous tone still images, part3: Extensions. Tech. rep., ISO/IEC 10918-3 and ITU Recommandation T.84, 1996.

[JPG02a] JPEG 2000 image coding system, part1. Final Publication Draft, ISO/IEC JTC 1/SC 29/WG 1 N2678, 19 July 2002.

[JPG02b] JPEG 2000 image coding system, part2. Final Publication Draft part 2, ISO/IEC JTC 1/SC 29/WG 1 N2679, 19 July 2002.

[JPG02c] JPEG 2000 image coding system, part3, cor. 1. Final Draft International Standard part 3, ISO/IEC JTC 1/SC 29/WG 1 N2705, 19 July 2002.

[JPG04] JPEG 2000 image coding system, part9. Final Draft International Standard part 9, ISO/IEC JTC 1/SC 29/WG 1 N3052R, 24 May 2004.

[KAK05] KAKADU. A comprehensive, heavily optimized, fully compliant software toolkit for jpeg2000 developers, version 4.5. <http://www.kakadusoftware.com/>, 2005.

[Kap95] V. Kaptelinin. A comparison of four navigation techniques in a 2d browsing task. In *Conference companion on Human factors in computing systems*, pp. 282–283. ACM Press, 1995.

[Kar03a] B. Karstens, R. Rosenbaum, and H. Schumann. Information presentation on mobile handhelds. In *Proceedings of IRMA*. May 2003.

[Kar03b] B. Karstens, R. Rosenbaum, and H. Schumann. Visual interfaces for mobile handhelds. In *Proceedings of HCII*. Crete/Greece, June 2003.

[Kar04] B. Karstens, R. Rosenbaum, and H. Schumann. *Information presentation on handheld devices*. Idea Group Publishing, e-commerce and m-commerce technologies edn., 2004.

[Kat91] S. Katz. *Film Directing Shot by Shot*. Michael Wiese Press, Studio City, California, 1991.

[Kay96a] V. Kayargadde and J. Martens. Perceptual characterization of images degraded by blur and noise: experiments. In *Journal of the Optical Society of America*, vol. 13 of 6, pp. 1166–77. 1996.

[Kay96b] V. Kayargadde and J. Martens. Perceptual characterization of images degraded by blur and noise: model. In *Journal of the Optical Society of America*, vol. 13 of 6, pp. 1178–88. 1996.

[Kea97a] T. A. Keahey. *Nonlinear Magnification*. Ph.D. thesis, Department of Computer Science, Indiana University, December 1997.

[Kea97b] T. A. Keahey and E. L. Robertson. Nonlinear magnification fields. In *Proceedings of the IEEE Symposium on Information Visualization*, p. 51. IEEE Computer Society, Washington, DC, USA, 1997.

[Kea98] A. Keahey. The generalized detail-in-context problem. In *Proceedings of the IEEE Symposium on Information Visualization*, pp. 44–51. IEEE Computer Society, Washington, DC, USA, 1998.

[Kea99] T. A. Keahey. Area-normalized thematic views. In *Proceedings of International Cartography Assembly*. 1999.

[Kea02] T. Keahey. Nonlinear magnification infocenter. <http://www.cs.indiana.edu/ tkeahey/research/nlm/nlm.html>, 2002.

[Khe04] A. Khella and B. B. Bederson. Pocket photomesa: a zoomable image browser for pdas. In *Proceedings of the 3rd international conference on Mobile and ubiquitous multimedia*, pp. 19–24. ACM Press, New York, NY, USA, 2004.

[Kim95] M.-B. Kim, Y.-D. Cho, D.-K. Kim, and N.-K. Ha. On the compression of medical images with regions of interest (ROIs). In *Proceedings of SPIE – Visual Communication and Image Processing*, vol. 2501 Part 1, pp. 733–744. Taipei, Taiwan, May 1995.

[Kim00] B. J. Kim, Z. Xiong, and W. A. Pearlman. Low bit-rate scalable video coding with 3-d set partitioning in hierarchical trees (3-d spiht). In *IEEE Transactions on Circuits and Systems for Video Technology*, vol. 10, pp. 1374–1387. December 2000.

[Kos01a] R. Kosara. *Semantic Depth of Field - Using Blur for Focus + Context Visualization*. Ph.D. thesis, Institute of Computer Graphics and Algorithms, Vienna University of Technology, Favoritenstrasse 9-11/186, A-1040 Vienna, Austria, 2001.

[Kos01b] R. Kosara, S. Miksch, and H. Hauser. Semantic depth of field. In *IEEE Symposium on Information Visualization*. San Diego, CA, USA, 22–23 2001.

[Kos02a] R. Kosara, S. Miksch, and H. Hauser. Focus + context taken literally. *IEEE Computer Graphics and Applications*, vol. 22(1):pp. 22–29, 2002.

[Kos02b] R. Kosara, S. Miksch, H. Hauser, J. Schrammel, V. Giller, and M. Tscheligi. Useful properties of semantic depth of field for better f+c visualization. *Proceedings of the Joint Eurographics–IEEE TCVG Symposium on Visualization*, pp. 205–210, 2002.

[Lai00] A. Laine. Wavelets in temporal and spatial processing of biomedical images. *Annual Review of Biomedical Engineering*, vol. 2:pp. 511–550, 2000.

[Lan06] T. G. Lane et al. Independent JPEG group software codec, version 4, internet distribution, V 6b. <ftp://ftp.uu.net/graphics/jpeg/>, 2006.

[Lat95] R. Latto. *The Artful Eye*, chap. The brain of the beholder, pp. 66–94. Oxford University Press, 1995.

[LEA05] LEADTOOLS. Raster imaging pro SDK. <http://www.leadtools.com/>, 2005.

[Lec03] V. Leck. xguide - personalized mobile information systems. In *Mobile Computer, technical report INI-Graphics-NET*. 2003.

[Lee90] H.-C. Lee. Review of image-blur models in a photographic system using principles of optics. *Optical Engineering*, vol. 29(5):pp. 405–421, 1990.

[Leu94] Y. K. Leung and M. D. Apperley. A review and taxonomy of distortion-oriented presentation techniques. *ACM Transactions on Computer-Human Interaction*, vol. 1(2):pp. 126–160, 1994.

[Li99] J. Li, H. Sun, H. Li, Q. Zhang, and X. Lin. Vfile - a virtual file media access mechanism and its application in jpeg2000 images browsing over the internet. In *ISO/IEC JTC 1/SC 29/WG 1 N1473*. 22 November 1999.

[Li01] W. Li. Overview of fine granularity scalability in mpeg-4 video standard. In *IEEE Transactions on Circuits and Systems for Video Technology*, vol. 11. March 2001.

[Lie97] H. Lieberman. A multi-scale, multi-layer, translucent virtual space. In *Proceedings of the IEEE Conference on Information Visualisation*, p. 126. IEEE Computer Society, Washington, DC, USA, 1997.

[Lin55] E. H. Linfoot. Information theory and optical images. In *Journal of the optical society America*, vol. 45, pp. 808–819. 1955.

[Lin01] E. Lin, C. Podilchuk, T. Kalker, and E. Delp. Streaming video and rate scalable compression: What are the challenges for watermarking. In *Proceedings of SPIE – Security and Watermarking of Multimedia Contents III*, vol. 4314, pp. 116–127. 2001.

[Liu02] L. Liu and G. Fan. A new method for jpeg2000 region-of-interest image coding: Most significant bitplanes shift. In *Proceedings of the 45th IEEE International Midwest Symposium on Circuits and Systems*. August 2002.

[Liu03a] H. Liu, X. Xie, W.-Y. Ma, and H. Zhang. Automatic browsing of large pictures on mobile devices. In *ACM Multimedia*, pp. 148–155. 2003.

[Liu03b] H. Liu, X. Xie, W.-Y. Ma, and H. Zhang. Mobipicture: browsing pictures on mobile devices. In *ACM Multimedia*, pp. 106–107. 2003.

[Liu03c] L. Liu and G. Fan. A new jpeg2000 region-of-interest image coding method: Partial significant bitplanes shift. In *IEEE Signal Processing Letter*, vol. 10, pp. 35–39. 2003.

[LIZ05] LIZARDTECH. Geoexpress with MrSID. <http://www.lizardtech.com/>, 2005.

[LM02] J. Le Moigne, N. Laporte, and N. S. Netanyahu. Enhancement of tropical land cover mapping with wavelet-based fusion and unsupervised clustering of sar and landsat image data. In *Proceedings of SPIE – Image and Signal Processing for Remote Sensing VII*, vol. 4541, pp. 190–198. 2002.

[Loh84] H. Lohscheller. A subjectively adapted image communication system. *IEEE Transactions on Communications*, vol. 32:pp. 1316–1322, December 1984.

[Lok95] I. Lokuge and S. Ishizaki. Geospace: an interactive visualization system for exploring complex information spaces. In *Proceedings of the SIGCHI conference on Human factors in computing systems*, pp. 409–414. ACM Press/Addison-Wesley Publishing Co., New York, NY, USA, 1995.

[LTI05] Leadtools image service. Whitepaper, Lead Technology, 2005.

[Lu02] A. Lu, C. J. Morris, D. S. Ebert, P. Rheingans, and C. Hansen. Non-photorealistic volume rendering using stippling techniques. In *Proceedings of the conference on Visualization*, pp. 211–218. IEEE Computer Society, Washington, DC, USA, 2002.

[Lue02] D. Luebke, B. Watson, J. D. Cohen, M. Reddy, and A. Varshney. *Level of Detail for 3D Graphics*. Elsevier Science Inc., New York, NY, USA, 2002.

[Lur05a] LuraTech. LuraWave JP2. <http://www.luratech.com>, 2005.

[Lur05b] LuraTech. LuraWave JP2 geo edition. <http://www.luratech.com>, 2005.

[Mac05] J. Macnicol, J. Arnold, and M. Frater. Scalable video coding by stream morphing. In *IEEE Transactions on Circuits and Systems for Video Technology*, vol. 15, pp. 306–319. February 2005.

[Mal89] S. G. Mallat. A theory for multiresolution signal decomposition: The wavelet representation. *IEEE Transaction on Pattern Analysis and Machine Intelligence*, vol. 11(7):pp. 674–693, 1989.

[Mal92] S. Mallat and S. Zhong. Characterization of signals from multiscale edges. In *IEEE Transactions on Pattern Analysis and Machine Intelligence*. 1992.

[Man99] M. K. Mandai, F. Idris, and S. Panchanathan. Image and video indexing in the compressed domain: a critical review. *Image Vision Computing Journal*, vol. 7(17):p. 513 Ů 529, 1999.

[Map06] MapViewer. Oracle. <http://www.oracle.com/technology/products/mapvie-wer/>, 2006.

[Mar80] D. Marr and E. Hildreth. Theory of edge detection. *Proceedings of the Royal Society London*, vol. B207:pp. 187–217, 1980.

[Mar02] P. Marziliano, F. Dufaux, S. Winkler, and T. Ebrahimi. A no-reference perceptual blur metric. In *IEEE International Conference on Image Processing*, vol. 3, pp. 57–60. 2002.

[Mar04] P. Marziliano, F. Dufaux, S. Winkler, and T. Ebrahimi. Perceptual blur and ringing metrics: Application to JPEG2000. *Signal Processing: Image Communication*, vol. 19(2):pp. 163–172, Feb 2004.

[McE95] A. M. McEachren. *How Maps Work: Presentaion, Visualization, and Design*. The Guilford Press, 72 Spring Street, New York, 1995.

[Mee03] J. Meessen, T. Suenaga, M. I. Guerrero, C. D. Vleeschouwer, and B. Macq. Layered architecture for navigation in jpeg 2000 mega-images. In *Proceedings of the 4th European Workshop on Image Analysis for Multimedia Interactive Services*, pp. 92–95. April 2003.

[Mee05] J. Meessen, J.-F. Delaigle, L.-Q. Xu, and B. Macq. Jpeg 2000 based scalable summary for understanding long video surveillance sequences. In *Proceedings of Electronic Imaging - Image and Video Communications and Processing*. January 2005.

[Mil98] F. W. Miller, P. J. Keleher, and S. K. Tripathi. General data streaming. In *Proceedings of the 19th IEEE Real-Time Systems Symposium*, pp. 232–241. 1998.

[Mis95] K. Misue, P. Eades, W. Lai, and K. Sugiyama. Layout adjustment and the mental map. *Journal of Visual Languages and Computing*, vol. 6(2):pp. 183–210, 1995.

[Mow87] P. H. Mowforth, J. Jelinek, and Z. P. Jin. An appropriate representation for early vision. *Pattern Recognition Letters*, vol. 5(2):pp. 175–182, 1987.

[MOX05] Remote image transmission system. Whitepaper, Moxa Technologies Co., Ltd., 2005.

[MPE93] Information technology: Coding of moving pictures and associated audio for digital storage media at up to about 1.5mbits/s, international standard, part 2: Video. Final, ISO/IEC 11172-2, 1993.

[MPE95] MPEG-2 information technology - generic coding of moving pictures and associated audio information: Video. Final, ISO/IEC JTC 1 13818-2, 1995.

[MPE02] MPEG-4 overview (V.21 Jeju Version). Final, ISO/IEC JTC 1/SC 29/WG 11 N4668, March 2002.

[MSM05] 3D DEM Pro. <http://www.msmacrosystem.nl/>, 2005.

[Mus05] G. Muskett. The use of visual perception in the interpretation of mycenaean art. In *Proceedings of SEEING THE PAST: Building knowledge of the past and present through acts of seeing*. Stanford University, CA, 2005.

[Nal86] V. S. Nalwa and T. O. Binford. On detecting edges. *IEEE Transactions on Pattern Analysis and Machine Intelligence*, vol. 8(6):pp. 699–714, 1986.

[Ngu01] A. Nguyen, V. Chandran, S. Sridharan, and R. Prandolini. Importance coding in jpeg2000 for improved interpretability. In *Proceedings of Image and Vision Computing New Zealand (IVCNZ)*. Dunedin, New Zealand, November 2001.

[Ngu02a] A. Nguyen, V. Chandran, and S. Sridharan. Jpeg2000 region of interest coding - a hybrid coefficient scaling and code-block distortion modulation method. In *Proceedings of the Fourth Australasian Workshop on Signal Processing and Applications (WOSPA)*. Brisbane, Australia, December 2002.

[Ngu02b] A. Nguyen, V. Chandran, S. Sridharan, and R. Prandolini. Progressive coding in jpeg2000 - improving content recognition performance using rois and importance maps. In *Proceedings of the European Signal Processing Conference (EUSIPCO)*. Toulouse, France, September 2002.

[Ngu03a] A. Nguyen, V. Chandran, S. Sridharan, and R. Prandolini. Guidelines to using region of interest coding in jpeg 2000. In *Proceedings of the International Symposium on Digital Signal Processing and Communication Systems (DSPCS)*. Gold Coast, Australia, December 2003.

[Ngu03b] A. Nguyen, V. Chandran, S. Sridharan, and R. Prandolini. Importance prioritisation coding in jpeg2000 for interpretability with application to surveillance imagery. In *Proceedings of Visual Communications and Image Processing (VCIP)*, vol. 5150, pp. 806–817. Lugano, Switzerland, July 2003.

[Nis98] D. Nister and C. Christopoulos. Lossless region of interest with a naturally progressive still image coding algorithm. In *Proceedings of ICIP*, vol. 3, pp. 856–859. 1998.

[NS997] A taxonomy of multiple window coordinations. Tech. rep., University of Maryland, Computer Science Department, C. North and B. Shneiderman, 1997.

[Ols00] C. Olston and A. Woodruff. Getting portals to behave. In *Proceedings of the IEEE Symposium on Information Visualization*, pp. 15–26. 2000.

[Ort97] A. Ortega, F. Carignano, S. Ayer, and M. Vetterli. Soft caching: Web cache management for images. In *IEEE Signal Processing Society Workshop on Multimedia*. Princeton, NJ, June 1997.

[Owe01] M. J. Owen, A. K. Lui, E. H. S. Lo, and M. W. Grigg. The design and implementation of a progressive on-demand image dissemination system for very large images. In *Proceedings of the 24th Australasian conference on Computer science*, pp. 148–155. IEEE Computer Society, Washington, DC, USA, 2001.

[Par02] K. Park and H. Park. Region-of-interest coding based on set partitioning in hierarchical trees. *IEEE Transactions on Circuits and Systems for Video Technology*, vol. 12(2):pp. 106–113, February 2002.

[PEG05] Pictools epic, advanced image compression&editing SDK. <http://www.pegasusimaging.com>, 2005.

[Pen93] W. Pennebaker and J. Mitchell. *JPEG Still Image Data Compression Standard*. Van Nostrand Reinhold, New York, 1993.

[Pla95] C. Plaisant, D. Carr, and B. Shneiderman. Image browsers: taxonomy, guidelines, and informal specifications. *IEEE Software*, vol. 12(2):pp. 21–32, 1995.

[PNG04] Information technology - portable network graphics (png): Functional specification. Tech. rep., ISO/IEC 15948:2004, March 2004.

[POL05] Polaris - interactive database visualization. <http://graphics.stanford.edu/projects/polaris/>, 2005.

[Poo00] S. Pook, E. Lecolinet, G. Vaysseix, and E. Barillot. Context and interaction in zoomable user interfaces. In *Proceedings of the working conference on Advanced visual interfaces*, pp. 227–231. ACM Press, New York, NY, USA, 2000.

[Pra01] W. K. Pratt. *Digital Image Processing: PIKS Inside*. John Wiley & Sons, Inc., New York, NY, USA, 2001.

[Pre70] J. M. S. Prewitt. Object enhancement and extraction. In B. S. Lipkin and A. Rosenfeld, editors, *Picture Processing and Psychopictorics*, pp. 75–149. Academic Press, New York, 1970.

[Ram00] S. Raman, H. Balakrishnan, and M. Srinivasan. An Image Transport Protocol for the Internet. In *8th International Conference on Network Protocols*. Osaka, Japan, October 2000.

[Rau96] U. Rauschenbach, R. Schultz, and H. Schumann. Quality and resource controlled transmission of images. In *Proceedings of the Eurographics Workshop on Multimedia*, pp. 32–43. Springer-Verlag New York, Inc., Secaucus, NJ, USA, 1996.

[Rau97] U. Rauschenbach and H. Schumann. Adaptive image transmission. In *WSCG'97 Winter School of Computer Graphics, Plzen, Czech Republic*. 1997.

[Rau98a] U. Rauschenbach. Progressive image transmission using levels of detail and regions of interest. In *Proceedings of the IASTED Conference on Computer Graphics and Imaging*. Halifax, Nova Scotia, Canada, June 1-4 1998.

[Rau98b] U. Rauschenbach and H. Schumann. Flexible embedded image communication using levels of detail and regions of interest. In *Proceedings of the workshop on Interactive Applications of Mobile Computing*. Rostock, Germany, November 24-25 1998.

[Rau99a] U. Rauschenbach. The rectangular fisheye view as an efficient method for the transmission and display of large images. In *Proceedings of IEEE ICIP*. 1999.

[Rau99b] U. Rauschenbach and H. Schumann. Demand-driven image transmission with levels of detail and regions of interest. *Computers and Graphics*, vol. 23(6):pp. 857–866, December 1999.

[Rau00] U. Rauschenbach. *Bedarfsgesteuerte Bildübertragung mit Regions of Interest und Level of Detail für mobile Umgebungen*. Ph.D. thesis, University of Rostock, 2000.

[Rau01a] U. Rauschenbach, S. Jeschke, and H. Schumann. General rectangular fisheye views for 2D graphics. *Computers & Graphics*, vol. 25(4):pp. 609–617, 2001.

[Rau01b] U. Rauschenbach, R. Rosenbaum, and H. Schumann. A flexible polygon representation of multiple overlapping regions of interest for wavelet-based image coding. In *Proceedings of IEEE ICIP*. Thessaloniki, Greece, October 7-10 2001.

[Ris02] T. Rist and P. Brandmeier. Customizing graphics for tiny displays of mobile devices. In *Journal Personal and Ubiquitous Computing*. 2002.

[Rob63] L. G. Roberts. Machine perception of three-dimensional solids. Tech. Rep. 315, Lincoln Lab, MIT, Lexington, MA, May 1963.

[Rob98] M. E. Robers, L. P. Kondi, and A. K. Katsaggelos. SNR scalable video coder using progressive transmission of DCT coefficients. In *Proceedings of SPIE – Visual Communications and Image Processing*, vol. 3309, pp. 201–212. 1998.

[Roe00] M. C. Roetgens. Magic lenses ® als Benutzerschnittstellenwerkzeuge.   <http://wwwcs.uni-paderborn.de/cs/ag-szwillus/lehre/vw/seminare/magiclenses/magiclenses.htm>, 2000.

[Ros01] R. Rosenbaum. Verfahren zum dynamischen, priorisierbaren und wahlfreien Zugriff auf Bildbereiche in JPEG2000-komprimierten Bildern sowie darauf aufbauende Client-Server-Architektur, Patent, amtliches Anmeldekennzeichen: 10138532.3, 2001.

[Ros02] R. Rosenbaum and H. Schumann. Flexible, dynamic and compliant region of interest coding in JPEG2000. In *Proceedings of IEEE ICIP*. Rochester, N.Y., September 2002.

[Ros03a] R. Rosenbaum and D. S. Taubman. Merging images in the jpeg2000 domain. In *Proceedings of VIIP*. September 2003.

[Ros03b] R. Rosenbaum and D. S. Taubman. Remote display of large raster images using jpeg2000 and the rectangular fisheye-view. In V. Skala, editor, *Journal of IEEE WSCG*, vol. 11, pp. 387–393. UNION Agency, February 2003. ISSN 1213 - 6972.

[Ros03c] R. Rosenbaum and C. Tominski. Pixels vs. vectors: Presentation of large images on mobile devices. In *Proceedings of the international Workshop on Mobile Computing*. June 2003.

[Ros04a] R. Rosenbaum and H. Schumann. Limited spatial access in jpeg2000 for remote image editing. In *Proceedings of VIIP*. September 2004.

[Ros04b] R. Rosenbaum and H. Schumann. Remote raster image browsing based on fast content reduction for mobile environments. In *Proceedings of EG-Multimedia*. October 2004.

[Ros04c] R. Rosenbaum and H. Schumann. Transcoding jpeg2000-streams for modern image browsing techniques. In *Proceedings of VIIP*. September 2004.

[Ros04d] R. Rosenbaum and C. Tominski. Presenting large graphical contents on mobile devices - performance issues. In *Proceedings of IRMA*. May 2004.

[Ros05a] R. Rosenbaum and H. Schumann. Grid-based interaction for effective image browsing on mobile devices. In *Proceedings of SPIE Electronic Imaging – Multimedia on Mobile Devices*. January 2005.

[Ros05b] R. Rosenbaum and H. Schumann. Jpeg2000-based image communication for modern browsing techniques. In *Proceedings of SPIE Electronic Imaging – Image and Video Communications and Processing*. January 2005.

[Ros06a] R. Rosenbaum and H. Schumann. Jpeg2000-based viewer guidance for mobile image browsing. In *Proceedings of IEEE MultiMedia-Modeling*. January 2006.

[Ros06b] R. Rosenbaum, C. Tominski, and H. Schumann. *Graphical Content on Mobile Devices*. Idea Group Publishing, encyclopedia of e-commerce, e-government and mobile commerce edn., 2006.

[Ros07a] R. Rosenbaum and H. Schumann. Interfaces for mobile image browsing. In *Proceedings of Electronic Imaging - Multimedia on Mobile Devices 2007*. January 2007.

[Ros07b] R. Rosenbaum and H. Schumann. Smooth transitions for mobile imagery browsing. In *Proceedings of Electronic Imaging - Multimedia on Mobile Devices 2007*. January 2007.

[SAG05] SAGE. <http://www.cs.cmu.edu/Groups/sage/sage.html>, 2005.

[Sai96a] A. Said and W. Pearlman. A new fast and efficient image codec based on set partitioning in hierarchical trees. *IEEE Transactions on Circuits and Systems for Video Technology*, vol. 6(3):pp. 243–250, June 1996.

[Sai96b] A. Said and W. A. Pearlman. An image multiresolution representation for lossless and lossy compression. In *Transactions on Image Processing, vol. 5, pp. 1303-1310*. 1996.

[Sal00] D. Salomon. *Data Compression: The Complete Reference*. Second edn., 2000.

[Sam84] H. Samet. The quadtree and related hierarchical data structures. *Computing Surveys*, vol. 16(2), 1984.

[San84] A. Sanz, C. Munoz, and N. Garcia. Approximation quality improvement techniques in progressive image transmission. *IEEE Journal on Selected Areas in Communications*, vol. SAC-2(2):pp. 359–373, March 1984.

[San00] D. Santa-Cruz, T. Ebrahimi, J. Askelöf, M. Larsson, and C. Christopoulos. JPEG 2000 still image coding versus other standards. In *SPIE's 45th annual meeting, Applications of Digital Image Processing XXIII*, vol. 4115 of *Proceedings of SPIE*, pp. 446–454. San Diego, California, August 2000.

[San04a] V. Sanchez, A. Basu, and M. K. Mandal. Prioritized region of interest coding in jpeg2000. *IEEE Transactions on Circuits and Systems for Video Technology*, vol. 14(9):pp. 1149–1155, 2004.

[San04b] M. B. Sandler and D. Black. Loss resilient, scalable audio compression and streaming. In *Proceedings of the European Workshop on the Integration of Knowledge,Semantic and Digital Media Technologies*. 2004.

[Sar93] M. Sarkar, S. Snibbe, O. Tversky, and S. Reiss. Stretching the rubber sheet. In *Proceedings of the ACM Symposium on User Interface Software and Technology*. 1993.

[Say00] K. Sayood. *Introduction to data compression, 2nd edition*. Morgan Kaufmann Publishers Inc., San Francisco, CA, USA, 2000.

[SC99] D. Santa Cruz, T. Ebrahimi, M. Larson, J. Askelöf, and C. Christopoulos. Region of interest coding in jpeg2000 for interactive client/server applications. In *IEEE Third workshop on multimedia signal processing*, pp. 389–394. September 1999.

[SC02] D. Santa-Cruz, R. Grosbois, and T. Ebrahimi. Jpeg 2000 performance evaluation and assessment. *Signal Processing: Image Communication*, vol. 17(1):pp. 113–130, January 2002.

[Sch96] M. Schneier and M. Abdel-Mottaleb. Exploiting the jpeg compression scheme for image retrieval. In *IEEE Transactions on Pattern Analysis and Machine Intelligence*. 1996.

[Sch00] H. Schumann and W. Müller. *Visualisierung - Grundlagen und allgemeine Methoden*. Springer Verlag, Heidelberg, 2000.

[Sch03a] T. Schütze. *Bildkomposition durch Transkodierung von JPEG2000-Datenströmen für mobile Umgebungen*. Master thesis, University of Rostock, March 2003.

[Sch03b] Schulzrinne, Casner, Frederick, and Jacobson. RTP: A transport protocol for real-time applications. *RFC 3550 Internet-Draft*, July 2003.

[Sec04] A. Secker and D. Taubman. Highly scalable video compression with scalable motion coding. In *IEEE Transactions on Image Processing*, vol. 13. August 2004.

[See04] T. Seebahn. *Effiziente Speicherung von Motion-JPEG2000-kodierten Bildsequenzen*. Master thesis, University of Rostock, November 2004.

[Sha48] C. Shannon. A mathematical theory of communication. *Bell System Technical Journal*, vol. 27:pp. 379–423, 623–656, 1948.

[Sha93] J. Shapiro. Embedded image coding using zerotrees of wavelet coefficients. *IEEE Transactions on Signal Processing*, vol. 41(12):pp. 3445–3462, Dec 1993.

[Sha96] J. Shapiro. Apparatus and method for emphasizing a selected region in the compressed representation of an image. U.S. Patent 5,563,960, October 1996.

[She96a] B. Shen and I. K. Sethi. Convolution-based edge detection for image/video in block dct domain. In *Journal of Visual Communications and Image Representation*. 1996.

[She96b] B. Shen and I. K. Sethi. Direct feature extraction from compressed images. In *SPIE – Storage and Retrieval for Image and Video Databases IV*. 1996.

[She99] K. Shen and E. Delp. Wavelet based rate scalable video compression. In *IEEE Transactions on Circuits and Systems for Video Technology*, vol. 9, pp. 109–122. February 1999.

[Shi99] Y. Q. Shi and H. Sun. *Image and Video Compression for Multimedia Engineering*. CRC Press, Inc., Boca Raton, FL, USA, 1999.

[Shn96] B. Shneiderman. The eyes have it: A task by data type taxonomy for information visualizations. *Proceedings of the IEEE Symposium on Visual Languages*, pp. 336–343, 1996.

[SI02] Z. Shu-Iong. Image fusion using wavelet transform. In *Proceedings of Geospatial Theory, Processing and Applications*, vol. 34. 2002.

[Sig97]   A. Signoroni and R. Leonardi. Progressive ROI coding and diagnostic quality for medical image compression. In *Proceedings of SPIE*, vol. 3309, pp. 674–685. 1997.

[Sku03]   A. Skupin and S. Fabrikant. Spatialization methods: A cartographic research agenda for non-geographic information visualization. In *Cartography and Geographic Information Science*, vol. 30, pp. 9–119. 2003.

[Smi93]   B. C. Smith and L. A. Rowe. Algorithms for manipulating compressed images. In *IEEE Computer Graphics and Applications*. 1993.

[Smi96]   B. C. Smith and L. A. Rowe. Compressed domain processing of jpeg-encoded images. In *Real-Time Imaging*, vol. 2, pp. 3–17. 1996.

[Smi98]   R. B. Smith, R. Hixon, and B. Horan. Supporting flexible roles in a shared space. In *Proceedings of the 1998 ACM conference on Computer supported cooperative work*, pp. 197–206. ACM Press, 1998.

[SMP05]   Pocketmap 3D. <http://www.pocketmap.com/>, 2005.

[Spe82]   R. Spence and M. Apperley. Data base navigation: An office environment for the professional. In *Behaviour and Information Technology*, pp. 43–54. 1982.

[Spe93]   R. Spence. A taxonomy of graphical presentation. In *Conference companion on Human factors in computing systems at INTERACT93 and CHI93*, pp. 113–114. ACM Press, New York, NY, USA, 1993.

[SPF05]   Spotfire. <http://www.spotfire.com>, 2005.

[Sta02]   J. Stastny. Image processing by using wavelet transform. In *Journal Electronic letters*. 2002.

[Sta03]   J. Stasko. Cs 7450 – information visualization. <http://www.cc.gatech.edu/classes/AY2003/cs7450_spring/>, February 2003.

[Ste95]   T. Stephenson and H. Voorhees. Imacts: an interactive, multiterabyte image archive. In *Proceedings of the 14th IEEE Symposium on Mass Storage Systems*, p. 146. IEEE Computer Society, Washington, DC, USA, 1995.

[Sto94]   M. C. Stone, K. Fishkin, and E. A. Bier. The movable filter as a user interface tool. In *Proceedings of CHI*, pp. 306–312. Boston, MA, 1994.

[Sto03]   M.-A. Storey. Information visualization & knowledge management, course notes, 2003.

[Str97]   J. Strom and P. Cosman. Medical image compression with lossless regions of interest. *Signal Processing*, vol. 59:pp. 155–171, June 1997.

[Str02]   T. Strothotte and S. Schlechtweg. *Non-Photorealistic Computer Graphics: Modeling, Rendering and Animation*. Morgan Kaufmann, 1 edn., June 15 2002.

[Sue03]   T. Suenaga, J. Meessen, and B. Macq. Jpeg2000 over mail protocol. In *Proceedings of SPIE – International Conference on Applications of Digital Image Processing*. August 2003.

[Suh02]   B. Suh, A. Woodruff, R. Rosenholtz, and A. Glass. Popout prism: adding perceptual principles to overview+detail document interfaces. In *Proceedings of the SIGCHI conference on Human factors in computing systems*, pp. 251–258. ACM Press, New York, NY, USA, 2002.

[Sva05]   C. H. Svanberg. Ericsson fourth quarter report 2004. 2005.

[Tai02]   H.-M. Tai, M. Long, W. He, and H. Yang. An efficient region of interest coding for medical image compression. In *Proceedings of the EMBS/BMES Conference*, vol. 2, pp. 1017 – 1018. 2002.

[Tan79]   S. Tanimoto. Image transmission with gross information first. In *Computer Graphics and Image Processing*, vol. 9, pp. 72–76. January 1979.

[Tau94]   D. S. Taubman. *Directionality and Scalability in Image and Video Compression*. Ph.D. thesis, University of California, Berkeley, 1994.

[Tau99]   D. Taubmann. High performance scaleable image compression with EBCOT. In *Proceedings of the IEEE International Conference On Image Processing*, vol. 3, pp. 344–348. August 1999.

[Tau01]   D. Taubman and M. Marcellin. *JPEG2000: Image compression fundamentals, standards and practice*. Kluwer Academic Publishers, Boston, November 2001.

[Tau02a] D. Taubman. Remote browsing of jpeg2000 images. In *Proceedings of ICIP*, pp. I: 229–232. Rochester, N.Y., September 2002.

[Tau02b] D. Taubman and M. Marcellin. Jpeg2000: Standard for interactive imaging. In *Proceedings of the IEEE*, vol. 90, pp. 1336–1357. August 2002.

[Tau03a] D. Taubman and R. Prandolini. Architecture, philosophy and performance of jpip: internet protocol standard for jpeg2000. In *Proceedings SPIE Symposium on VCIP*. Lugano, Switzerland, July 2003.

[Tau03b] D. S. Taubman and R. Rosenbaum. Rate-distortion optimized interactive browsing of jpeg2000 images. In *Proceedings of IEEE ICIP*. September 2003.

[The00]   G. Theo and W. M. Arnold. Pictoseek: combining color and shape invariant features for image retrieval. *IEEE Transactions in Image Processing*, vol. 1(9):pp. 102–119, 2000.

[The05]   The Center of perceptual Systems.   University of Texas, Austin. <http://www.cps.utexas.edu/>, 2005.

[The06]   The MapPoint Web Service. Microsoft ®. <http://www.microsoft.com/mappoint/products/webservice/>, 2006.

[Thi04]   J. Thie and D. Taubman. Optimal erasure protection assignment for scalable compressed data with small packets and short channel codewords. *EURASIP Journal on Applied Signal Processing Ǔ Special issue on Multimedia over IP and Wireless Networks*, (2):pp. 207–219, February 2004.

[Ton04]   H. Tong, M. Li, H. Zhang, and C. Zhang. No-reference quality assessment for jpeg2000 compressed images. In *Proceedings of ICIP*, pp. 3539–3542. 2004.

[Twe97]   L. Tweedie. Characterizing interactive externalizations. In *Proceedings of the SIGCHI conference on Human factors in computing systems*, pp. 375–382. ACM Press, New York, NY, USA, 1997.

[Ven05]   R. F. i Ventura, P. Vandergheynst, and P. Frossard. Low rate and flexible image coding with redundant representations. *IEEE Transactions on Image Processing*, February 2005.

[Vet95]   M. Vetterli and J. Kovacevic. *Wavelets and subband coding*. Prentice Hall, Englewood Cliffs, NJ, USA, 1995.

[Vir02]   Virtual Network Computing. RealVNC. <http://www.realvnc.com/>, 2002.

[VRM97] VRML the virtual reality modeling language. Tech. rep., ISO/IEC 14772-1:1997, 1997.

[Wal91]   G. K. Wallace. The jpeg still picture compression standard. *Communications of the ACM*, vol. 34(4):pp. 30–44, 1991.

[Wan02a] Z. Wang, S. Banerjee, B. Evans, and A. Bovik. Generalized bitplane-by-bitplane shift method for jpeg2000 roi coding. In *Proceedings of IEEE ICIP*. Rochester, N.Y., September 22-25 2002.

[Wan02b] Z. Wang and A. Bovik. Bitplane-by-bitplane shift (bbbshift)- a suggestion for jpeg2000 region of interest coding. In *IEEE Signal Processing Letters*, vol. 9. Rochester, N.Y., September 22-25 2002.

[Wan02c] R. Want, T. Pering, G. Danneels, M. Kumar, M. Sundar, and J. Light. The personal server: Changing the way we think about ubiquitous computing. In *Proceedings of the 4th international conference on Ubiquitous Computing*, pp. 194–209. London, UK, 2002.

[War95] C. Ware and M. Lewis. The dragmag image magnifier. In *Conference companion on Human factors in computing systems at CHI*, pp. 407–408. ACM Press, New York, NY, USA, 1995.

[WES04] Command and conquer. <http://www.westwood.com>, 2004.

[Wie01] K. J. Wiebe and A. Basu. Improving image and video transmission quality over ATM with foveal prioritization and priority dithering. *Pattern Recognition Letters*, vol. 22(8):pp. 905–915, 2001.

[Woo86] J. Woods and S. O'Neil. Subband coding of images. *IEEE Transactions on Acoustics, Speech and Signal Processing*, vol. 34:pp. 1278–1288, October 1986.

[Wu02] T. Wu, A. C. Miguel, E. A. Riskin, A. E. Mohr, R. E. Ladner, and S. Hauck. Protecting regions of interest in medical images in a lossy packet network. In *Proceedings of the SPIE – Medical Imaging: PACS and Integrated Medical Information Systems*, vol. 4685, pp. 137–148. 2002.

[Xie05] X. Xie, H. Liu, S. Goumaz, and W.-Y. Ma. Learning user interest for image browsing on small-form-factor devices. In *Proceedings of the SIGCHI conference on Human factors in computing systems*, pp. 671–680. ACM Press, New York, NY, USA, 2005.

[Xio99] Z. Xiong, K. Ramchandran, M. Orchard, and Y. Zhang. A comparative study of dct- and wavelet-based image coding. In *IEEE Transactions on Circutis and Systems for Video Technology*, vol. 9. August 1999.

[Yin04] X. W. Yin, A. C. Downton, M. Fleury, and J. He. Multi-component document image coding using regions-of-interest. In *Document Analysis Systems*, pp. 158–169. 2004.

[Yu02] W. Yu, R. Qiu, and J. E. Fritts. Advantages of motion-jpeg2000 in video processing. In *Proceedings of VCIP*, pp. 635–645. 2002.

[Yu04] Z. V. A. Yu, W.; Sahinoglu. Energy efficient jpeg 2000 image transmission over point-to-point wireless networks. In *Global Telecommunications Conference (GLOBECOM)*. November 2004.

[Zha96] J. Zhao, Y. Shimazu, K. Ohta, R. Hayasaka, and Y. Matsushita. A jpeg codec adaptive to region importance. In *Proceedings of the fourth ACM international conference on Multimedia*, pp. 209–218. ACM Press, New York, NY, USA, 1996.